REDISCOVERING TRAVEL

ALSO BY SETH KUGEL

Nueva York:
The Complete Guide to Latino Life in the Five Boroughs
(with Carolina González)

Toulouse, France.

REDISCOVERING TRAVEL

A Guide for the Globally Curious

Seth Kugel

LIVERIGHT PUBLISHING CORPORATION
A Division of W. W. Norton & Company
Independent Publishers Since 1923
New York   London

Rediscovering Travel is a work of nonfiction. Certain names have been changed.

Manufacturing by LSC Communications, Harrisonburg
Book design by Lovedog Studio
Production manager: Anna Oler

Library of Congress Cataloging-in-Publication Data

Names: Kugel, Seth, author.
Title: Rediscovering travel : a guide for the globally curious / Seth Kugel.
Description: First edition. | New York : Liveright Publishing Corporation,
   [2018] | Includes bibliographical references.
Identifiers: LCCN 2018028589 | ISBN 9780871408501 (hardcover)
Subjects: LCSH: Travel. | Tourism. | Kugel, Seth—Travel.
Classification: LCC G155.A1 K836 2018 | DDC 360.4/819—dc23
LC record available at https://lccn.loc.gov/2018028589

Liveright Publishing Corporation
500 Fifth Avenue, New York, N.Y. 10110
www.wwnorton.com

W. W. Norton & Company Ltd.
15 Carlisle Street, London W1D 3BS

1 2 3 4 5 6 7 8 9 0

To B and D

CONTENTS

Chapter 1
REDISCOVERING TRAVEL   3

Chapter 2
ORGANIC EXPERIENCES   23

Chapter 3
WHY WE TRAVEL   53

Chapter 4
TECHNOLOGY AND TRAVEL   103

Chapter 5
RISK AND TRAVEL   159

Chapter 6
PEOPLE AND TRAVEL   185

Chapter 7
MONEY AND TRAVEL   223

Chapter 8
BAD INFLUENCES, GOOD TRAVELERS   243

EPILOGUE   271

Acknowledgments   277

Appendix 1: TRAVEL MODE   281

Appendix 2: A MINI-GUIDE TO RISK
ASSESSMENT AND REDUCTION   287

Notes   297

REDISCOVERING TRAVEL

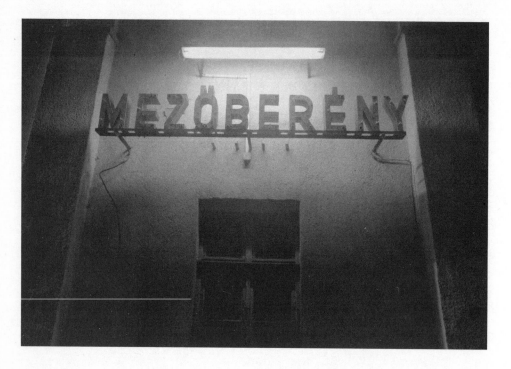

Train station in Mezőberény, Hungary.

Chapter 1

REDISCOVERING TRAVEL

Stenciled in white block letters on a dreary cement wall in Mezőberény, a tidy but fraying town of twelve thousand in the hyperbolically named Great Hungarian Plain, appeared the word:

SZESZFŐZDE

Hours earlier, in the overcast predawn hours of a nippy January day, I had stumbled off the Bucharest-to-Budapest train to see what it would be like to spend the weekend in the opposite of a tourist destination. Mezőberény was not just absent from guidebooks. It did not have a single restaurant, hotel, or activity listed on TripAdvisor, something that cannot be said for Mbabara, Uganda, or Dalanzadgad, Mongolia. I did have some info on the town, thanks to its municipal website: Resident József Halász had recently celebrated his ninetieth birthday.

Or that's what Google Translate told me. Hungarian is a Uralic language, more closely related to the output you might get falling asleep on a keyboard than to English or German or French. That makes even basic comprehension a challenge, as I found as soon as I rushed from the train to the station's restrooms and faced the urgent need to choose between two doors: *FÉRFI* and *NŐI*. The authorities had apparently saved a few forints by not splurging on stick-figure signs.

The day had been born cold and gray and stayed that way as I walked through the town, slowly getting my bearings, intrigued by the prewar, pre-Communist homes and the more than occasional bike rider—there were almost more bikes than cars—who waved hello. But then a winter drizzle took up, causing an abrupt decline in the number of cyclists even as the number of wandering American visitors held steady at one. To me, a travel day that turns rainy is like a piece of chocolate I've dropped on the floor: It's significantly less appealing, but I'll be damned if I'm going to throw it away.

It was in the first minutes of rain that I came across the stenciled sign on an otherwise residential street. Beyond the wall, down a cracking, now puddle-pocked driveway, were a dozen or so plastic barrels lined up like nuclear-waste drums. Beyond them, maybe a hundred feet from where I stood, was a one-story L-shaped building. What was this place? Well, SZESZFŐZDE, apparently. But what was that?

In the old days (say, 2009), I would have pulled out an English-Hungarian phrase book or pocket dictionary, but instead I activated international roaming on my phone, carefully spelled out S-Z-E-S-Z-F-O-Z-D-E, and tapped Go.

The less-than-lightning speed of Great Hungarian Plain mobile service provided a dramatic pause. And then came my answer:

DISTILLERY

You don't say.

I would have guessed PRIVATE PROPERTY maybe, or DANGER—STAY OUT, or MIND YOUR OWN BUSINESS YOU MEDDLING FOREIGNER! But a distillery? A wave of adrenaline washed down my torso as my lips curled into a dumb-luck smile.

Two rather gruff-looking men emerged from the door—the older one smoking a cigarette and wearing a sweater and work-stained trousers that suggested Warsaw Pact 1986 more than European Union 2014. I waved to them, pointed to the bulky Canon 7D hanging from my neck, and then to the building. Old-school Google Translate.

They waved me inside and gave me a tour.

* * * *

Even for a travel writer, the idea of landing in a small town with no known attractions and no known English speakers, where I had not a single contact and no idea where I'd be sleeping, was nerve-wracking. The fact that I had to write a first-person column about the experience for the *New York Times* a week later added to the pressure. In three and a half years as the "Frugal Traveler," I had never been shy about pointing out my shortcomings; if my weekend in Mezőberény was a miserable failure, the world would know.

I had been an unlikely choice for the column to begin with. As a longtime freelancer for the *Times,* I had written almost entirely about New York City. Of the dozen or so destination stories I had been assigned, most were about the Dominican Republic, Mexico, or Brazil—countries I knew well and where I spoke the language. (The two exceptions were Philadelphia, where I also spoke the language, and Curaçao, where I did a great job of lying on the beach.)

For a job in which dinner-party acquaintances and Twitter followers alike expect you to spout infallible advice about Roman ruins and Tokyo *takoyaki* off the top of your head, I was pathetically traveled. I had never set foot in East or South Asia. I had spent a total of a week in Europe since my junior semester abroad in Paris, nineteen years earlier. Even in the far more familiar Western Hemisphere, I was a renowned bungler. My first column recounted how I almost had to cancel my debut trip after leaving my passport on a men's room paper-towel dispenser in the São Paulo airport. (Someone turned it in to lost and found, thus saving my trip—and perhaps my career—though plenty of readers wrote in to ask how such a numbskull had gotten the job.)

According to my editor, I was chosen because he liked "writers who traveled, not travel writers." I had spent the previous two years covering every corner of Brazil as a freelance correspondent. But introducing yourself as a reporter makes travel far easier, grabbing people's attention and opening many doors. The Frugal Traveler column is different: Under strict orders from my far wiser predecessors, I didn't tell anyone I met on the road that I worked for the *Times* or that I was even a writer (until afterward, if I needed to use their names). I was expected to make friends and have adventures on the basis of my own extroverted personality.

And though I am extroverted—quite so, in fact—among friends or speaking to a crowd or interviewing a source, striking up conversations with strangers for no reason whatsoever always felt to me like that first jump off the dock into a cold New England lake.

Even by the Hungary trip, four years into the job, approaching strangers still made me nervous. But at least I had raised my game from utterly pathetic to awkwardly mediocre, and had learned that Mezőberény was just the kind of place where jumping into the lake would likely pay off.

One of my most ironclad rules of travel is this: The number of visitors a place receives is inversely related to how nice locals are to those visitors. Mezőberény, as far as I knew, had received precisely no foreign tourists ever. It was the anti-Paris, and this distillery the anti-Louvre.

People who inhabit the still-plentiful tourist-free swaths of the planet tend not only to be just nicer, but more curious. They say a bear in the wild is just as scared of you as you are of it. I say people in places where outsiders rarely go are just as curious about visitors as visitors are about them. The question is not why the distillery workers invited me—a camera-toting, gibberish-talking stranger— in for a tour, it's why wouldn't they? If it were me, I'd be thinking: "What is this odd foreigner doing outside our szeszfőzde with a camera? Wait till I tell the kids! And by the way, isn't it about time we took a break?"

❊ ❊ ❊ ❊

Once they waved me into the ancient but fully functioning distillery, the men let me take pictures as they gave me a vaguely intelligible lesson via pointing, expressive looks, and smartphone-translated Hungarian, on how *pálinka*—Hungarian fruit brandy— was made. Those barrels I had seen outside, it turned out, were full of fermenting pear and grape and apple juices. Inside, it was distilled somehow through a looping and tangled system of pipes running out of tin tanks up and along the walls. It looked like the laboratory of a mad scientist with a penchant for tacky linoleum flooring.

As they led me around, I engaged in that most intrinsic of travel activities: trying to see the world from the vantage point of someone utterly different from me. What was their life like? Had they traveled? Who were their parents and grandparents? The language barrier that did not allow them to answer did not stop me from wondering.

I also hoped to engage in that second-most intrinsic of travel activities: souvenir hunting. So I asked to buy some brandy. What better souvenir than one that comes with a story? But they refused to sell me any—or even let me taste a drop.

In another setting, perhaps, this would have annoyed me. Here, it created a whiff of intrigue. Was my request culturally inappropriate? Had they simply not understood what I wanted? Did their bosses keep such a close watch on the inventory that they would notice a missing nip?

After soaking in every rusty detail and every glint of pride in the men's tired eyes, I typed "Come visit me in New York" into Google Translate—laughs all around—then headed back onto the drizzly streets of Mezőberény, utterly elated.

*　*　*　*

What was so great about this moment? Sure, the *szeszfőzde* was a neat little story for friends, and in my case, worth a few paragraphs in the newspaper. But wasn't it just a grimy business making local hooch in a town that even most Hungarians would classify as the middle of nowhere? It was because I discovered it. Not a discovery in the sense of a cure for AIDS or a previously undiscovered species of poison-spitting neon frog the size of a pinky nail. Perhaps it was not earth-shattering, but it was 100 percent unexpected, 100 percent real, and 100 percent mine.

Discovery used to be the lifeblood of travel, at least for those who shunned tour-bus groups and all-inclusive resorts. We used to leave home knowing relatively little about our destination—perhaps with some highlighted guidebook pages denoting major attractions and local tipping etiquette, a list of tips culled from well-traveled friends, or articles copied and pasted into a Word document. And for the ambitious, a notional feel for the local history or culture gleaned pre-trip from a historical novel.

Beyond that, we were on our own. Paper guidebooks frozen in time helped us along, as did pamphlets and paper maps from tourist information booths and tips from a hotel concierge. Earlier this century, Google searches in internet cafés lent a hand. But otherwise, there was no choice: You decided what to do with your own eyes and ears, by wandering, by initiating human-to-human contact. Tips came from hearing fellow travelers' stories over hostel or (non-Air) B&B breakfasts, entering a shop to ask directions and ending up in a conversation with the owner, or catching a whiff of fresh bread or sizzling chilies and following your nose.

Of course, all that still happens today—but only if you really go out of your way to make it happen. Not only is nearly every place in the world documented to within an inch of its life, but that documentation—which comes dressed as both fact and opinion—is overwhelmingly and immediately available, thanks to pervasive technology. That's great for many things in life—medical information, how-to videos, shorter commutes. But don't we travel to break our routine? To experience the unexpected? To let the world delight us?

If we do, we have a funny way of showing it. We pore over online reviews for weeks, plan days down to the half hour, and then let GPS and the collected wisdom of the unwise lead us blindly. We mean well—no one wants to have a romantic dinner go wrong or to get lost and miss out on a "must-see attraction" or to risk chaos by failing to keep the kids entertained for three minutes.

But isn't that just a digital version of the old-fashioned group tour? Well, almost, except that on the bus tour, you actually get to meet the person whose advice you're taking.

That's why I believe it is time we rediscover travel, and recognize the value of what an overdocumented world has taken away: the delight of making things happen on your own.

✳　✳　✳　✳

Is it possible that stumbling upon a dank distillery might be just as thrilling as a tour of one of the world's great monuments? Did the surge of emotion I felt when the word *distillery* popped onto my screen match what I felt when I first glanced up at the ceiling of the Sistine Chapel?

Probably not, although I remember the distillery moment quite precisely and barely recall what I felt at the Sistine Chapel. Why? Because although Michelangelo's prophets and sibyls and biblical re-creations are several trillion times lovelier than rusty pipes in a concrete building reeking of fermented fruit, I had seen them before in photos, heard professors talk about them, and read other travelers' accounts as I sought the best times to avoid crowds.

Expectations were high. At the Vatican, anything short of a life-changing epiphany would have been a disappointment, and it's pretty hard to have life-changing epiphanies while surrounded by crowds pretending to have life-changing epiphanies. It was, of course, a worthwhile experience and would have made for incredible Instagram fodder if only I had gone a few years later. But by now the live experience has merged with the images implanted in my brain long before my visit (and after, via #SistineChapel).

* * * *

Why the szeszfőzde workers wouldn't sell to me was a mystery. In fact, it was the third mystery I had encountered during my first four hours in town.

The first came moments after I relieved myself in the *férfi* room in the Mezőberény train station and emerged into the misty morning. On a sign outside the station was what appeared to be a tourist information map. Its very existence was unexpected—if TripAdvisor wasn't here, could tourism exist? But the more confounding issue was why the welcome messages were written in three languages (none of which was English). *Wilkommen* gave away one as German; *Köszöntő*, with its overload of diacritical marks, had to be Hungarian. The third language's greeting was *Pozdravenie*, which I didn't recognize at all.

This completely fascinated me. German, I knew, was a second

language in much of central Europe. Hungarian, of course. But what was the third language? I didn't think I'd ever seen a trilingual tourist map anywhere in the world where one of the three languages wasn't English. A few taps of the smartphone and the answer emerged: Slovak. Come again? Slovakia bordered Hungary to the north, but Mezőberény was much closer to Romania to the east (where my train came from) and even Serbia to the southwest. Mystery number one remained unsolved.

There was another surprise: Spread across the map were thirty-nine points of interest. I didn't know what any of them were, since I can't read Hungarian, German, or Slovak, but there was clearly more to this little town than you'd ever think from its dot on the map and its forlorn train station with stick-figure–free restrooms. I had been tricked into assuming that if the English-language internet didn't have much to say about a place, nothing was there.

I did recognize one word on the map, right in the center of town: szálló—hotel. That was good news. I snapped a photo of it to find my way there.

Few people were out, giving me the chance to observe the town before it observed me. Like many travelers, I find the first few moments in a new country or city strange and disorienting. Things look and sound and smell different, humans dress different, sometimes even the dogs bark different. The neurons start to fire in the part of your brain that handles "We're not in Kansas anymore" circumstances. And there's an added touch of excitement or panic when you have no guide, no language skills, no hotel reservation, and no idea what is going to happen—if anything is going to happen at all.

Every little detail helps. A scrap metal heap? There's some industry here. A sign that reads CARGILL behind a barbed-wire fence? There's probably something agricultural in that warehouse. Closer to town, the agro-industrial started giving way to residential and even commercial; I saw an ETTEREM, a restaurant of sorts—so I knew I wouldn't starve. And wait, were those . . . bike lanes? That was most unexpected—I had erroneously associated bike lanes exclusively with places like Scandinavia and Holland and Portland,

Oregon. Why would there be bike lanes in small-town Hungary? Wait, why would there not be? Was I suffering from anti–ex-Soviet-bloc prejudice?

A left turn at a traffic circle brought me past a cryptic sculpture of three girls huddled together on the right, a supermarket on the left. And beyond was surely the most majestic edifice Mezőberény had to offer: a two-story mansion with elegant arched windows and a Juliet balcony over a carved wooden front door: the Berény-Szálló.

And then, something else unexpected: Though it was not yet 7 a.m., and still just before sunrise, two young men were drinking beer by the entrance. I greeted them and found they spoke English surprisingly well. Had I underestimated the provinciality of the town? No (not yet anyway), they turned out to be medical students visiting from Budapest, in town for a pig-killing.

Hmm, promising. I began to drop hints that I would like to be invited.

"But the pig is already dead," one said. They were back for a break.

That jibed with my limited knowledge of ritual pig slaughters—get them killed early so that their many component parts can be dressed and cooked over the course of the day, much of it for immediate consumption.

Pork is my weakness. In the past, my online dating profile has read, "If pork shoulder were a vegetable, I could be a vegetarian." And "immediate" is my favorite kind of consumption. But in the time it took to reserve a room for the evening and leave my bags in storage, the medical students had disappeared, perhaps to stuff sausages.

That was depressing, but also instructive, I thought: In many parts of the world, an out-of-place foreigner would have been instantly invited to join. Were Hungarians different? (Or, perhaps I should say, more like New Yorkers?)

The whereabouts of this pig-killing became mystery number two. Looking for it struck me as an excellent excuse to walk around town, after stopping by the local bakery for a black *kávé*—a rare decipherable Hungarian word—and a chocolate snail pastry.

I asked the drowsy woman behind the counter (who got by in English) whether there was anything interesting to see in town.

She answered with a look.

"Nothing?" I interpreted.

"Nothing."

Even without evidence to the contrary—there was a pig-killing somewhere, plus quite a scrap-metal heap—eleven thousand people glommed together anywhere must by the very nature of human society have created something that outsiders perceive as interesting, even if those who live there do not consider it so. A family's laundry drying on a clothesline, for example, can reveal the locally prevalent style of undergarments.

So I set out walking around town, sniffing for roasting offal, assembling bits of information, and waving to people on bikes— most of whom were elderly, though I wasn't sure whether that meant the elderly of Mezőberény like to ride bikes, or that no one else is up before eight on a Saturday. Actually, many dogs were up, greeting me from front yards with the friendly yips of the small-town canine. (Rural dogs bark frantic alarms, and city dogs are far more nonchalant.)

And then, eventually, I came to the *szeszfőzde*, where the refusal to sell me *pálinka* become the third mystery of the day. A little more wandering brought me to a place called the Burger Box, whose sign read 0–24 NONSTOP (Hungarian was getting easier by the minute). A burger place is always a good spot to see just how far American values have penetrated other lands, and by American values I mean ketchup, mustard, and relish. None of those words appeared on the undecipherable menu—I recognized only "paprika."

It was the perfect excuse to talk to the lone other customer, a forty-year-old man named Gabor, who told me in remarkably good English that he had stopped by for a snack on his way to German class.

I probably should have asked how his Slovak was, but instead I inquired about which burger he was having.

"I make myself," he said, meaning he custom-ordered. I asked him to order two—and we chatted. He was excited to hear I was from New York, which did not surprise me—people are so excited

to meet someone from New York that I often recommend that anyone from within a few states away introduce themselves as, say,
"from Pennsylvania, which is near New York."

But Gabor had actually been there. I asked him when.

"Bin Laden."

"2001."

"Yes."

"Before or after?"

"I saw the hole."

I asked him where else he had been. Washington, he said—a reasonable choice for a tourist, and Richmond, Virginia, he added—not
so much. It turned out he had gone to the United States on a whim
and ended up working for a housekeeping service in Richmond.

The burger was terrible—the kind of grayish ground meat that
could push anyone closer to pork-shoulder-excluded vegetarianism.
But if one of the reasons we travel is to better understand how the
world works, then meeting a former Richmond, Virginia, house-
keeper eating a custom-ordered chili-cheeseburger on his way to German class is, to me, just as good as any critically acclaimed museum.

I'd given up on the pig slaughter, so after bidding *auf Wiedersehen*
to Gabor, I figured I'd go to church. Not for the reasons tourists usually go to churches—to feign interest in frescoes and icons—and not
for spiritual guidance, but to meet people.

As a secular Jew, I've been to synagogue maybe a half-dozen
times in my life: a wedding here, a bar mitzvah there, once to interview an Argentinian rabbi in the Bronx. But as a lone traveler, I've
been to church dozens of times, because church is the most intimate
part of people's lives that is open to the public, and welcoming by
mandate. "You shall treat the stranger who sojourns with you as the
native among you, and you shall love him as yourself," says Leviti-
cus 19:34. And, in my experience, Christians of every stripe follow
that to the letter . . . as long as you catch them in services.

I found a Catholic church on the way back to town, but mass
wasn't until 5 p.m., almost six hours away. So I kept walking and
stumbled across the town museum, the OPSKK Museum Collection, in an old-fashioned, very yellow home. It was my lucky day,

or, more specifically, my lucky two hours: What seemed to be the town's most legitimate tourist attraction was open only on Saturdays from 10 a.m. to noon.

The museum was no Louvre, but you could take that two ways: It was not one one-millionth as impressive. But it was not one-billionth as crowded. And, unlike the staff at the Louvre, which is polite because politeness is in their job description, a young, wispy-bearded man named Zsolt was downright thrilled—or perhaps shocked—to see me. I was, he said in halting English, the first guest in three weeks. He waived the entrance fee (out of kindness, I thought at first, though in retrospect it must have saved him from some sort of accounting procedure at the end of his shift) and took me on a tour.

There is not a soul reading this book who cares about Mezőberény's history (don't lie!), nor did I until I arrived in town. But now I was eager to hear anything that might help figure out this place. The house where we stood, Zsolt told me, was once the residence of the family who had helped "re-birth" the town in the early nineteenth century. It later became a school, and then a library, before becoming a museum.

In the backyard was a memorial to Mezőberény's Jews taken away during the Holocaust and never heard from again. Inside, Zsolt showed me an exhibition of work by a local embroiderer, and some wacky artifacts, including an ancient, enormous water carbonation machine—a refrigerator-size SodaStream. Finally, we entered an area full of more quotidian objects, including a four-poster bed, household goods, and family portraits. It was the Slovak room, he said.

Aha! Slovak! That could not be a coincidence, but Zsolt's English didn't prove up to the task of explaining.

✳   ✳   ✳   ✳

I returned to the church at 4:54 p.m. and found the gate locked, lights out. Finally, an older woman opened the doors and people started to filter in, mostly her non-English-speaking demographic. A young organist greeted me in English, but she soon disappeared to man the pipes.

I had settled in, still mildly uncomfortable, when three twenty-somethings took a pew a few rows in front of me. Target spotted. Once mass ended, I made a beeline for them and was delighted to find that their English was excellent. One had recently graduated as a lawyer, another was an economics student at the English-language Central European University in Budapest, founded by George Soros.

I asked them about the town history, eager to pick up where Zsolt's English left off. They obliged. Sometime before the end of Ottoman rule in 1699, the original town was destroyed. An eighteenth-century effort to repopulate brought in not just Hungarians but Germans and . . . Slovaks! (Mystery 1, check.)

They gave me a restaurant recommendation for that night, a spot on the edge of town, Tópart Vendéglő, that I could never have found myself. And they suggested I take a bus to some famed thermal baths in a nearby town.

Eventually, I told them about my visit to the *szeszfőzde* and asked where I could buy *pálinka*. Balázs, the economics student, said the place to get good *pálinka* was actually his godfather's house. "You know," he said, "I am thinking we should go knock on his door and see if he has some to try."

Funny, I was thinking the same thing. There is no better travel moment than being invited to someone's home in a strange, faraway land. So we went and knocked on the door. After a lengthy delay, Zsuzsi, his godmother, answered, frumpily dressed in furry slippers and seemingly exhausted despite the early evening hour.

Balázs translated. "She asks you to pardon her appearance," he said. "She was at a pig-killing early this morning."

I asked Balázs whether there were normally multiple pig-killings on Saturdays. He asked Zsuzsi. "She says this was one with some doctors from Budapest."

It had occurred on a farm outside of town, which made sense, and meant my search had been futile. (Mystery 2, solved.) But I did score an invitation to come back the next day to buy some *pálinka* from István, Balázs' godfather.

I said good-bye to everyone, walked to the restaurant, and ordered the house special pork croquettes and a soup. The meal was nothing to write home about, much less mention in a book—let's just say it was heavy and Hungarian and the noodles in the soup strongly resembled maggots. But the waitress, who was chattily stretching her English to the absolute limit, mentioned that the place was also an inn, with three bedrooms upstairs. She insisted I see them, for they were special; each was decorated in the style of one of the ethnic groups that founded the town: Hungarian, German, and Slovak. She also told me that the statue I had seen downtown, the three huddled girls, represented the unification of the three groups.

It had been an extraordinary day: a predawn arrival, a mysterious tourism sign, a scrap-metal heap, a missed pig slaughter, a distillery tour, a burger with a new friend, a museum all to myself—and all before noon. Then Catholic mass, a history lesson, an invitation to buy *pálinka*, a traditional dinner with maggot pasta, and a trinational bedroom tour.

* * * *

The next day, I set off to the famous bathhouse my new friends had recommended—which was pleasant enough, though the highlight was successfully navigating the two-leg intercity route via the Hungarian public bus system.

Afterward, I was really looking forward to my visit with István for my first mule-kicking slug of *pálinka*, but it was still bugging me that the *szeszfözde* staff wouldn't sell to me.

This time, the family was more prepared for visitors. István sat me down with some appetizers and then brought out his wares, in plastic bottles with felt-marker drawings indicating the fruit each spirit was made from—plum, grape, pear. But we were unable to converse at all. Zsuzsi, no longer in furry slippers, tried to communicate with me in German. Surprisingly, my viewing of World War II movies had equipped me to understand that their son was coming over, and that he spoke English.

The son, István Jr. ("István Small," his dad explained, with a brief and adorable stab at English), arrived with his wife and their five-year-old, who wore a powder-blue scarf with "Hello Kitty"—or at least a member of the same litter—on it. Meeting cute local kids is vital to the success of every trip. I tried on her scarf, which she found funny, though not nearly as entertaining as her discovery that she could speak to me in Hungarian and I could not understand her. I must have been the first foreigner she had ever met.

Not so István Small. He had lived for a year in Georgetown, South Carolina, making him an able translator. The conversation suddenly got quite sophisticated—Zsuzsi was a retired school-teacher and wanted to know about the American education system; she had heard that high school students in the United States could skip certain subjects if they wanted, and she was appalled to hear I had skipped physics to take Introductory Spanish. I asked them about life in the Soviet era, and they recalled getting their news from the Voice of America.

Then I asked to see where István distills his *pálinka*, assuming he was hiding a small moonshine-style still in a shed out back. "Oh, he doesn't make it himself," said the son. He explained that István ferments fruit juice in barrels and then takes it to a *szeszfőzde*, which finishes the job. And yes, it was *that szeszfőzde*. The workers wouldn't sell me *pálinka*, it turns out, because it was not their *pálinka* to sell.

The family invited me to a pig-killing the next day, but I was due back in Budapest for my flight home. It turned out a weekend was not quite enough time to see Mezőberény.

It's not everyone's thing to get off a train in a random Hungarian town and poke around for a few days. One person's adventurous weekend is another's forty-eight hours alone and confused in Hungarian Hicksville, sitting through an incomprehensible mass and hopping a public bus to a thermal bathhouse. What if I hadn't happened to stop by the museum during the only two weekly hours it was open? What if there had been no hotel?

You might even wonder what I found so appealing about a grungy local distillery. If I were so into spirits, why didn't I take the Buda-bike Lake Velence Wellness Tour, which stops off at a *pálinka* distillery, includes a free tasting, and is conducted in English?

Even more guaranteed would be a distillery tour back home. A press release I received a few years back from Sugarlands Distilling Company in Gatlinburg, Tennessee, made a double-first-on-TripAdvisor claim: It "leads all U.S. distilleries in five-star reviews," with 2,831, and was "currently ranked as the No. 1 Thing to Do" in town. (Sorry, Ripley's Aquarium of the Smokies.) You can even try all fourteen flavors of their moonshine, such as "Blueberry Muffin" and "Maple Bacon," just as they did during Prohibition.

Fourteen flavors is fourteen more than I tried at the *szeszfőzde*. Could 2,831 five-star reviewers be wrong? Not only is the *szeszfőzde* not the No. 1 "Thing to do" in Mezőberény, it is not even one of the thirty-nine points of interest on the Hungarian-German-Slovak map at the town train station. And though you're practically guaranteed a pleasant, seamless experience at Sugarlands, I can absolutely not guarantee that you'll be invited into any old *szeszfőzde* you come across in small-town Hungary.

But, of course, that's not the point. I wasn't even looking for a distillery; it was something that just happened on the way to not finding a pig-killing. Well, I made it happen. By forcing myself for the thousandth time to wander unknown streets, to tolerate uncomfortable moments, to thrive on unprocessed experiences and unvarnished attractions.

Admittedly, Hungary was not the first country where I had sought out a TripAdvisor-free town to visit. I had taken similar detours in Mexico, where I spoke the language, and Turkey, where hospitality levels are culturally off the charts, and both had gone great. Mezőberény was an uber-test of my discovery-based travel philosophy, a choice most travelers would not entertain, given their paltry vacation time, limited budget, and yen to see London or Rome or Yosemite National Park or the Great Wall of China.

That's perfectly reasonable. But even a tiny push toward spontaneity and discovery can improve just about any trip. Even to destinations where the scales are tipped toward footstep-following and prechewed adventure. Still, every tiny push is tough. Even for me, even closer to home, even where I speak the language and know which restroom to use.

✳ ✳ ✳ ✳

In 2013, I decided to rotate the classic coast-to-coast American road trip ninety degrees and drive from Baton Rouge, Louisiana, to Fargo, North Dakota. The idea was to linger in the states that most cross-country road-trippers sped through.

By one late afternoon in Kansas, I was behind schedule, worried about ticking off the long list of attractions and historic towns on my way to the bison herds of the Flint Hills, when I noticed a sign on the side of US 75: "Livestock Auction 6 p.m."

My thought process went something like this:

1. Hmm, never been to a livestock auction before.
2. No, I've got too much ground to cover, and the hotel room I reserved is still hours away.
3. I'll miss some great stuff tomorrow and my whole trip will be delayed and maybe I'll miss the bison and this article will stink.
4. It's probably a boring event anyway.

(By this time I have driven one mile past it.)

5. But, on the other hand, random stops have often worked before! I should be adventurous!
6. Or should I? Will I dare talk to anyone? I'm a middle-aged, strangely dressed New Yorker. I don't fit in there.
7. OH MY GOD I WILL BE SO UNCOMFORTABLE AND THEN I'LL REGRET WASTING MY TIME THERE AND THE TIME I LOST WILL MEAN I'LL HAVE LESS TIME TO SEE BISON WHICH COULD BE A LIFE-ALTERING EXPERIENCE!

(Two miles past it.)

8. But wait. The worst that could happen is I would be delayed half an hour. It's boring, I leave. Why am I being such a loser?

(I turn around, head back, park my car and nervously walk in the entrance.)

9. Oh, no, everyone is looking at me. I'm such an outsider.
10. What should I say to meet people? How about "I'm not from here, can I ask you why those kids are parading cows around the ring?"

After several false starts, I finally managed to approach someone. He was friendly and curious about what I was doing there. Others joined us, and I became a sideshow as the good people of Coffey County explained the cow parade. It was a highlight of their county fair, a "premium auction" in which bidders did not actually buy the animals but essentially donated a cash prize to the young participants, 4-H members ages seven to eighteen, who had raised them. The kids marched the steers and heifers (don't call them "cows," city boy) around a ring to the mesmerizing slur of an auctioneer's call.

I stayed only an hour or so, but it was so fascinating that days later I would divert from my route again to attend two county fairs in Minnesota, and then devote a column and a video to them. It has since become a staple of my travel advice that county fairs are one of the greatest travel destinations in the United States for anyone from a big city—or, even better, another country. When foreigners ask for advice for a summer trip to the United States, I always tell them there is nothing more American than a county fair.

*   *   *   *

Of course there have been trips where following my adventurous instinct turned out to be a cockamamie move that ruined the day or even my whole trip. For example . . . OK, so there was the time . . . wait, I can't even remember a single time. That's not because it always works out great, but because if it doesn't, what have you lost? An hour? A day? At worst, a weekend? And most of the time, it does work out, because the world is an interesting place and people are generally nice and even something half-good becomes great when you discover it yourself. And something half-bad can turn into a story you can tell for years to come.

When I urge you to "rediscover travel" in the coming chapters, it may sometimes sound like I'm nostalgic for a pre-smartphone, pre-TripAdvisor, pre–baggage fee world. But this is not an anti–travel industry or anti-technology screed. So many advances have been essential to and have greatly facilitated our ability to travel the world, and I'll get into them all. The explosive growth of airlines and sinking cost of fares over the last half-century have given expo-nentially more people the chance to travel, albeit uncomfortably. Technology used right is as much of a boon to travel as technology used wrong is its bane. Companies harnessing the sharing economy have brought travelers closer to the places they visit by helping them stay in real people's homes, connecting them to local events, and finding them independent tour guides. Sustainable travel initiatives have helped stem the impact of the travel hordes on our fragile envi-ronment and often even more fragile local cultures. And innovative tour operators have allowed us to see far more of the world than would have been possible, or safe, in the past.

Still, no matter how many well-meaning cogs there are in the international travel machine, the more you can replace them with the billions of normal people just living their lives out there, the better. They are the unwitting tour guides to our best travel experiences.

Nuveram's pistachio orchards in İntepe, Turkey.

Chapter 2
· · · · · · · · · · · ·

ORGANIC EXPERIENCES

I usually allotted four days of travel to a column; sometimes, when things went right, I gathered plenty of material with a day to spare. That happened in July 2011, in the city of Gaziantep, Turkey—just thirty miles from the Syrian border that has since become embroiled in a refugee crisis. Back then, however, the city was simply the under-the-tourist-radar center of Turkey's pistachio industry.

For someone with a sweet tooth the size of a *T. rex* incisor (i.e. me), this can best be understood by its residents' formidable per-capita consumption of honey-drenched, pistachio-studded baklava. After three days there, I had gorged on the stuff. But I also scored a tour of the Pistachio Research Institute by posing as a traveler fascinated by pistachios and even managed to make a few people laugh with my inside knowledge that the Turkish word for pistachio, *fıstık*, was slang for an attractive woman.

With a free day before my flight from Gaziantep to Istanbul, I decided to rent a car and drive ninety miles east to the city of Şanlıurfa, home to famous bazaars and thought to be the birthplace of the biblical Abraham. When I realized that much of the highway bisected pistachio groves, I felt the same nagging curiosity as when I pass a cluster of Bangladeshi immigrant businesses in Queens or a small village on the Rhine or a farmhouse along an Iowa highway. Who's there? What are their lives like? If I stopped in right now, what would I discover?

Usually, I keep on driving. Not only do I often need to be somewhere, but what would I say to these people anyhow? Even after years of finding myself in unfamiliar situations, my instinct is to avoid chatting up strangers.

But this time, suppressing self-doubt, I turned onto a dirt road that led, according to a sign, to three towns: Bağlıca, Güzelköy, and İntepe. An effectively drawn symbol warned the route would be bumpy.

I was suddenly in a different world, jolting past orderly rows of bushy green pistachio trees rooted in soil that crumbled in the piercingly dry heat. Bağlıca came first—and I wish I could say it was a picturesque village where gray-haired men drank tea in an Ottoman-era café in the shadow of an intricate seventeenth-century mosque. Instead, Bağlıca was one of those drab villages that perpetually disappoint those novice travelers whose romantic notions of poverty come with thatched roofs or carved sandstone or artisanal brick rather than cement block. Not a single human appeared, just agricultural equipment rusting alongside the road. There was not even a store where I might strike up a chat with the owner.

Despite its name ("Beautiful Village"), Güzelköy was equally unattractive, but at least there I encountered a live person emerging from a house. Spotting some turkeys (always fun to see in Turkey) pecking about, I got out of the car to take some photos. The man gave me a suspicious look and wrote down the number of my license plate as though I were a spy. Which, in a sense, I was. Good-bye, Güzelköy.

My luck changed at İntepe, which was slightly bigger (about five hundred inhabitants, I would learn later) and a bit less ugly (but not much). This time, I got out of the car to take a picture of some wandering geese, really just an excuse to see if anyone would talk to a total stranger taking pictures of geese. A man approached.

"Hello," I said, then broke out my sparse Turkish vocabulary: "English, no Turkish, tourist."

He was more interested in me than in my license plate, and thus began one of those improvisational sign-language conversations that are somehow decipherable, though it mainly consisted of pointing to my map and overenunciating the words *camera* and *tourist*.

Here's the translation into spoken conversation:

NUVERAM: My name is Nuveram. What are you doing here
in İntepe?

ME: I am a tourist named Seth. I was going to Şanlıurfa, saw
this town on a map, and decided to come to take photos of
fıstık.

NUVERAM: Are you hungry? Come to my house to eat.

ME: Nuveram, what a generous surprise!?

(I acted surprised, but I'd been angling for just such an invitation.)

İntepe had the same cement-block feel as Bağlıca, but Nuveram's
property was an antidote to the drabness. He led me through a carefully tended garden, past pomegranate trees and a hammock, and
into a living room without furniture: Rugs covered the floor, scarlet
cushions inlaid with intricate patterns lined the walls.

And I felt what many first-time visitors to New York City
report when they catch a glimpse of Fifth Avenue or stroll through
Central Park: I had stepped into a movie set. Of course, you don't
need an invitation to gain access to New York—Manhattan is a
22.8-square-mile film set. That's a good thing, because I doubt
that if you see Robert De Niro on a Tribeca street, a few words
of halting English and a few gestures will get you invited over.
(Though it's worth a try.)

So the feeling of stepping into the Danaoğlu family home—heck,
walking by his pomegranate trees—was every bit as thrilling to me
as taking in Niagara Falls or Notre-Dame de Paris. What was lost in
grandeur was made up for by admission into the family sanctuary of
someone with such a vastly different life experience. I was in a place
I couldn't have imagined that morning, or even one second before I
entered the property.

It used to be that entering "regular" people's homes depended on
the luck of bumping into generous souls like Nuveram. But these
days, many tour operators and hospitality services offer processed
versions of such experiences. That's not always bad—I've stayed in

Airbnbs around the world and entered homes from Swaziland to Rio de Janeiro on organized tours.

But it's not the same, for two reasons. First, because I had "discovered" the house. Second, because Nuveram didn't know I was coming, hadn't been paid, and didn't even have time to alert his wife or family. This is his house as it always was. And, presumably, my arrival was as much a novelty to his family as their home was to me.

It was, in other words, an organic travel experience. These days, we mostly associate the term *organic* with food. But to me, a shift toward discovery-based travel would have an obvious parallel with the organic food movement. Both push us away from consumption of processed products provided by an industry that does not always have the best interests of the customer at heart.

The organic food movement is, in part, an effort to go back to the time before hormones and pesticides and GMOs and factory farms and corn syrup and food processing plants. In many ways, organic food is what we used to just call *food*. But now, we go out of our way, often at great expense, to eat the way we used to.

Travel is not so different. A few years ago, it wasn't unusual to spend a morning wandering about a foreign town with no smartphone to tell you what to do, no service to create "authentic" experiences for you, and no particular goal in mind except to let discoveries happen. Today, we take fewer risks, often shying away from unsupervised adventure.

The parallel isn't perfect: Traveling organically doesn't cost more money—in fact, it costs less. But it does cost planning time and, even harder, requires courage. Then again, eating organically takes courage, too: You have to give up regular Doritos.

Doritos are terrible for me, but I love them. Why? Because some food engineer found just the right combination of salt, oil, cheese, and chemicals to sprinkle on a tortilla chip so that when I put one on my tongue my brain lights up with pleasure.

Organic food is often more expensive, harder to find, not nearly as shiny and beautiful, and occasionally much less delicious, but it's better for you in the long run. And a century of technological and culinary advances has made healthy eating far more enjoyable—few if any Americans were downing quinoa with coconut water in 1990, let alone in the nineteenth century, and knowledge of nutrition has advanced, even if some pay it little heed. Farmers of the nineteenth century wouldn't recognize today's farm-to-table organic meal as their food any more than the Chinese recognize the sesame chicken lunch special with pork fried rice down the block from my apartment as their native cuisine.

The travel industry, too, has developed cheaper, mass-produced products to be as tempting as possible to consumers, sometimes disregarding what is good for them. That has allowed more people to travel—just as more can afford mass-produced snack foods. And just as I still eat Doritos, I'm sure I'd also like the comfort of a bus tour that picks me up at my hotel at 9 a.m. and is led by a charismatic, knowledgeable guide who has processed the city into digestible chunks, with a dash of travel MSG. It's easy, it's delicious.

There's nothing wrong with a city tour once in a while, but it's bad for you in excess. Unlike Doritos, it will have no detrimental effects upon your health. Instead, it will just mean you missed a potentially better experience.

Many travel companies now realize they've gone too far to homogenize experiences and have set out to reverse-engineer spontaneity and fun that should come organically. Some large hotel operators even delve into their guests' social media accounts to create such "delight"—which became a travel-industry buzzword a few years ago. Here's some advice for the hospitality industry from an article on the site sproutsocial.com. It is quoting a Hyatt Hotels Corporation "social strategy and activation specialist": "Pay attention . . . for details that might explain why your guests are staying with you or opportunities to make someone's stay special." The specialist then describes what happened when staff at one Hyatt noticed that a guest had posted a sonogram from his wife's recent doctor's visit: They scrambled to put together a package of "various beers, bacon and other snacks with a handwritten note to congratulate the 'father-to-be.' "[1]

Here's how I see that playing out.

"Hey, Jim, how was your trip?"
"Great! I was missing my wife something fierce, but then my
hotel spied on my social media accounts and sent me some
bacon! It was like I was back with my family!"

Nothing wrong with food corporations or start-ups or ministries
of tourism or tour operators offering consumers what they want—but
also nothing wrong with consumers rejecting those offers. And even
if cooking at home is a luxury you don't have the time for, a vacation
may be the only time of your life when you have complete control over
every hour of your day to plan—or not plan—as you wish.

Traveling organically is certainly more challenging. My
communication with Nuveram and his family would have been far
easier with a guide to interpret, for example. But though conversations without one can be strained and less substantive, they have
their own appeal. Even the most minor mutual understanding can
bring smiles, and conversation always leads to efforts to find shared
humanity, rather than conflict.

So the two of us spoke about Turkish food (in that I listed the
dishes I had tasted—and rubbed my stomach to indicate I had loved
them). Other members of the family trickled in: his veiled, traditionally dressed wife Perihan, and then their adult children and grandchildren in Western clothing. It turned out to be school vacation,
and the extended family was in from the city.

Then came the food: a heaping plate of Turkish rice, grilled
chicken, wafer-thin bread, tomato and cucumber salad, two plates
of spicy green peppers, and no silverware. I realized it was all for
me, and I tried with hand signals to gather everyone together to eat
with me. No luck.

And thus the show began. Live, from İntepe: Foreigner Eats Turkish Food. Will he like it? Will he finish it? Of course, he won't. I
complimented Perihan profusely for her cooking wiles and gave the

international hand signal that guests seeking mercy from excessive generosity have long employed: If I eat all this, I will become fat! They all laughed, because when someone who doesn't speak your language makes even the worst joke, you must laugh. (It's in the UN Charter.)

Hand signals can only go on for so long, so the kids fetched their English-class notebooks.

First came the same conversation travelers from English-speaking countries have with eager beginning English students around the world:

YOU: "Hello."
KIDS: "Hello. How are you?"
YOU: "Fine, thank you. How are you?"
KIDS: "Fine, thank you. How are you?"

Cracks me up every time. Then they continued—"What is your name?" "Where are you from?" "How old are you?"—until the vocabulary well ran dry.

So we moved on to an area of international interest that does not require speaking the same language: soccer stars. They gave some names (Messi, Cristiano Ronaldo) and I gave my opinion (an uninformed thumbs-up). I was impressed they had heard of American forward Landon Donovan, though this was only a year after the 2010 World Cup in which he had scored three goals.

Then I showed them the photos I had taken in Gaziantep. (Digital photography is a great advance for telling people who don't speak your language about your trip.) Impressed with my camera skills—OK, probably just with my camera—they brought in a set of great-grandparents, 172 years evenly split between them, to be photographed.

One boy could say just two things in English: "perfect" and "I love you." But he stretched their usefulness impressively.

"İntepe, perfect?" he asked me.
"Evet, evet," I replied ("yes" in Turkish).
Then: "Turkey, I love you?"

Again: "Evet, evet!"

And: "America, I love you. Seth, I love you."

I'm welling up now just thinking about it. Not because it was an intercultural Kumbaya moment that portended world peace, but because it was a clever linguistic effort by a smart kid using his limited tools to get a point across. And I'll bet it was thrilling for him to make himself understood in a language he hears only in school and, perhaps, on YouTube.

The inflow of grandchildren and cousins continued as the afternoon went on, and among them virtually every minute of the visit was captured on cellphone video.

Eventually I was led to the house next door, home base for the musical side of the family. One of Nuveram and Perihan's sons broke out a stringed *bağlama* and sang. And then the kids took me on a tour of the town and neighboring orchards. Our exploration ended only when we reached a ridge and they stopped me. We could not go on, for there were snakes beyond. ("There are snakes beyond," by the way, is a very easy concept to get across even with no shared language.)

As I finally left around dusk, I got big hugs, kisses on the cheeks, and "I love yous" from the boys. From the girls, handshakes.

I had skipped out on Şanlıurfa—undoubtedly a marvelous city that I hope to visit someday—but had no regrets. Instead, I was thinking about how clearly I would remember the experience and almost certainly recount it to many people for years to come. I was sure Nuveram, Perihan, their children and grandchildren would remember the experience just as vividly, and tell many people about the tourist who wandered into their little dot on the map and spent the afternoon.

✳   ✳   ✳   ✳

When we take an organized tour that includes a visit to someone's home, or stay with a family on a homestay, or rent a room through Airbnb, we have come into contact with card-carrying members of the tourism industry who have, to a greater or lesser extent, packaged the world in the way they think we want to see it. The homes may be real, but the activities are transactions—the sellers are exposing their lives for money, like some sort of cultural stripper.

My visit to Nuveram's family house, on the other hand, had to be the event of the month, or year, even. For all of us.

And it proves that organic, discovery-based travel does not require heading to an unknown town for an entire weekend, though I'm apparently not against it. I risked at most an hour by turning off a highway down a dirt road lined with pistachio groves. But even if that seems, ahem, nuts, there are simpler ways.

✳ ✳ ✳ ✳

Let's take food—such a basic element of travel for so many of us. It can be tempting to plan out all meals in advance with a list of restaurants compiled from articles and rankings and (sigh) Anthony Bourdain episodes and narrowed down by user reviews and availability of reservations. You all but guarantee a steady flow of predictably above-par meals.

But read enough raves about any particular restaurant and you're much more likely to be disappointed if the meal was just "very good." You were expecting to bite into a lamb shank and see God.

Instead, consider the opposite strategy: You arrive in your destination with no list at all, ask fellow travelers and locals for advice, browse the menus posted in restaurant windows or simply peer through those windows to see whether a place looks fun.

Some meals would be duds. But the successes would be all the better for having come across them on your own. I'd argue that the very same dish tastes better if you have no idea what to expect. Sky-high expectations can make even a fine dinner disappoint, whereas an utter lack of expectations makes the same dishes a sublime surprise.

It's amazing how picky we can become when our standards are influenced by the praise of others. Imagine reading about an Amalfi coast restaurant where the celebrated chef frequently brings out the house-made limoncello and pulls up a chair to share a digestif with customers. You go and have a lovely meal, but that night the chef has to duck out early. What a disappointment! Or the chef appears with limoncello but sits down at another table. What a semi-disappointment!

Now, say you stumbled across this place, or you happened to meet one of the waiters at a bar the night before, or the owner of your *pensione* recommended it and called in your reservation. You have an unexpectedly incredible meal, and when the chef never comes out with the limoncello, you don't know the difference. And if the chef sits with you, well, then your trip is made.

There are lots of ways to detect the quality of a place without numbing your mind and your palate with online reviews.

There's a scene in the Netflix series *Master of None* where the main character, Dev, goes to Nashville on a date with newly single Rachel.

DEV: Want to get something to eat?

RACHEL: Sure, what about the place across the street?

DEV: Yeah, should I look it up on Yelp to see if it's any good?

RACHEL: Well, I mean, a large man is walking in there right now and he seems superexcited.

DEV: Yeah, I guess that kind of is like old-school Yelp, right?

In fact, it's the opposite of old-school Yelp. They have no idea what is going to happen when they go in (love the white barbecue sauce, it turns out) and are just going on their own instincts, not the (sometimes fake) evaluation of people they don't know, and who sometimes have a bone to pick.

A deep dive into the endless opinions available about a restaurant is a bit like reading multiple movie reviews before seeing a film—except that on your trip, you are the main character and have just created a real-life spoiler.

It's time we leave a bit more of our vacation to chance, take a few extra risks, welcome a bit of unease. In other words, escape the false premise of the modern travel industry: that travelers can experience exotic new lands with all the comforts of home because aside from a carefully monitored IV drip of novelty and exoticism, everything will be conveniently packaged, familiar, and controlled. In other words, exactly like the real world isn't.

* * * *

What was it like to live in a time when traveling meant arriving somewhere with next to no idea what you'd find?

You hardly need to go back to Columbus, although I'll come back to him later. Pick up any travel book written more than a century ago. At age twenty-one, Samuel Clemens found his way onto a steamship headed down the Ohio River and on to New Orleans, attempting to find his way to the Amazon. "I was a traveler!" he wrote (as Mark Twain) in an 1875 edition of the *Atlantic Monthly*. "A word had never tasted so good in my mouth before. I had an exultant sense of being bound for mysterious lands and distant climes which I have never felt in so uplifting a degree since."

Not long before that trip, Clemens had been a small-town kid whose connections with the outside world were the US Post Office Department, the books that lay past the pillared entrance of the Hannibal, Missouri, public library, and the steamships that plied the Mississippi. These days, "mysterious lands and distant climes" sounds more like a line from *Game of Thrones* than a description of modern travel, considering I can go onto Google Street View and tell you how many parking spaces there are in front of the municipal pool in Ulaanbaatar, Mongolia.

Places that are mysterious and distant these days—Somalia, say, or Taliban-controlled stretches of Afghanistan—are the exception. Not so much Siem Reap, Cambodia, where a few taps on my phone in New York on the autumn day I'm writing this reveal the temperature is eighty-two and falling, down from a high of ninety-three. (Humidity is 46 percent and winds are ten miles an hour out of the northeast. Sounds like a lovely breeze.)

There are things you can't know for sure about Siem Reap, now a budget traveler's paradise near the temples of Angkor. For example, how far is Bliss Villa, one of more than a hundred properties listed on hostelworld.com, from the backpacker main drag called Pub Street? Is it three minutes, as an Australian female (age range eighteen to twenty-four) would have it? Or five, as a British male (age range twenty-five to thirty) contends? Once you resolve that cliffhanger, perhaps you're wondering whether the Miss Wong Cocktail Bar is right for you? Lisa B, one of a thousand-plus TripAdvisor reviewers to chime in on the issue, says maybe so, if you enjoy a Sipsmith sloe gin. But not if you're a stickler for the moistness of barbecue duck pancakes, "which, unfortunately, were a bit dry."

Not that surprises aren't in store even in the most touristed Southeast Asian towns. Perhaps the chef was having an off night during Lisa B's visit, and a visit today would reveal the pancakes quite moist.

Modern-day coders are not at fault. Thanks to human nature, past visitors have been dulling our travel experiences since long before Lisa B went to Cambodia. "Language is a treacherous thing, a most unsure vehicle, and it can seldom arrange descriptive words in a way that they will not inflate the facts," wrote Mark Twain in *Following the Equator*, which recounts his 1895 tour of the British Empire.

He was speaking about his experience at the Taj Mahal:

> I had read a great deal too much about it. I saw it in the day-time, I saw it in the moonlight, I saw it near at hand, I saw it from a distance; and I knew all the time, that of its kind it was *the* wonder of the world, with no competitor now and no possible future competitor; and yet, it was not *my* Taj. *My* Taj had been built by excitable literary people; it was solidly lodged in my head, and I could not blast it out.[2]

In other words, he had read too much about it in TripAdvisor's nineteenth-century predecessor: books. Compare that to his experience at the mosques and tombs in Agra and Delhi on the same visit.

> By good fortune I had not read much about them, and therefore was able to get a natural and rational focus upon them, with the result that they thrilled, blessed, and exalted me. But if I had previously overheated my imagination by drinking too

much pestilential literary hot Scotch, I should have suffered disappointment and sorrow.[3]

Today, we have far more available to us than Twain did. Add to books and magazines user reviews, blogs, and sponsored content and it's too easy to feel a tinge of disappointment if something is merely awesome and not as life-changing as billed, be it Niagara Falls or a pizza slice.

This is not to say you shouldn't go to Siem Reap or the Taj Mahal, or pose with a stone-faced member of the Queen's Guard in London.

Or fight past crowds to get to the *Mona Lisa*. Just don't do it because you want to check it off a list or post a selfie on social media. Do it because you're a huge da Vinci fan, or study facial expressions for a living, or did a report on it in fifth grade.

The Louvre once determined that 80 percent of its seven million annual visitors come principally to see the *Mona Lisa*. Why? Because its artistic quality so outshines the thirty-eight thousand other pieces on display? Because a passion for Renaissance art is embedded in their DNA? Not a chance—and it's highly unlikely 5.6 million people all got the same elementary school assignment.

It's because it's famous. And, as a result, it's bound to disappoint most who see it, much as the Taj Mahal disappointed Mark Twain. They've simply heard or read too many raves. (Darkened by varnish and cracked with age, it would probably disappoint da Vinci himself.)

How do famous attractions become famous anyway? The Taj Mahal's fame was probably unavoidable, given its scale and grandeur. Not so the *Mona Lisa*.

La Gioconda, as the painting was originally known, was well regarded by aficionados by the time Twain passed through Paris on the world tour that produced his most famous travel work, *The Innocents Abroad*. But it was no Taj Mahal. Twain swung through the Louvre without mentioning it. Forty years later, in 1907, it garnered but a two-sentence mention in the 470-page Baedeker guide to *Paris and its Environs*.

Mona's rise to Taj Mahal status began in 1911, when she caught her big break: She was stolen. Vincenzo Peruggia's heist made headlines worldwide, and voilà! Everyone had heard of her. SOME JUDGES REGARD THE PAINTING AS THE FINEST EXISTING, the *New York Times* instructed its readers in an extended headline. And thus it was imprinted in our great- and great-great-grandparents' brains as the greatest work of art in the world. They passed that status down to us, stripped of its origin story.

When I saw her back in my college days, I didn't know she had been stolen. Now that I know, I kind of want to see her again.

✳ ✳ ✳ ✳

Not everything can be a discovery. Some information, some details make travel better. Background reading is a notable example. Hype is not. Nor is blindly following guidebook recommendations at the expense of adventure. Guidebooks are great as supplements to discovery: What is this church we've come across? Look it up and see if it's famous! But they do not work as replacements for it. People have known this for more than a century—well, fictional Miss Bartlett from E. M. Forster's *Room with a View* did, at least.

In the classic novel, the clever British writer Eleanor Lavish chides Lucy for assiduously studying from a guidebook while on a family trip in Florence.

"Tut, tut! Miss Lucy!" says Miss Lavish. "I hope we shall soon emancipate you from Baedeker. He does but touch the surface of things. As to the true Italy—he does not even dream of it. The true Italy is only to be found by patient observation."[4]

She ends up seizing Lucy's guidebook and abandoning her in the Santa Croce basilica. Lucy tears up. How can she observe frescoes with no tome to explain their significance? And how will she find her way back to the *pensione*? But then "the pernicious charm of Italy worked on her, and, instead of acquiring information, she began to be happy."

Guidebooks have improved over the decades, helped along by men the likes of Eugene Fodor and by tire companies the likes of Michelin. But in 1957, a GI with a law degree from Yale published an entirely new kind of travel guide. The spare but cheery first edition of Arthur Frommer's *Europe on 5 Dollars a Day* was a hit, and soon hundreds of thousands of young Americans were packing it and subsequent editions alongside their Kodachrome film and American Express travelers checks, and lugging their nonrolling suitcases off to the Old World.[5]

It's hard to imagine in today's world of hipster hostels and sub-$500 transatlantic flights, but young Americans traveling Europe on a shoestring is a relatively modern phenomenon. Before World War II, most travelers to Europe went by boat on journeys that lasted months, and weren't cheap. But now a generation of postcard-writing, pre-hippie, proto-backpackers was hopping on and off trains across Europe, with Frommer's book as their Bible.

Mr. Frommer, however, was much more concise than God.

In his first edition, nine pages sum up London. Munich and Rome get eight; Venice, seven; Florence, Vienna, and Nice, five each. There's just one page on Madrid, the city where, he wrote, "the rocket tempo of the 20th century never reached." Paris is covered in twelve pages—not even one page per arrondissement!—including three spare maps that could have been drawn on a cocktail napkin.

Frommer's Paris advice is almost entirely focused on where to sleep and eat. In the entire section, he gives just two sightseeing tips, both budget-oriented: (1) "[Watch] the passing parade on the Champs-Elysées . . . the best form of entertainment in Paris," for the price of just one cup of coffee, because no French waiter will kick you out of a sidewalk café for lollygagging; (2) "Schedule your trip to the Louvre for a Saturday, when no admission is charged."[6]

It's not that Frommer didn't expect you to see the sights, he just figured you'd find them yourself. They appear only as cameos. Your dollar-a-night hotel has no shower? Try the twenty-cent municipal bathhouse that he notes is next to Notre Dame. (BYO soap.) Want "a very fine, yet inexpensive, restaurant"? That's Aux Cinq Pains d'Orge at 29 rue Surcouf, near the Eiffel Tower.

Although Frommer's guidebooks did expand in following years, they kept the same philosophy. "In the early days Frommer's edict was rather sensible," John Wilcock, who wrote for the company in the 1960s, once told me. "Don't waste time writing essays, we don't want silky prose. We want prices, what time the bus leaves, and that kind of stuff, and that was very sensible. It was all to the point that you couldn't really afford to give space over to fancy writing, you needed it for facts."

In 1957, Arthur Frommer found you a place to sleep and a cheap meal, told you which day to go to the Louvre, and abandoned you (poor thing), to the streets of Paris. In 2018, TripAdvisor lists more than 1,200 "Things to do" in Paris. The current No. 75, Père-Lachaise Cemetery, has more than 5,000 reviews, should you want to spend hours reading the opinions of people you don't know on whether you should visit a cemetery that was far beyond the scope of Frommer's guide and miles outside its cocktail-napkin maps.

As a result, generations raised on Choose Your Own Adventure books are now letting unscientific Top-10 lists, bloviating TripAdvisor reviews, TV stars, and blogger-marketers choose our adventures for us. Even those who boast of "winging it" often depend on apps to point the way, quite literally, in the case of Google Maps, to the next highly rated stop.

✳   ✳   ✳   ✳

TripAdvisor is not the problem. It can be an extraordinary—even revolutionary—tool, when used properly and sparingly. I'll get to that. The problem is the way travelers use it: dutifully following it around like a long-winded and frustratingly contradictory tour guide.

Nor are smartphones the problem. I admire travelers who leave theirs at home, but their ranks are thinning. The world doesn't work anymore without one, as proven by the near-total absence of pay phones and the usefulness of WhatsApp and other messaging apps abroad. (And translation apps may be the greatest gift to travelers since rolling suitcases.)

But we can recapture the spirit of those who depended on that 1957 edition of *Europe on 5 Dollars a Day*. Frommer provided the basics: Here's a reasonable budget, here's how you find the trains, here's a hand-drawn map of Rome, here's how you say, "That's too

expensive" in Greek, here are five Madrid hotels that are too expensive for you (all the rest are fine). Now get to it!

How would most travelers react today if they woke up pulling
into the Copenhagen train station with nothing but Arthur Frommer's two-page city summary to work from? Panic, I'd guess. But
much like Miss Lucy when she finds herself minus her Baedeker in
Santa Croce, they would wipe away their tears and go out and discover Denmark.

Again, by "discover" I do not mean being the first person somewhere, or even the first outsider. Discovery is not a fact, it's an experience. There's a place you didn't know existed, and then, suddenly,
you do. And you found it by taking the long route, peering around
corners, knocking on doors, talking to strangers on buses. And so
it's yours.

That doesn't mean you should hit the road with no plan whatsoever, though that can work if you're traveling alone or with like-
minded adventurers. It just means you dare to adjust your plans
when an intriguing possibility materializes, and make those plans
flexible in the first place. Jam-packed schedules in foreign places are
not just bad for discovery, they're nonsensical unless you thrive on
stress and failure.

Some things, of course, have to be planned. You're not going to
get to the crown of the Statue of Liberty, for instance, without a
reservation made months in advance. When I'm preparing for a trip,
I make a big list of everything I want to do in each city or region,
checking to see whether anything needs to be scheduled ahead of
time. But beyond that, I mostly wing it, sitting down each morning
to set a loose agenda I hope to abandon in pursuit of the unexpected.
I also try to leave a day open for exploring a lesser-known neighborhood or region. When I do, it's almost always the best day of the
trip, maybe because I can truly relax, without feeling any pressure
to love the Venus de Milo or Pike Place Market or whatever other
tourist attraction people come from far and wide to see.

A few years ago, I presented my travel philosophy to a group in
Manhattan. I had done my usual bit about avoiding processed experiences and valuing spontaneity, showing slides of what could hap-

pen: my lunch with an elderly Lebanese woman, the isolated beach I found at the end of an unmarked path in Albania, the jail-cell–like hotel room where I was forced to sleep when my Guatemalan bus driver decided to end the day's run in his hometown, not my destination. (Spontaneity is more delightful if you're the spontaneous one.)

Then came a comment from a middle-aged man who said he'd love to travel like me, "but I only have two weeks of vacation a year. I need nothing to go wrong."

I get it. But there is time for spontaneity in every trip, even a day trip. What matters is not how long your detour is, but that you're willing to detour at all. A young backpacker on a gap year might drop everything for a month; a couple traveling for a month might spare a few days; a family on a Disney cruise might skip a guided "Port Adventure" and have an adventurous afternoon in port.

And everyone can fit in microadventures—say, ordering a menu item you've never heard of. If you hate it, you still have a story to tell: Who knew lamb kidney with fried crickets would be disgusting? If you love it, you might learn later that everyone else in the world already knew what a Reuben sandwich was. Who cares? That day, *you* discovered it.

But if it is something unusual, even better. "Anything is potentially an attraction," wrote social theorist Dean MacCannell in his seminal 1976 book, *The Tourist: A New Theory of the Leisure Class*. "It simply awaits one person to take the trouble to point it out to another as something noteworthy, or worth seeing."

The middle-aged man who needed everything to be perfect was out of luck, anyway. Eliminating all traces of spontaneity won't do the trick, because no trip is ever perfect. Ever heard of rain? Flat tires? Lost luggage? Food poisoning? Unless you're taking a helicopter to a private jet to Disney World, travel takes place in the real world.

✳   ✳   ✳   ✳

It's not the same real world as it was in Arthur Frommer's time—the rocket tempo of the twentieth century may not have reached Madrid by 1957, but the homogenization of the twenty-first century sure has by 2018—at least if the fifty Starbucks locations that have opened there since 2002 are any indication.

You can avoid Starbucks, of course, but there are other ways globalization has affected travel that are difficult to avoid. I hadn't really thought about this until a trip to, of all places, the *Kunstkamera*, the museum in St. Petersburg most famous for Peter the Great's collection of deformed fetuses preserved in formaldehyde.

They are as abominably tantalizing as advertised. But I was far more struck by the halls that make up the "Collections on the Culture and Life of the Peoples of the World," with their life-size figures of Aleuts, Bedouins, Sumatrans, Samurai, and many other groups wearing what my twenty-first-century self processed as "historically accurate native costumes"—the kind you might see locals wearing at annual festivals or shows performed for tourists.

It wasn't the display itself, but rather the age of the collection, dating back to the nineteenth century. Somewhere between the Mapuche people of Chile and the Aleuts, it hit me that at the time the outfits were likely first displayed—and even well into the twentieth century—much of what I was seeing had not been festival attire, it was what people actually wore in daily life around the world.

This is still true in a handful of places—the riotously colorful woven shirts, pants, and wraparound skirts of the Kaqchikel Maya in Guatemala come to mind, as does standard dress in conservative Muslim places like Gaziantep. For the most part, though, the worldwide wardrobe uses the same building blocks. The world is still a fascinating place, but—sartorially, anyway—it is significantly less fascinating than it used to be. We have become a T-shirt planet. The same process has seen Doritos and Snickers follow Colgate toothpaste and Coca-Cola into corner shops in most of the world, and sprinkled Zaras and Starbucks throughout trendier neighborhoods from Mumbai to Buenos Aires.

Whether globalization is good or bad for human existence is up for debate, but there's no way it's good for travelers. In part, that's because our willpower weakens when we're on unfamiliar ground. We know we shouldn't eat a hamburger in Rome, yet after an exhausting day lost in the streets and bored in a museum, a sign that promises McDonald's, 5 minuti, and even has an arrow to point you in the right direction, can be very tempting. When you wake up jetlagged and bleary-eyed in a strange country where you don't speak a word of the language, it feels a lot safer to go to the Starbucks on the corner (or on the next one) rather than gamble on a tiny bakery. That little place might have become a morning ritual you'd remember for years—but no, you seem to have forgotten that even if no one speaks English, *coffee* (or *kofi* or *cafea* or *kavé*) is practically a universal word.

Clothing, food and drink, stores—entire communities—can feel eerily familiar no matter where in the world you are. I'm all for that at airports, where any way of reducing misery is welcome, even if it's a KFC at the Sultan Hasanuddin International Airport in Makassar, Indonesia, during a six-hour layover. (Tasty potatoes, by the way.) But elsewhere, more and more peculiarly wonderful places are suddenly less peculiar and less wonderful.

See if you recognize the newly cool neighborhood described in this paragraph from the old Surfacing column of the *New York Times* travel section:

BISTROS AND BOUTIQUES ADD LIFE
WHERE GRIT ONCE PREVAILED

_____ used to have a terrible reputation. After most factories shut down in the mid-1900s, it was left a gritty district of discount shops and greasy spoons. But as residents move to this side of the river to escape downtown's escalating rents and tourism, the area has become a blue-collar hybrid with yoga studios and bistros joining longtime establishments along the main drag. A wave of new art galleries, trendy boutiques and Brooklyn-style lofts stuffed with architects and social media types has followed, along with a remarkable influx of young creative types, restaurateurs and hoteliers. As a result, the

neighborhood has been reborn as a hip enclave better known for its indie culture and fine dining.[7]

Sound familiar? Your city probably has a neighborhood like this,
as does the city you plan to visit next summer. In fact, I cobbled
the paragraph together from multiple Surfacing columns. The headline is about the Detroit–Shoreway neighborhood in Cleveland; the
first sentence describes Praga, in Warsaw; the second is Saint-Henri,
Montreal. The third is West Asheville, North Carolina, and then it's
on to the Ninth Square in New Haven (with an added clause about
Karaköy in Istanbul). We finish up in Duxton Hill, Singapore.

These neighborhoods, which count Williamsburg, Brooklyn,
as at least indirect inspiration, have become tourist magnets, and
why not? Their contours are instantly recognizable, and within that
comfortable cocoon, chefs and artisans and vintage-shop owners
have added local inspiration. It's not that different from going to
McDonald's in Peru and being intrigued by the packets of spicy *aji
amarillo* sauce available alongside ketchup.

The *Times* column often read—for the format has now changed—
as a parody of itself, but you can hardly blame the writers. (Including me. My occasional contributions to the column included this
line about a nightspot named Astronete in São Paulo: a "straight-
out-of-Williamsburg bar run by a Brazilian couple who once lived
in Brooklyn.")

Other publications also give the people what they want. Guess
where a *Condé Nast Traveler* found such a transformation: San Juan,
Puerto Rico. What? Hipsters in San Juan? Can you believe it? (Yes.)

Here's the dramatic story:

A writer finds himself on a "deserted street in the industrial neighborhood of Santurce."[8] He must duck under a highway overpass to
get there. Oh, no! But it's all worth it, for guess what he finds?

"The buoyant sounds of music and laughter, transforming what
had seemed like a foreboding backstreet I'd mistakenly entered into
a place of mystery and possibility, of a good time about to be had."

The mystery slowly unravels: a salad that contains organic

greens from a farmers' market, a cocktail inspired by a tacky tropical drink but reinvented with a more sophisticated flair. What clientele could possibly inhabit such a place? Why, it's "a group of young and stylish strangers" who "soon felt like old friends." Nearby, housing projects had been converted into . . . wait for it . . . "condominiums for the moneyed residents who had discovered the neighborhood."

He visits another neighborhood in San Juan that shows signs of being the next new thing. It's Bushwick, er, I mean Villa Palmeras, which is "still plagued with poverty and violence." He orders a traditional Puerto Rican meal of fried steak and plantains, but wait! The owner takes him to the roof to show off the new organic garden he had installed over the previous year. "It's important to know where my food comes from," says the proud fellow.

In closing, the author reflects: "I could have been back in Brooklyn, with one notable exception: Less than a mile away I was able to find a nearly empty stretch of beach, where, in the shade of a palm tree, I happily passed out."

Now, do the restaurants sound good? They do. Has this writer done a good job on his assignment? He has. But what is it saying? That the ideal travel destination is somewhere rapidly transforming into what you are used to back home, but with a beach?

As I planned a trip to South Africa in 2014, I realized I would have about twenty-four hours between arrival in Johannesburg and my drive to Kruger National Park. Visiting an enormous city for the first time and staying just a day can be overwhelming, so I decided to find a specific place to focus on. What made the most sense was to go to the place that I had heard the most about—Soweto, the township where the anti-apartheid movement got its start in a 1976 uprising. The movement, which finally succeeded in ending the openly racist system in 1994, was probably the most constantly covered international news story of my childhood and twenties, outlasting even the Cold War. It seemed worth a day's visit.

Not everyone thought so. I sent my whole South Africa itinerary to a friend of a friend in Johannesburg. He thought it was great, except the Soweto part. Every journalist writes about Soweto and eats in Wandie's Place and visits the museum, he said, and it was getting dull. "We strongly suggest you reconsider and rather stay in Braamfontein or the newly revamped, up-and-coming Maboneng area . . . . [They] are still up and coming, urban renewal vibey spots (think Dumbo Brooklyn about 8–10 years ago)."

Braamfontein was a walkable neighborhood of hipster shops and restaurants, he added; Maboneng was full of art galleries and had the only independent cinema in town, and Sunday rooftop salsa.

In other words, I should fly fourteen hours from New York to Johannesburg to see a South African version of Brooklyn. If I timed it right, I could dance to a music genre created by Puerto Rican and Cuban musicians in Spanish Harlem. (See chapter 7 for how my trip to Soweto went.)

You don't even need the *Times* or a friend of a friend to find a place to sip a latte and peer out the window at cutting-edge street art whose creator can no longer live in the neighborhood. There's a crowdsourced app for that, subtly named "Where is Williamsburg?" It will find you Williamsburg-like neighborhoods anywhere from Yaoundé, Cameroon, to Christchurch, New Zealand, to Tehran.

Even places that have incredible attractions sometimes aren't recognized until the hipsters move in. I moved to Queens in 2006, attracted by the polyglot population and ridiculously cheap restaurants run by an amalgam of humanity. I liked the fact that, as Manhattan burst with new chain stores and Brooklyn with kale, Queens reminded me of how things were in the "old days" (which to me was the 1990s). So, after years of telling everyone how great Queens was, it was thrilling to hear that Lonely Planet had named Queens its No. 1 "best in the U.S." destination for 2015.

Then I read the article.

Queens, New York's largest borough, is also quickly becoming its hippest, but most travelers haven't clued in . . . yet. With microbreweries springing up, new boutique hotels, a reinvented seaside at Rockaway, a world-class art scene, and a truly global food culture, 2015 is the year to try Queens.[9]

Microbreweries, boutique hotels, a "reinvented seaside"—code for a hipsterized beach. Alas. At least they included the "truly global food culture," which in my neighborhood alone has Indians, Bangladeshis, Russians, Colombians, Peruvians, and Mexicans among others cooking in unpretentious locales that you know aren't pulling punches, since they have to please the toughest critics—their compatriots. There are more than a dozen Nepalese and Tibetan restaurants within two blocks of my subway stop. But now that Queens has microbreweries, it's finally worth a visit?

T-shirt planet has also given us certain terms that now pop up so much in travel promotion that their meanings have been diluted. Dubbing a hotel *boutique* used to signify a one-off high-end experience. Now it could be just about anything, even a chain—as long as it's not a Sheraton or Marriott or youth hostel and has at least one wall of exposed brick or a print by a local artist in each room.

Artisanal is another one. The word, which once meant "made in a traditional or nonmechanized way," has now become so meaningless that the McDonald's "artisan grilled chicken sandwich" is served on an "artisan roll." It's doubly artisanal!

The word has also popped up in places that you wouldn't expect. There's a fairly ordinary pizza place on the narrow pedestrian tourist street of La Ronda in Quito, Ecuador, which prominently calls itself "artisanal," just as a bakery called "The Bakery," in a small town in Panama, has a sign boasting its "artisanal bread." But really, what nonchain pizzeria or tiny local bakery would ever be nonartisanal?

Still, words matter less than substance. And when globalization brings big business and international chains to historic city centers, what's lost is immeasurable. On January 1, 2015, rent-control laws ended in Spain, resulting in the much-lamented closing of what Barcelona's *El Periódico* newspaper editorial called "the undeniable protagonists of the Catalonia capital's urban landscape."[10] It meant that shops like a toy store called El Palacio de Juguete, which had been in the same family since 1936 and had paid a thousand euros in rent, was replaced with a Geox, the Italian shoe brand, which paid around thirty-five thousand euros a month, according to a *New York Times* report. A study in 2016 found that 90 percent of the stores along the city's major arteries belonged to multinationals, chains, or franchises. "A tourist from Madrid, Paris or Sevilla won't buy products they can get in their own city," the editorial concluded.[11]

Perhaps residents of Madrid, Paris, or Sevilla have begun to go farther afield—to Lisbon. Someone is, because tourism in Lisbon has been booming, so the chains have hightailed it there as well. The cover story in the February 15–21, 2017, issue of *TimeOut Lisbon* was "30 Historic Shops of Lisbon You Have to Visit Before They Close." It's not just shops, of course. Apartment-rental services in cities around the world have turned what once were residential buildings into virtual hotels, leaving some neighborhoods feeling oddly like cultural amusement parks.

There are some good things about globalization. I admit to loading up on Zara T-shirts when I ran low on laundry in Lisbon. It can also be charming to try local restaurants that fancy themselves to be serving American food; on a family trip to Athens in the mid-1980s, a hamburger I ordered (surely to my parents' chagrin) turned out to be a literal "ham" burger, with egg. Similarly charming was the laundry truck that drove by me in tiny Alausí, Ecuador, equipped with an ice-cream-truck–style music system. I couldn't help but sing along with the words, to the bemusement of a woman selling me ice cream. "Oh, give me a home, where the buffalo roam. . . ." Globalization bloopers can be a blast.

✳ ✳ ✳ ✳

If you already value spontaneity and steer clear of every McDonald's and Williamsburg in the places you go, great. Now step it up a notch. Baseball players and concert violinists and chefs and surgeons can always improve. Why can't travelers?

I'm far from the traveler I want to be. After years of great adventures, I'm still apprehensive—always—when I see a chance to deviate from plans. Do I really dare talk to that stranger, or knock on that door, or turn down that dirt road, or go into that quirky restaurant, or accept that invitation? What if I'm thrust into an uncomfortable social situation? What if I miss out on a life-changing experience where I was originally headed?

So I've created a two-part rule for when opportunities arise.

1. If there are no safety risks involved, always do it.
2. If there is some perceived danger—say, entering a stranger's house or getting on a motorbike—double-check you're not conflating physical danger with social discomfort or fear of missing out on something else. If you are, see number one.

Still, I break these rules all the time. This book is full of adventures in odd places with eccentric personalities with whom I had the courage to strike up conversations. What I don't mention are the far more frequent times that I chickened out and went to a museum.

✳ ✳ ✳ ✳

Mary Kingsley, a nineteenth-century British traveler, was much more daring than both you and I—something I say with great confidence, even though I don't know who you are.

At age thirty-one, Ms. Kingsley had inherited some money from her father and found herself "in possession of five or six months which were not heavily forestalled."[12]

That's when she made her first of two solo trips to West Africa via steamship, despite a doctor's warning that it was "the deadliest spot on earth." She noted that the first line that appeared in a French phrasebook for use in Dahomey was "Help, I am drowning." Soon afterward came: "Why has this man not been buried?"

"Is the tip included?" apparently did not make it.

Kingsley was off to see a world that Europeans knew virtually nothing about, unless they happened to be missionaries or colonial officials. Everything she encountered was new and unexpected. She was overwhelmed by the offerings at the market in Freetown, Sierra Leone ("things one wants the pen of a Rabelais to catalogue," she wrote). She canoed among crocodiles in the mangroves ("a pleasure to be indulged in with caution"). She sought out villages of Bioko island's little-understood Bubi people, very literally off the beaten trail. ("For many a merry hour have I spent dodging up and down a path trying to make out at what particular point it was advisable to dive into the forest thicket to reach a village.")

That's where she leaves me in the dust. But we have one thing in common: the belief that overplanning travel was not just pointless but counterproductive. She ridiculed and largely dismissed the advice she sought from travelers who had been to West Africa before her: "I think many seemed to translate my request for practical hints and advice into an advertisement that 'Rubbish may be shot here,'" she wrote. Much of it, she complained, could be categorized as "dangers," "disagreeables," and "diseases," as well as "things you must take."

She gave no quarter to these doomsayers and overpackers, and upon arrival soon realized that most of what they said (and what she had read) was wrong or didn't apply to her: "One by one I took my old ideas derived from books and thoughts based on imperfect knowledge and weighed them against the real life around me, and found them either worthless or wanting."

Substitute "websites" for books and "user reviews" for imperfect knowledge and her words would hold up well today.

Kingsley's travels served for much more than adventure: She wrote books and did the lecture circuit back home, inserting barbed critiques of colonialism into her talks. Credit that to her tendency to dismiss what had been documented by other Europeans and to push forward into places she knew nothing about. My detour down the dirt road to İntepe was the extremely minor-league equivalent of her diving into the forest thicket to find a Bubi village—places that were unknown to us but that we deemed worth the risk. Of course, in my case the risk was missing out on a cool city, and for her it was her life. She would eventually die of typhoid while serving as a nurse in the Second Boer War in South Africa.

* * * *

We each have our own tolerance for adventure. That means that though we all could benefit from upping our discovery game and striving for organic travel experiences, we should each do it at our own pace. One low-grade option, for example, is simply to pledge to talk to at least five strangers a day.

For people willing to go a bit farther, try this. On your next trip—let's say it's two weeks—cook up a list of ten things you really want to do, culled from whatever sources you would normally use— guidebooks, articles, YouTube, TripAdvisor, seventh-grade French (*Allons aux Champs-Elysées!*). They can be as clichéd or as critically acclaimed as you want. Spend as much time seeing them as you want—no rush. The rest of the time—and there will be plenty more time—plan as you go, seeking advice from fellow travelers or pursuing whatever catches your eye. In whatever time is left over from that, just wander.

Travelers who strike out on their own, whether for a day or a week or an hour—or even for thirty seconds to stop someone and ask for a recommendation—begin to feel that they are participating in the life of a place rather than just observing it as they pass through. And that makes for a different kind of trip.

A red panda at the Chongquing Zoo.

. . . .

Chapter 3

WHY WE TRAVEL

At 5 a.m. on January 31, 2013, a Yangtze riverboat strewn with spit-out sunflower-seed shells deposited several hundred Chinese passengers and me at Chongqing, then a twenty-million-person megalopolis I had not heard of a month earlier. After meeting my Couchsurfing hosts—a magazine editor named Yang Yang, her mother, her grandmother, and her young daughter—and taking a nap, I bundled up and set out on my own for the city zoo, eager to see the giant pandas it was famous for.

They were OK. But the real highlight was seeing the distantly related red pandas. Ever seen one? I hadn't. They are fox-colored, raccoon-size, ring-tailed weasel cousins with Photoshopped panda faces. I promptly declared them the cutest creatures on earth.

The real lowlight was wiping my nose and having the tissue turn black. Ever done that? I hadn't. Moments earlier, I had thought my snot was freezing—but when the feeling crescendoed into a thousand microscopic thorns, I finally pulled out my tissue and wiped to see if I was bleeding. Chinese scientists had recently named Chongqing one of the ten most polluted cities on earth.

Yang Yang would take me to her favorite lookout spot that afternoon to show off the fast-growing skyline of her mammoth city—only to find it all but invisible through the soot.

✳ ✳ ✳ ✳

Almost four years later, I opened the *New York Times* at my breakfast table in Queens and spotted a story from India: TWO CHILDREN, ONE RICH, ONE POOR, GASPING FOR AIR IN DELHI'S SMOG.[1]

It was a story of suffering in a faraway place that I would typically have read a few lines of, thought, "How awful," and moved on to local news or the crossword. But this time, I had a flashback—to red pandas and a black tissue. The smog-choked cities of Asia had been utterly theoretical to me in the past, but now even my superficial experience was enough to spur me to keep reading, to make two families' struggles feel real, to empathize just a tiny bit more.

✳ ✳ ✳ ✳

People generally prefer to stay put.

Around ten thousand years ago, human beings started abandoning their nomadic hunting-and-gathering ways to settle into agrarian societies. For millennia thereafter, travelers left home to trade, wage war, or please their deities. But travel for the sake of travel was not even really a thing until the twentieth century. A few Ancient Greeks went to see Egypt; Romans with means would head to the coasts until their road system and economy faded with the empire. In the mid-1600s, moneyed Englishmen started taking what would be dubbed the Grand Tour of Europe, visiting the great cultural sites of Western civilization and hobnobbing with local aristocrats (as well as good amounts of what-happens-on-the-continent-stays-on-the-continent drinking, gambling, and what was then known as whoring). When Thomas Cook and others established the modern travel industry in the second half of the nineteenth century, a growing number of people from across social classes took to trains and steamships of their own volition, but it was still a tiny minority of humanity.

Even now that so many of us crave travel, our deep desire to stay put is also evident, as Netflix replaces movie theaters and Amazon Prime devastates local shopping malls. And even when we do travel, despite great advances in technology—stagecoaches and schooners to SUVs and Airbus A340s—we still complain bitterly. Removing our shoes for airport security is torture, even as we voluntarily kick off our shoes to put our feet up on the sofa.

So what explains why we are willing to prepare three-ounce bottles of every necessary liquid, leave our homes vulnerable to burglars and burst pipes, suffer jet lag and sunburn and sudden-onset diarrhea?

If we were all to brainstorm a list and put it on a dry-erase board, it might look like this:

To get away
To see the world
To bond with family
To help others
To relax and drink margaritas

I'm up for all of them, down to the margaritas—as long as we can exclude the syrupy, hangover-inducing kind served at all-inclusive resorts.

But it's not just those five. The way leisure travel developed over time is curious, and, like the history of everything else, influences us more than we realize.

It's not an innate human desire, like eating or sex or keeping warm in the winter—or having sex to keep warm in the winter when there's nothing to eat. It's not even an ancient construct evidenced across human societies, like art or cuisine or religion or sport or coming-of-age rituals. Instead, it's an almost entirely modern—largely but not entirely Western—concept that emerged only when the conditions were right.

Not to say people didn't previously make their way long distances, of course. But travel for its own sake was rare, and what motivated it easier to explain. Migration is older than our species and its motive is hard-wired: survival. Business travel was around long before the Silk Road, and its objective almost equally ancient: profit. War, imperialism, and exploration—or often some combination of the three—had obvious, if often dark, incentives. Taking the family to Yosemite or the girlfriend to Paris, however, is a human construct that had its start much more recently and unnaturally.

Unbeknownst to most (and certainly to me before I took up the travel column), scholars have been batting around questions about leisure travel for decades. Are humans naturally nesters or explorers? How are vacations associated with social status? Why do we take so many pictures on the road? When did we stop looking at the beach as the edge of an evil, child-swallowing, monster-inhabited ocean and start seeing it as a place to frolic, relax, and get a tan? Can a semester abroad make you a better person?

I will devote the rest of this chapter to some of the personal, societal, and historical reasons we travel—some of which we are conscious of, others of which we may not be, and not all of which are good.

But first, a definition: What counts as travel to the travel industry and what I'm counting as travel for this book are not precisely the same. Business trips don't count. Nor do trips to the beach or to your cabin in the woods if the principal purpose is to escape and rest. I fully support such outings—in fact, I could sure use a long weekend in the Bahamas right about now. But I'd call it something more akin to "remote relaxation."

On the other hand, many things that are not literally vacations count as travel here. Semesters and sabbaticals abroad are obviously travel. But even a mandatory visit to the in-laws, or a friend's wedding in the most ordinary of places (say, a suburban Marriott), can be injected with elements of travel.

In short, I am defining travel as "visiting places far from home primarily for the purposes of leisure." But leisure is too broad. Let's break it down. Why do we travel?

TO FIGURE OUT THE WORLD

My travels, and perhaps yours, are fueled largely by curiosity about the diverse ways human beings live and the places they inhabit—not to mention the vast and often beautiful places they don't.

I will (God willing) never fully comprehend the suffering of that Indian family whose baby vomits through the night into the poisoned air. But a visceral if brief experience in a city where breathing literally hurts and cityscapes vanish behind a gray curtain did connect me, however insignificantly, to a faraway place.

That, of course, was not my specific objective of the two weeks I spent in China. If spending two weeks traveling up the Yangtze in commuter boats with no guide and no Mandarin is not your cup of 茶, I get it: Every traveler's curiosity manifests itself differently. I also can't drive by a big apartment building anywhere without wondering who lives in each apartment, what they do for a living, what they are cooking in the kitchen, and when someone last had sex there (in the apartment, not the kitchen). A nature lover may be more consumed by dreams of seeing Antarctica. A poet may aspire to visit the desk where Chilean Nobel laureate Pablo Neruda penned:

I want
To do with you what spring does with the cherry trees.[2]

Those are just different manifestations of our thirst for understanding and adventure—notably more romantic ones, I might add, than hankering for data on the sexual habits of unseen strangers.

My two weeks traveling solo up the Yangtze by train, overnight boat, and hydrofoil were not particularly enjoyable. Too many lonely days without a proficient English speaker in sight, too many nights on rock-hard mattresses the Chinese somehow favor. But to me, China had long been the most mysterious country in the world. I imagined correctly that the trip would both answer questions I had long pondered and pose many more that I didn't know I had.

A tourist cruise up the Yangtze—timed to pass through all of the famed Three Gorges in the daylight, would have been more scenic and easier, with softer (cleaner) beds and a guide to take the edge off cultural and linguistic misunderstandings. But what fun is that?

The daytime hydrofoil I took from Badong to Fengjie, towns with few tourist attractions and fewer tourists, did pass through the Wu Gorge—the only one I'd catch. Most of the Chinese passengers acted like Staten Island Ferry commuters passing the Statue of Liberty, protected from the cold and the view in an indoor cabin. But a handful—mostly kids—braved the cold on a tiny deck to watch.

As I took pictures of the sheer-faced cliffs rising from the river's edge and gazed at occasional barges bearing automobiles or heaps of something earthy, the kids found a new attraction: me. They tried, quite charmingly, to connect. A nine-year-old named Liu Wei offered a bite-size Dove chocolate; an older boy gave me potato chips. Wang Jun Peng, a ten-year-old in a puffy silver coat and Angry Birds face mask, had a more complex interchange in mind. He held up a one-yuan bill and asked me something in Mandarin.

I tapped open Google Translate on my phone, switched the keyboard setting to Chinese, and handed it over. If you have never seen a Chinese speaker use a smartphone, it is mesmerizing. As Jun Peng typed in Roman letters, an array of characters popped up that matched what he typed. ("M-A" produces sixty-seven ideograms and two horse emojis, for example.) Soon, he handed the phone back to me.

"Do you have US dollars?"

Ah, so he wanted a real live greenback. I didn't have any singles, so I handed him a twenty from my wallet. But I would want that back, so I knelt down to unzip my suitcase, where I knew I had some loose coins floating around. I used to love foreign coins as a kid; maybe Chinese kids do as well.

Not nearly as much as they love peering into strangers' bags, it turns out. A crowd of kids (plus a few adults) rushed up behind me, craning their necks. What mysteries might a foreigner's suitcase contain? I pulled open the flap to reveal nothing but rumpled T-shirts, dirty socks, and a toiletry kit—much of it likely made in China—but it didn't matter. They were wowed.

It was not the first time in my trip that I had encountered curious Chinese trampling Western privacy boundaries. Ten days earlier, security guards at the entrance to the Shanghai Museum exhibits had shown a similar disregard for my privacy. When they insisted I run my rather large camera bag over to the checkroom, one held onto my passport. When I returned, maybe two minutes later, he and another guard were taking a break and eagerly flipping through the pages of the document.

I gave them a quizzical "Should you really be doing that?" look. But, far from embarrassed, they were beaming.

"We like your passport!" one exclaimed.

To be fair, my passport really is likable. It is worn and faded and has Mozambican and Russian and Bolivian visas and extra pages added to accommodate stamps in many shapes and sizes and shades and alphabets.

A crowd of inquisitive children jostling to look into my bag was exactly what I did not know I had come to China to experience: a people that had evolved along a separate branch of the cultural evolutionary tree, by far the biggest of the very few modern nations never colonized by Europe. I had read that their "Canton System," which survived until 1842, had sharply curtailed interactions between foreigners and Chinese, restricting contact to a small portion of Guangzhou, formerly known in the West as Canton. It was long illegal to teach Chinese to foreigners.

The resulting cultural differences were starker than I had imagined. I spent a week in South Korea on my way back, and, on my first day wandering around Seoul, I had the unexpected feeling that culturally, I was more than halfway home.

The Chinese recognize this more than I did. That same year I was there, 2013, the Chinese government undertook a campaign to teach its exploding number of outgoing tourists and students to avoid behavior that could be perceived as rudeness and loudness by receiving countries. I might have benefited from a parallel campaign to teach American visitors not to look ignorant in China. In Shanghai, I stupefied a Chinese street vendor with my inability to count to ten on one hand, as the Chinese do. He had perfectly understood my gesture for "How much are these gloves?" but I stared blankly when he answered with a one-handed signal that looked like a pointed gun. He surely thought I was a simpleton for not knowing the sign for what more than a billion of his compatriots would instantly recognize as "8."

Then there was my ignorance in matters of hygiene. Boarding a large commuter boat from Fengjie to Chongqing in the middle of the night, I bought a third-class ticket and received along with it a cabin number on a slip of paper. But in the room I found a family of six plus a cat occupying the two bunk beds. Surely I had the wrong cabin. I returned to reception and showed the Google-Translated Chinese character for "full" to a worker. She gave me a dubious look, walked me back to the cabin, barged in, and offered a stern lecture to the family. Two children promptly abandoned one of the lower bunks, leaving me with a slept-in bed, no change of sheets provided.

I was just as perplexed by regularly occurring extreme acts of generosity. Arriving one night in Badong, a particularly grimy river town utterly free of tourists, I managed to check into a gaudy, modernish hotel meant for Chinese business travelers. The next morning, nervously eager to see the city, I asked a middle-aged woman at reception for a Google-Translated breakfast suggestion. Instead of typing an answer, she simply dialed up her English-speaking son in Beijing and handed me the phone.

"Do you choose beef noodles or lamb noodles?" he asked.

"Lamb noodles."

"I must warn you, they are very spicy!"

"No problem."

"OK, my mom will show you where."

She sure would! Even though she was the only staff member in the lobby, she abandoned her desk, led me to her car, zoomed me up the zigzagging road that led from the port to higher ground, parked, went in the restaurant with me, ordered my noodles, waited as I ate, and drove me back to the hotel.

China was largely crime-free—for undemocratic reasons, perhaps, but eliminating one stress for foreign visitors. It also busted stereotypes as often as it confirmed them. Yang Yang's four-generation, all-female family living under one roof was not at all what I expected, and it baffled me that they welcomed a strange American man into their home. Yang Yang spoke good English and was an extraordinarily generous host, taking me to her magazine's pre–Chinese New Year party and on several trips around the city. I had not expected such generosity and openness—any more than I had expected dirty sheets, red pandas, and an utter lack of privacy.

❋ ❋ ❋ ❋

For me, and perhaps for others, the constant itch to go somewhere comes in part from the frustration that our worldview is largely shaped by the thin sliver of Earth we inhabit for most of the year—geographically, professionally, socioeconomically—and the knowledge that so many other slivers exist that we could never see.

In this sense, travel is an imperfect substitute for what many of us dream of doing: to live somewhere radically different, to inhabit an entirely separate patch of this planet long enough to know it intimately. Long enough to learn not just how to order espresso but also to practice a new language, make friends, figure out supermarkets, navigate new kinds of bureaucracy, and grow accustomed to regular power outages. Long enough to realize that our abstract generalizations of entire peoples—such as "incredibly friendly" or "so rude"—exist only in the Jamaicas and Parises of our glossily simplistic imaginations.

Or simply to drop everything and travel the world. But despite the online infestation of "I did it and so can you" stories found in blogs and Instagram accounts and YouTube channels, most of us have nowhere near the level of financial stability or youth or lack of responsibilities to make either a sabbatical abroad or a nomadic life a practical possibility. Even for some of us who can—like me, who through my late twenties and thirties was largely single and, as a freelance journalist, could have easily moved abroad—it can be hard to pull the trigger. (I finally pulled it at thirty-eight, moving to São Paulo for two years.)

So we travel in fits and starts, where we can fit it in. We do it, in large part, for positive reasons. But not entirely.

TO BOOST OUR SOCIAL STANDING

We travel at least in small part to shape what people think of us. Everybody gets a kick out of announcing where they're off to and regaling friends with stories upon their return. Not you? Yeah, right—imagine how different your next trip would be if you were forced to undertake it in secret. You tell no family, friends, or coworkers where you're going. You post nothing on social media while you're gone, send no texts or emails or postcards to anyone. You bring back no gifts, nor do you tell a single story about your adventures—for the rest of your life.

Part of our reasoning is the widespread notion that being well traveled is an essential part of being a complete person. Look-at-me travel is deeply embedded in (at least Western) society. "A man who has not been in Italy, is always conscious of an inferiority, from his not having seen what it is expected a man should see," is an oft-quoted line from James Boswell's 1791 *Life of Samuel Johnson*, echoing one motivation of the Grand Tourists.[3]

Many people—and plenty of Italian tourism boosters—stop quoting there. But Boswell goes on:

> The grand object of travelling is to see the shores of the Med-iterranean. On those shores were the four great empires of the world: the Assyrian, the Persian, the Grecian, and the Roman. All our religion, almost all our law, almost all our arts, almost all that sets us above savages, has come to us from the shores of the Mediterranean.

In other words, there are simply things one must see to be a sophis-ticated person. Johnson's words are easily condemned, Western civ-ilization vs. the savages, and all, but to this day, Rome and Athens rank high on the "What? You've never been to ____?" list, alongside Paris, New York, the Grand Canyon, and, these days, Thailand.

Pressures can vary among different slices of society. Sometimes ethnicity or ancestry or geography creates a sense of obligation, whether the connection is more concrete (the Puerto Rican who has never been to Puerto Rico, for instance) or more spiritual (the Jew who has never been to Israel). In wealthier tiers of tropical locales, having seen snow can be seen as a divider of the worldly and the provincial.

And of course, once you get somewhere, the pressure doesn't end. Go to Paris without seeing the Louvre? Barcelona without gawking at Gaudí's Sagrada Família? Bali without eating suckling pig at the restaurant Anthony Bourdain crowed about?

Since 2014, I've hosted "Amigo Gringo," a YouTube channel to help Brazilians visiting New York navigate the city and the culture.

Commenters repeatedly ask me, "I only have three days in New York—what are the 'must-sees'?"

There are no "must-sees" in New York, I reply (and reply and reply). What you should do depends entirely on what interests you. Why anyone who hates museums would force themselves through an afternoon at the Met is beyond me.

No one has described the tyranny of the must-see better than writer Alain de Botton in *The Art of Travel*, as he recounts an outing in Madrid where he finds himself being lectured by the pages of a Michelin guidebook that rated attractions with a star system:

> The explorers who had come before and discovered facts had at the same time laid down distinctions between what was significant and what was not—distinctions that had, over time, hardened into almost immutable truths about where value lay in Madrid. The Plaza de la Villa had one star, the Palacio Real two stars, the Monasterio de las Descalzas Reales three stars, and the Plaza de Oriente no stars at all.
>
> Such distinctions were not necessarily false, but their effect was pernicious. Where guidebooks praised a site, they pressured a visitor to match their authoritative enthusiasm, and where they were silent, pleasure or interest seemed unwarranted.[4]

De Botton was more enthusiastic about other elements of life in the city. "I had three-star levels of interest in the underrepresentation of vegetables in the Spanish diet," he wrote, "and the long and noble-sounding surnames of ordinary citizens."

We're a little bit less stodgy than in the Michelin guide days, but no less judgmental. Monuments seem to matter less, cool neighborhoods and innovative restaurants more.

There's a sketch from Porta dos Fundos, a Brazilian YouTube channel exponentially more popular than mine, that captures this. Cíntia is back in Brazil after three years in New York and bumps into her friend Luiza, who wants to know whether she went to Sashima, a three-table Japanese restaurant with a seventy-five-year waitlist run by a North Korean refugee. Or Belly's, where customers must bring their own ingredients and act as chef while the owner sits on a couch and says, "Cook for me, bitch." When Cíntia admits she missed them, Luiza says derisively, "You might as well have stayed in Brazil."

It might sound like I'm urging everyone to strike out on their own, abandoning anything ever listed in any guidebook. But the too-cool-for-school travelers who avoid all clichés are themselves the ultimate cliché; "off the beaten path" is now among the most beaten of paths. In other words, there is nothing new under the sun, not even lying on the beach in the rain. Whatever it is you want to do or wherever it is you want to go (unless it's, say, being the first person to skate-board to the North Pole in a bikini) someone's done it before you.

Letting what society expects of you influence how you budget your precious travel time is foolish. Alas, most of us let it happen subconsciously—and subconscious foolishness may be even worse. One seemingly innocent way this happens is when we decide to make a list.

TO CHECK BOXES

Around the time people started posting their "selfies" to "social media," another phrase was coined that crystallized a different ages-old reason for travel—the "bucket list."

A to-do list for life was not new, of course, but the concept of applying it to travel came to a head with Patricia Schultz's block-buster *1,000 Places to See Before You Die*, which she called a "life list." But it wasn't until 2007 that the term spread, when Morgan Freeman's and Jack Nicholson's characters in *The Bucket List* met as hospital roommates and set off to get tattoos and go skydiving before they died. A decade later, countless travelers have compiled lists of places they want to go, whether or not they are in imminent danger of kicking the bucket.

I think dreaming about places you want to visit is a fantastic use of free time, and keeping a list of them as a planning tool is great.

But like people who count how many countries they've been to, people with a bucket list of destinations can be tricked into feeling that the mission is simply to check them off, not to experience them. It also implies that there are places one needs to visit in order to have lived a complete life, which sounds like a Grand Tour/Baedeker-inspired concept.

Ironically, neither *1,000 Places* nor *The Bucket List* endorses such a philosophy. Much of Schultz's book is quite personal—listing not places all humans must see before they die but rather her ideas of the kinds of places one should visit. It includes, for example, the Burgh Island Hotel in Bigbury-on-Sea in Devon, England, which is so far out of the way from anywhere as to be wholly incompatible with going just to check it off a list. (Come in August for the heather on the moor, she advises.) Freeman's lists are experiential, not destination-based: "Witness something truly majestic," "Drive a Shelby Mustang."

A travel bucket list that reads like that sounds great: "Spend enough time in a Swiss village that every shop owner greets me by name," "Be able to answer 'yes' when someone asks, 'Do you know your way around India?'" "Pick three friends I've made in hostels and visit them in their hometowns."

But few published travel lists are good models. An article with a title like "Top 17 Beaches in the World" would make a futile bucket list, if for no other reason than such a list is impossible to compile accurately, and whoever takes it literally is a sucker. (I once tried to prove this by walking the entire length of the forty-one-mile shore of the virtually unknown Brazilian state of Piauí in search of its best beaches. It took four exhausting days and was still inconclusive.)

Appearing on a list can also imply that certain destinations are hot. I have one requirement before I do any radio or TV show or podcast: Do not ask me to list what destinations are trending that year. To me, the only reason to know what destinations are hot is to avoid them. There are exceptions, of course, such as places where something special is happening that won't be there forever. I'd certainly recommend you go to the World Cup if you have the money.

That explains the value in the perennially popular *New York Times* Places to Go lists that come with each new year. They don't claim to be a "Best Places in the World list," but rather a list of places where things are happening or changing or improving. In the past, those have included Malta's capital celebrating its 450th birthday, Cincinnati for its three new theaters, and Mozambique now that it has decriminalized homosexuality.

Another kind of list-checking travel that has emerged in recent years is perhaps the most asinine of them all: the quest to visit every country in the world. To my perennial dismay, those engaged in this ultimate of ego stunts are celebrated with breathless media coverage.

The pointlessness of such an accomplishment is so transparent it can almost be proven mathematically.

To begin with, there is little agreement on how many countries there actually are, making the goal slippery. Perhaps the closest we can come to an official list are members of the United Nations General Assembly, of which there are 193. But that excludes Taiwan and the Vatican, each quite formidable tourist destinations. (Let's not even get into Palestine.)

Second, it's nonsensical to give each country equal status. In the UN General Assembly, every member gets one vote, but that's the result of a political compromise and clearly not ideal, considering China's population is more than 35,000 times that of Monaco, and Russia covers 280,000 times the territory of San Marino. Can you really apply the same rules to travel, where your choices are (mostly) independent of geopolitical considerations? That would make touching down in the tiny island nations of Nauru, Tuvalu, and Kiribati more valuable than visiting the far larger and more diverse islands of Bali, Java, and Sumatra within Indonesia, a single nation. And technically, a beach getaway to the French territory of Guadeloupe would exempt you from ever visiting Paris.

Visiting every country in the world over a period of, say, five years, is a waste of time, not to mention carbon emissions. Someone who spent that same time living a year each in Spain, Turkey, Nigeria, Mexico, and Japan has my respect. They've actually seen the world.

Luckily, the every-country-on-Earth club is small. But when we ask someone, "How many countries have you been to?" or boast of our own numbers, we fall into the same trap. Imagine doing that with mountains. Someone asks two friends how many they've climbed. The first lists twenty-three that have gently sloping trails to pleasant views at the top. The second answers, "Oh, just one, Everest."

I despise being asked how many countries I've been to, preferring to shock people with the places I have never been. I'm a travel writer who hasn't set foot in India. Can you believe it? I can. When I get a question like "What are your top Vietnam recommendations?" I take great pleasure in saying, "Couldn't tell you." Of course, I'd love to go, but no more than I'd love to go to many parts of Italy and France and Chile and South Korea and South Africa that I've never seen, and I've been to those countries multiple times. I've never been to the Grand Canyon, either, or to Las Vegas, and would not go out of my way to visit either one (or both, which could be done in a weekend with the help of a helicopter). Disagree? Fine, then you go.

TO GET SOME SUN AND SEE THE VIEWS

A day at the beach wasn't even a thing—at least in Western society—until the mid-eighteenth century. Before that, the ocean was perceived as a dangerous place, full of menacing sea monsters, as any old *mappa mundi* worth its salt will show. Before the nineteenth century, dips in the ocean for purposes other than leaping from a sinking ship (or walking the plank) were few: swimming for pleasure gained acceptance only in the 1860s and 1870s. And even when doctors in Victorian novels recommended walks in the salty air and dips in the frigid waters, that was largely about strolling fully clothed and wading out of "bathing machines," carriagelike dressing rooms that rolled up to the shore and even into the water to screen scantily clad bathers from prying eyes.

Exposing skin in order to darken it was unthinkable before doctors discovered that sunlight was a Vitamin D booster, and tanning for aesthetic purposes took off after Coco Chanel appeared in Paris in the 1920s with an accidental tan and her fans seized on her darker skin as a fashion trend. The bikini didn't go mainstream (or get its name) until the 1940s, in part thanks to the need to conserve fabric during World War II, a classic lemonade-from-lemons story.

Heading to the Caribbean to sprawl on beaches and avoid falling coconuts also got a late start. Europeans and New World colonists certainly wouldn't have wanted to go to Jamaica in 1780, when fun stuff like malaria and yellow fever killed 42 percent of the men in the British 85th Regiment, which had arrived just that year. British troops still died at a 12 percent clip between 1817 and 1836. (Newly arrived slaves, ironically, fared "better," benefitting from certain immunities gained in Africa.) Tropical vacations in the Caribbean got their first big boost with the 1890 Jamaica Hotels Law, which promoted standards in the construction of tourist-worthy hotels. Things really got rolling after World War I, and by the time I was growing up, even one visit was not enough—at least according to a literal interpretation of the "Come Back to Jamaica" ad campaign.

These days, the century-plus effort to market Caribbean beach vacations can only be seen as a resounding success: They are the default winter trip for much of cold-weather America. Nothing wrong with getting away from the cold, if that's what your inner travel spirit prioritizes. But I suspect some portion of the two and a half million Americans who head to the Caribbean each winter do so in part because it's what society (largely in the form of Corona ads) tells them to do.

Sometimes, marketing magic can create demand out of thin air. Or turquoise waters.

I almost choked on my breakfast the first time I saw an ad in a São Paulo newspaper for resorts in Punta Cana, Dominican Republic. Why would Brazilians, with their 4,500 miles of coastline, travel so far?

A popular Brazilian travel website described the appeal like this:

> Think of a beach like those in Northeast Brazil, long, crannied, framed by endless palm trees and coral reefs—except with the white sands and turquoise blue sea of the Caribbean. Welcome to Punta Cana.[5]

So, it's like our beaches, but the colors are nicer? More recently,

Brazilian YouTubers and other celebrities have been popping up there as well, almost certainly as part of marketing campaigns. As a result, more and more Brazilians dream of taking a seven-hour flight to stay in an isolated resort where no one speaks their language rather than making a much shorter trip to beaches most of the world drools over.

Our love of nature in general is also, in part, an invention. National parks were created in the United States in part to heal the country after the Civil War, not because of growing demand for sleeping under canvas near grizzly bears. At least by then, people had begun to value hiking up a mountain and basking in their reward—a sweeping view of the countryside below. But that, too, has not always been a thing. "Before the mid-eighteenth century," wrote Eric Zuelow in *A History of Modern Tourism*, "people simply did not go into the mountains if they could help it."[6]

The Alps, wrote British sociologist John Urry, "had been regarded as mountains of immense inhospitality, ugliness and terror" in the eighteenth century.[7] In those days, people climbed mountains largely for the same reason chickens cross the road—to get to the other side. Occasionally, it was for religious or ritualistic purposes. It should be noted that millennia earlier, when Moses climbed Mount Sinai to receive the Ten Commandments, no Israelite went, "Hey, let me come along, I bet the view is awesome from up there!"

BECAUSE WE CAN

Well into the nineteenth century, travel was horrifyingly rough. In Europe and the United States, getting around for all but the richest meant traveling over rutted roads that jolted stagecoaches and the spines within. Their suspension systems were "reminiscent of creative medieval torture tools," Zuelow told me, noting that "all but the very wealthy were condemned to spend their nights in overcrowded and flea-infested inns." And it was painfully slow—Edinburgh to London was four days by horseback or ten by stagecoach.

Sea travel wasn't much better—all but the rich traveled steerage, which meant suffering for weeks in a cramped, hot, often disease-ridden environment. Until steamships cut transatlantic travel to, at best, five days, crossing the Atlantic took weeks (or months). But with annual leave not yet invented, people probably didn't have the time to go anyway.

The steam engine changed all that, albeit gradually, and by the mid-nineteenth century it was possible for far more people to get out of town. English labor organizations seized upon early rail travel to invent the package trip; Thomas Cook and others expanded on it in the 1840s. But these early excursions were not billed as leisure travel. Niagara Falls was seen as a tool to turn American atheists into believers, and Cook's early excursions took English workers to temperance rallies—though most probably would have preferred a stop at a Hungarian distillery. Those pretenses soon disappeared, but as any accountant who has attended a "conference" in Oahu can tell you, couching leisure travel as something more dignified is still very much with us today.

By the 1850s, English agencies were running trips into the Continent and mass tourism had begun. Half a century later, automobiles ushered in the era of family tourism. Though the steam and internal combustion engines proved vital to democratizing travel, a less-polluting innovation also helped: the weekend. The Industrial Revolution helped extend the traditional Christian day of rest into two.

About a century later, air travel traced a parallel route. Getting from London to India between world wars had meant fourteen layovers. By the 1950s and 1960s, air travel had become far more efficient, and it has grown (and grown cheaper) since. And even with today's shrinking seats and all-out wars for space in overhead compartments, it's still far better than the stagecoach.

Parallel to increased comfort and efficient transport was reduced risk. "One of the things [Cook] knew, which was absolutely crucial, was to reduce the anxiety and risk when people were out of their homes," John Urry told me in a 2014 interview. (He died in 2016.)

Communications have also changed and encouraged travel. Wifi connections greet travelers around the world, encouraging a warier crowd to stray farther from home. The internet was hardly the first breakthrough. When the telegraph arrived in Cairo in the nineteenth century, it was seen as a boon for tourism, since Europeans wouldn't feel entirely cut off from home.

Crossing borders has become much less of a hassle—as confirmed by anyone who used to have to pull out a passport in the middle of the night every time their train crossed a border in Europe. For countries that do require visas, those are quite often available via the internet or for purchase upon arrival. To see how much easier it has become for Americans and Europeans to travel abroad than in the days when visas and bureaucratic border crossings made travel less attractive, look no further than the visa process required for many non-Europeans who want to visit the United States. They must get to, and pass, an in-person interview at an often distant American consulate or embassy—a huge disincentive.

TO EXPLORE (AND EXPLOIT?)

Modern travel is deeply influenced—whether we like it or not—by the explorers and conquerers and crusaders and pilgrims and biologists and missionaries—and even anthropologists—who made it around the world before leisure travelers could, and frequently without the best of intentions.

We have adopted their language—we "explore," "discover," and seek the "exotic"—and sometimes also their venturing-into-the-unknown attitude. We jot down stories of cultural mishaps, dangers, and derring-do in our travel journals as though we were scribes on Vasco da Gama's first voyage to India.

And even though we of course denounce and distance ourselves from the sins of past centuries—conquest, colonialism, slavery—sometimes our travel patterns seem unsettlingly similar.

Here we come to the ultimate man of controversy, Christopher Columbus, hero to generations of American schoolchildren but now a symbol for many people of the destruction and conquest of the Americas by rapacious European powers.

Whether we admire Columbus as brave and resourceful or abhor the conquest and destruction he caused, his writings show him to have been both subjugator and tourist.

"The Admiral says that he never beheld such a beautiful place," according to the journal of his first voyage, "with trees bordering the river, handsome, green and different from ours, having fruits and flowers, each one according to its nature." If you've ever been to a bustling market in a faraway place, you probably know the feeling. In the Bahamas, he described fish "so unlike ours that it is wonderful. Some are the shape of dories, and of the finest colors in the world, blue, yellow, red, and other tints, all painted in various ways, and the colors are so bright that there is not a man who would not be astonished, and would not take great delight in seeing them."[8] With just the slightest editing, that's pretty good copy for a snorkel-rental website.

And, early on, when natives fled a village in fear of the arrival of white men, he insisted his crew leave the villagers' belongings untouched—not even "a pin."

We know the other side of it, of course. The slaughters began later, but even on his first trip he seized natives to turn them into interpreter-slaves, and, pretty fish notwithstanding, he communicated his broader mission to King Ferdinand and Queen Isabella as such: "If devout religious persons were here, knowing the language, they would all turn Christians," he wrote. "Thus your highnesses should resolve to make them Christians, for I believe that, if the work was begun, in a little time a multitude of nations would be converted to our faith, with the acquisition of great lordships, peoples and riches for Spain."

It's not hard to draw parallels to travel today.

Of course, missionaries still exist, although their agenda can be as much or more about personal growth or volunteer work rather than evangelism.

Destruction of traditional culture and exploitation of local resources in the name of capitalism don't strike me as that much better than doing it in the name of Christianity or gold. Developers have certainly had a hand in turning fishing villages into beach resorts that mine their gold not from the sand but from the credit cards of visitors. The process may be more gradual, and the displaced may receive adequate compensation and/or employment in some cases, but the transformation can be dramatic. Cancún and Punta Cana were unknown, sparsely populated fishing areas before developers, with the support of tourism officials, started building in the 1970s. Now they receive millions of tourists a year at their international airports.

Most travelers are not developers. But how many of us, encountering an isolated beach in a tropical land, do not at least think about moving there, or opening up a B&B or surf shop? Travel writers like me live to write about such places, often drawing developers and putting at risk the traditional lifestyle.

Being served by low-paid workers of color can also sometimes smack of the colonial era. When Columbus arrived at one island, "the people all came to the shore, calling out and giving thanks to God. Some of them brought us water, others came with food." When I read that passage, I was reminded of how Polynesian resort employees lined up on the beach to greet backpackers arriving via catamaran, or how traditionally dressed indigenous performers danced when a trainload of tourists arrived at the Sibambe stop after heading down the Nariz del Diablo mountain in Ecuador. None of this was "bad," per se, but it does play into what travelers dream of upon arrival in an "exotic" land.

In another Columbus throwback, the travel industry (and many travelers) fetishize the idea of untouched indigenous cultures. In some places, demand to experience this aboriginal world inspires Disney-like shows to meet travelers' expectations. Though by any measure Swaziland is one of the more traditional African countries (it has a polygamous king!), that's not enough for many visitors. So they flock to the Mantenga Cultural Village, an attraction that replicates how the Swazi people lived in the 1850s. Presumably, visitors know that they are not seeing a real-life village. Yet many don't bother specifying in their social media posts that this is not modern life. "Meet our new friend Nikiwe!" wrote one Instagram poster, who posed with a traditionally dressed girl at Mantenga. "She and others performed native welcome songs and dances for us." Another visitor posted a picture of a man in traditional dress in front of a hut and wrote simply: "#tribes in #africa #swaziland."

Travelers also expropriate resources. Açaí, the Amazonian palm fruit now considered a "superfood," was just a cheap, caloric staple of local diets when it became a fad among surfers and jiujitsu practitioners in Rio late in the twentieth century. By the early twenty-first, an American traveler had discovered açaí bowls on a trip to Brazil, soon founding Sambazon and exporting it to the United States; many other entrepreneurs followed suit. By the time I got down there to do a story in 2009, foreign demand had caused the price to rise locally, forcing some poorer residents to substitute other foods. Journalists have described similar increases in the price of quinoa in the Andes.

Companies that produce and export such superfoods pretty much all claim to do so sustainably and to support local farmers. Their claims certainly have more validity than Christian explorers' efforts to save "savage souls," but even the best-intentioned of entrepreneurs are not perfect, and their efforts often have unexpected consequences.

More alarmingly, the rape and slavery of the age of exploration have echoes today in sex tourism. You don't have to search too long online to find videos of creepy old white guys having sex with suspiciously young prostitutes in faraway lands. More on that in chapter 6.

It should be noted that just decades after the age of exploration kicked off, Renaissance writers were promoting travel for noble reasons that still ring true today. Michel de Montaigne, the sixteenth-century French philosopher, championed journeys not by armed galleon but by horseback:

> Travel seems to me a beneficial exercise. The soul finds continual exertion, observing unknown, novel things. And I know no better school . . . than to propose incessantly the diversity of so many other lives, fancies and customs and to make one taste such perpetual variety of human nature. The body is neither idle nor toiling, and this moderate agitation holds one's attention. I stay on my horse without dismounting—as colicky as I am—without getting bored, for eight to ten hours.[9]

We still travel to break up our monotonous lives, to learn, to see others who are different from us. Montaigne makes an argument not for passive travel but for travel that keeps you "neither idle nor toiling." The modern-day version of his horse might be a bicycle, since touring by bicycle also allows us to feel a part of the world we travel through—enduring the bumps in the road and the gusts of heat, hearing birds and catching whiffs of cooking.

In a 1625 collection of essays, English statesman Francis Bacon—who had traveled through Europe in his youth, well before the Grand Tour took off—recognized the importance of breaking out of one's bubble. In "Of Travel," he gives advice to a figurative traveler that still serves us today. I will translate four particularly relevant passages into contemporary terminology.[10]

> Let [the traveler] sequester himself, from the company of his countrymen, and diet in such places, where there is good company of the nation where he travelleth.

Avoid hanging out with fellow travelers or expats. Don't eat in touristy restaurants.

> Let him, upon his removes from one place to another, procure recommendation to some person of quality, residing in the place whither he removeth.

Before you go, ask your friends and acquaintances for local contacts.

> When a traveller returneth home, let him not leave the countries, where he hath travelled, altogether behind him; but maintain a correspondence by letters, with those of his acquaintance, which are of most worth.

When you meet someone great, be sure to friend them on Facebook and stay in touch—at least via pithy annual birthday messages.

> And let his travel appear rather in his discourse, than his apparel or gesture; and in his discourse, let him be rather advised in his answers, than forward to tell stories; and let it appear that

he doth not change his country manners, for those of foreign parts; but only prick in some flowers, of that he hath learned abroad, into the customs of his own country.

Don't come back to work wearing saris or anoraks or native charms or crowing about the "new you." Rather, make the "old you" better by integrating the best of the cultures you have experienced into your life. And don't drone on about your adventures.

Travel in Bacon's and Montaigne's day was difficult. Free potato chips on Jet Blue were still centuries off. But they all traveled long before any organized travel industry existed; no concocted tours, no "cultural villages," no international hotel chains or fast-food restaurants or soda companies. Their travels were effortlessly organic in a way that many travelers today must take great pains to find.

FOR "AUTHENTIC" EXPERIENCES

Many travelers strive to see real life, to experience places as they really are, rather than in a version put on for tourists.

Though most travelers and travel marketers see *authenticity* as a desirable trait, the term—and sometimes the idea—has drawn criticism. In part, that's because it is more frequently applied to experiences removed from our own—often in non-Western cultures. You are certainly more likely to see *authentic* attached to experiences in Native American reservations or African villages than in an outing in London or Washington. ("To your left, observe the authentic lobbyist on his way to an authentic meeting with an authentic senator.")

The authenticity debate has been bandied around for a long time by those who study tourism.

In *The Tourist*, Dean MacCannell makes much of tourists' "fascination for the 'real life' of others." Among tourist attractions, he specifically counted "decay, refuse, human and industrial derelicts, monuments, museums, parks, decorated plazas and architecture shows of industrial virtue."[11] But not all such attractions are equal. The closer they are to unaltered real life—the parts not usually shown to outsiders—the better.

Watching poor people has also long held a special, and especially cringeworthy, appeal. Here's how the *Milwaukee Sentinel* described New York City's Spanish Harlem in 1979:

> Groups of unemployed youths—unemployment among the young runs as high as 40%—congregate on street corners. Children are seen playing in small, fenced-in lots. Mangy dogs lie in the doorways of abandoned and crumbling buildings.

Not an unusual story for the era, except that the article ran in the newspaper's travel section. It was the description of the Penny Sightseeing Company's tour of Harlem.

MacCannell described six levels of travel authenticity, from the staged to the pure.[12]

1. The "front region," which he describes as "the kind of social space tourists attempt to overcome or to get behind."
2. A touristic front region—a place with cosmetic changes to make it seem more genuine. He gives the example of a seafood restaurant with a fishing net hanging on the wall.
3. A front region that is a simulated back region. Colonial Williamsburg, for example, or, nowadays, an Airbnb property that the owner bought purely as an investment but is decorated like a local, lived-in home.
4. A "back region" that is "open to outsiders." His examples include a magazine exposé, but to me this might include the streets of an untouristy neighborhood.
5. A "back region" that may be "cleaned up or altered a bit" because tourists occasionally make their way there. A real Airbnb apartment fits in here, as does the Louis Armstrong House Museum near my home in Queens—the actual house the legendary trumpeter lived in for three decades,

preserved mostly unchanged by his wife until, upon her death, it became a museum.

6. The true back region: real, unaltered life.

The travel industry has grown (like a weed) since the original edition of *The Tourist* came out, and efforts to simulate authenticity have grown more sophisticated.

We have open kitchens in hip restaurants, backstage and behind-the-scenes tours, access to "real" places and experiences through services like Airbnb.

And the commodification of these "back regions" turns them into semifront regions that are at least partly staged. Line cooks in an open kitchen don't curse (or cough near your food) as much as they might if left alone. The Rockettes' dressing rooms surely don't look the same when a crowd of tourists is allowed to peek in. And Airbnb owners do not leave their underwear on the floor or dirty dishes in the sink, and even have been known to remove family photos (or put up family photos, if they're offering one of the growing number of investment properties as faux homes).

As Elizabeth Becker describes in *Overbooked: The Exploding Business of Travel and Tourism*, French authorities realized that French people acting French was of substantial value—a crucial but intangible attraction worth preserving—and made an effort to do so. That strikes me as a win-win, but not all efforts are. The town of Kidlington, England, started receiving regular busloads of Chinese tourists in 2016 after Chinese tourist agencies decided the everyday life there—Kidlingtonians walking their dogs and putting out their trash, in other words, being Kidlingtonian—was a worthy attraction.

As the travel industry co-opts private life and packages it for travelers—not a bad thing, necessarily—it ups the ante for those of us looking to see real life. And that frequently comes at some cost. That's the instinct, for example, that makes people seek out exchange programs or homestays.

A YMCA-run exchange program took me to a village in western Kenya when I was fifteen. It was perhaps my most formative early travel experience. But I do remember some "authentic" disappointments. My roommate Brian and I were assigned to a rectangular metal structure that resembled a Western house, not the circular, thatched-roof huts assigned to many of our friends. In the house's defense, it was inhabited by wasps and spiders and featured a scary-looking portrait of Uganda's then-strongman Idi Amin, but it did not match my image of an African home that the years of *National Geographic* magazines on my shelf had shown me. Nor did the devout Christianity of our hosts, nor the Coca-Cola sold in a village store.

Yet of course it was authentic—for I was visiting in 1985, not 1885, when perhaps I would have found a village that hewed closer to my fantasy. (At least there wouldn't have been Coke, which wasn't invented until 1886.)

The irony in seeking out such fake authenticity should be clear. Yet since we are surely all looking to avoid touristy restaurants, cheesy tours, and caricatured presentations of modern culture, perhaps we should shed the word *authenticity* altogether and make it our goal to encounter stuff that's as close to real life and as removed from the travel industry as possible. In other words, to travel organically.

There are exceptions, especially when the real life we seek is historic. In that case, we will need the travel industry to provide great attractions both famed—like Colonial Williamsburg—or hidden, like the Museum of Comtois Homes in eastern France, a collection of centuries-old homes from across the region that were carefully moved to a rolling plot of land in Nancray.

But those places are advertised as history. It is when we conflate history, fantasy, and reality that we err as travelers. Or, alas, as travel journalists. Perhaps no incident while working as the Frugal Traveler galled me more than the publication of misleading *National Geographic*–like images to accompany my article about two nights spent in the Baliem Valley in Papua, Indonesia. I trekked up narrow mountain trails to spend the night in Dani villages where neither cell signals nor motor vehicles can reach. Despite my explicit instructions for how to reach the same villages I had visited, the photographer who was sent after me decided not to make the climb. Instead, he stayed at the valley's most luxurious hotel and shot a Papuan ceremony put on for tourists. The photos that reached the editors were of near-nude Dani people adorned with feathers, face paint, boar tusks protruding from nostrils.

The villages where I spent the night were hardly modern. Residents still slept grouped by gender, not marriage. But even during an elaborate funeral ritual I was fortunate enough to witness—the one that included that pig-killing via poison arrow—the villagers did not paint their faces or perform nearly naked. Instead, they wore the authentic modern garb known as T-shirts. The exception that proved the rule was a man wearing little more than a penis sheath. He was a very elderly man clinging, seemingly, to a fading tradition.

I saw the photos on the photographer's Instagram feed ("On location in #Papua, photographing the #Dani tribe") and immediately wrote to my editor:

"Saw nothing like this in my time with the Dani people in Papua. Couple of old guys still dress like this, but without the makeup. I know this sort of pic is going to be very tempting to run in my article . . . but my guess, this is part of something put on for tourists. Just planting this thought in your mind for when photos are picked."

No luck. The *Times* published the photographer's images with this misleading if not literally inaccurate caption: "One of the elders in the Dani compound in his full ceremonial dress, which is used for weddings, funerals and other significant dates."[13] Perhaps somewhere. But not in the village I was in or the funeral I was at. Such "authenticity"—selling disappearing traditions as daily life—would undoubtedly stick in the minds of readers, some of whom might have followed in my footsteps and been at least slightly disappointed to see these unauthentic photos of what was—to me, anyway—one of the most memorable destinations of my life.

Gary Arndt, a renowned and tireless travel photographer and blogger, captured the authenticity trap perfectly on his blog *Everything Everywhere* (as well as on *theAtlantic.com*):[14]

The problem stems from the expectations people have before they go. When I was in Samoa, I was talking to a woman from New Zealand who had been driving around the islands. She sounded disappointed and a little bit upset that Samoans had television sets. She lamented the destruction of the Samoan lifestyle and blamed it on Western countries. She then went into a rant about how wonderful it was being able to live a self-sufficient life in a village.

I pointed out the inconvenient fact that Samoa is not in fact self-sufficient in food. No Pacific country is. The most popular foods are instant noodles and corned beef. The biggest part of the Samoan economy is income sent home from Samoans living abroad. The current population of Samoa would be almost impossible to sustain by methods used in the 19th century. . . .

Her Samoa was closer to the Samoa of the 19th century or the Samoa of Margaret Mead. She was denied her authentic cultural experience because Samoans (how dare they!) were watching TV and using electricity. Samoans just weren't Samoan enough for her. Even though she would never state it as such and would bristle at the accusation, she wanted Samoa to be a cultural zoo where she could go and look at the locals doing their cultural thing.

The problem of course wasn't with Samoa. It was with the woman.

Gary goes on to point out that although we delight in restaurants in our own countries that serve non-Western cuisine, we are appalled when we see McDonald's, Burger King, or Starbucks all over developing countries we visit on vacation. It is a huge mistake—an utter misunderstanding of authenticity—to pretend we are visiting a civilization that has had no contact with our own world. Instead of looking for authenticity in isolation, we must understand that our world's fascinating interconnectedness is the ultimate authenticity, and that its absence is an equally intriguing exception.

TO FIND CONNECTIONS

Alain de Botton awakens after a first night at a beachfront hotel in Barbados. He makes his way to a chair at the edge of the sea and finds a view straight out of a brochure—jungle-covered hills, sand stretching out in the distance to the tip of the bay, coconut trees angling toward a turquoise sea. Yet he can barely appreciate it—he has a sore throat from the flight and is stressed because he had forgotten to tell a colleague he would be away. "A momentous but until then overlooked fact was making itself apparent: I had inadvertently brought myself with me to the island."[15]

We often set off on trips imagining we will escape the pressures of home. But total escape is a fantasy, even more so for those with a lot to escape from. Travel plans that are open to finding connections have a far better chance of success than often-futile attempts to disconnect.

One great form of connection that has become increasingly popular in recent years is the search for family history, whether through living relatives or dead ancestors. We see this everywhere, for reasons both historically meaningful (African Americans on journeys to West Africa, for example) or practical (Italian Americans heading to their great-grandfather's hilltop village to seek the baptismal records in order to stake a claim to European citizenship).

But connections crop up whether you're expecting them or not, and they also surprise you along the way. In 2014, I visited an eco resort in the Surinamese Amazon run by a man named Nelson Tiapoe. Nelson regularly led tours of a nearby Maroon village founded by descendants of African slaves who had escaped into the jungle in the seventeenth and eighteenth centuries. He told me of a visiting Ghanaian couple who had shed tears at scenes of the Maroon mothers washing clothes in the river as their children frolicked nearby. Never before had they seen such an African scene outside of Africa, they told him. Nelson, himself a Maroon who had grown up in Suriname's far-off coastal capital, imparted a memorable lesson in things being more connected than they seem. On a hike through what seemed to me like a primeval rain forest across the river from the village, he pointed out proof that it was not—in the form of a mango tree. Mangoes are not indigenous to the Amazon, he noted, so a Maroon settlement must have existed there at one point. (It was, in fact, the former site of his grandparents' home.) How long had I been visiting the tropics without knowing mangoes were not native to South America? How many forests had I visited and simply assumed they had been there forever?

I was feeling about as disconnected as a person could be as I wandered the city of Yichang before the first leg of my Yangtze boat trip, and that was a good thing. But so was walking into a café where I was practically pounced on by a bubbly teenaged girl named Kiki, eager to practice her English. No need, she was fluent, and she told me of her plans—more like dreams, they seemed to me—to go to university in Canada.

We followed each other on Instagram, but I don't remember seeing her at all until, a couple of years later, she became impossible to miss in my feed. There she was—dressed in lingerie on Canadian rooftops, at stripper-pole class, in confoundingly fashionable outfits, with accompanying captions written in clever if occasionally mysterious prose and occasionally thanking professional photographers. There were occasional references to exams and pictures with studious-looking friends; she had clearly made it to college. I had met a future social media star.

Connections can also be humbling. In northern Lebanon, I spent a night with a Christian Lebanese family in the sleepy coastal town of Anfeh. My host, Marie-Josée Anjoul, invited me to join the family for services at Notre Dame du Gardien, a Byzantine-era Greek Orthodox church.

But entering the ancient structure, I felt a wallop of cognitive dissonance: The walls were covered with inscriptions in Arabic, and I thought: Wait, were these people Muslims or Christians? The moment was brief, and followed with a wave of embarrassment. As a good post–September 11 New Yorker, I know full well that *Arab* is a geographical and linguistic designation, not a religious one. But apparently, I was not as enlightened as I'd thought. I had brought myself with me, but I would take a better self home.

For decades, I have gleefully made fun of tourists who visit New York for their obsession with squirrels. I wrote an article about it in the *Times* in 2003, for a Brazilian publication in 2011, and produced a video about it in 2014. In between, I poked fun at every foreign tourist delighting in our city's rats-with-tails population.

Then, in 2015, the penny dropped. Visiting the Ubud Monkey Forest in Bali, I was as enchanted with the monkeys as were my fellow foreigners, in what could be the most touristy place in Indonesia. The locals around me could scarcely be bothered, yet there I was, gawking like a Chilean in Central Park. I can no longer mock squirrel-worship in New York: There but for the grace of a suburban American childhood go I.

TO FEEL SUPERIOR

Of the words we use to describe why we travel, *off the beaten path* is a stale cliché, *authenticity* a dicey concept. But nothing is more galling to me than the faux gem: "Are you a traveler or a tourist?"

You have almost certainly heard this question, although it's possible you've only seen it emblazoned on the image of a backpacker trekking through the Rockies on your most annoying friend's social media feed. Or as the subject of a banal quiz on HuffPost or Matador Network or LifeBuzz.

It is barely a question at all, but rather a tool for shallow self-affirmation, as much an attempt to simplify an entangled, multilayered concept as its binary brethren, "Am I a good person?" and "Am I a racist?"

Wait, let me guess. You are a good person, you're not a racist, and, of course, you're a traveler off for an adventure that will test your limits, uncovering deep personal truths and achieving self-realization! I mean, what else would you be doing on that one-week getaway to Cinque Terre?

Like good and evil or tolerance and racism, *traveler* and *tourist* are the two ends of a continuum. Where each one stops and the other begins is subjective. But—and this is quite a coincidence— individuals tend to draw the line in such a way as to put themselves on the good, nonracist, traveler side of it.

I will not speak to your evilness or racism. But according to the oldest reference I can find that defines *traveler* and *tourist*, you're almost definitely a tourist. It came in Paul Bowles's 1949 novel *The Sheltering Sky*. Here's how protagonist Port Moresby distinguishes the two:

> He did not think of himself as a tourist; he was a traveler. The difference is partly one of time, he would explain. Whereas the tourist generally hurries back home at the end of a few weeks or months, the traveler, belonging no more to one place than to the next, moves slowly, over periods of years, from one part of the earth to the other.[16]

I can think of a handful of people who have been on the road for years, and they're very admirable. But they are almost certainly not you.

To me, calling yourself a traveler implies your superiority to others—such as the retiree group shuffling off a tour bus, or the family who stops in a touristy Latin Quarter café for Cokes, or the couple who stay in a downtown hotel, while you like to score Airbnbs in a "genuine" part of town. Such thinking is pointless and offensive. No one goes on a trip to be a caricature. People are doing their best, operating within their own constraints. And surely there are others looking down on you in the same way.

Take New Yorkers. We love to make fun of tourists, their fascination with Times Square, their helplessly square outfits, the plastic knife and fork they consider appropriate for the eating of pizza. Yet at the same time we celebrate ourselves as the most tolerant people in the world. An Afghan woman wearing a burka in the subway and a lesbian couple sitting hand-in-hand in a park are seen as symbols of our acceptance and diversity. A tackily dressed Midwesterner blocking the sidewalk in SoHo? Out with you!

Not much has changed since 1976, when Dean MacCannell first observed: "The rhetoric of moral superiority that comfortably inhabits this talk about tourists was once found in unconsciously prejudicial statements about other 'outsiders,' Indians, Chicanos, young people, blacks, women."[17]

This prejudice against tourists—I'd call it *tourism*, if the term weren't already taken—is pernicious. Yet it's difficult to resist. I often criticize the hostel circuit as a mobile party bubble of young and not particularly intrepid adventurers. On a homestay in Lake Atitlan, Guatemala, I snootily dismissed the Israeli backpackers I saw in the next town, clustered in a café and smoking pot. I was different when I was their age, I thought, boasting (to myself) of having trudged an alternative path through Europe during my junior year in Paris with my buddy Dave, avoiding other Americans and speaking stilted French to each other. But I had no idea what those Israelis did when they were out of my sight—or the day before or after I met them—or whether, who knows, this was their well-earned break after completing their military service, or in an isolated Himalayan village learning Nepalese.

"The touristic critique of tourism is based on a desire to go beyond the other 'mere' tourists to a more profound appreciation of society and culture," wrote MacCannell, nailing me thirty-five years before the fact. "Sightseers are motivated by a desire to see life as it is really lived, even to get in with the natives, and at the same time, they are deprecated for always failing to achieve these goals."[18]

Perhaps not all tourist-travelers desire this deeper involvement. But those of us who seek it need to lay off the deprecation of those on the tour bus or in the tourist trap. Let he that hath never sought refuge in a foreign McDonald's cast the first McNugget.

A more accurate contrast than *traveler* versus *tourist* would be *traveler* versus *vacationer*. Vacationers want to escape, to relax, to eat well, and to get massages by their cabana's private plunge pool. Travelers want to see, to learn, to grow, to understand, to experience. Writer and philosopher Roman Krznaric distinguishes between time off and time on. Travelers like him treat their trips as "time on, an integral part of our lives. . . . We may well return in an altered state, having discovered worlds which appear on no maps, and in no guidebooks." Vacationers are taking "time off."[19]

TO TAKE PICTURES

Another clue to why we travel can be wrangled out of the activity we associate most closely with being on the road: diarrhea. Just kidding! It's photography.

It's hardly possible for most of us to imagine traveling without taking photos. Levels of obsession vary: I've been obsessed with photography since I took an ice-cream-sandwich–shaped 110 camera to London at age eleven, and I've got the albums (you definitely don't want to see) to prove it. Others let their travel partners do the honors, but few would visit a faraway place and come home with no visual record.

Few people alive today can remember a time when taking your own pictures while on vacation was not yet affordable: the 1935 Sears, Roebuck Catalog listed an Eastman Brownie camera for $2.65, equivalent to less than $50 today.

What does our long obsession with travel photography tell us about travel? Does taking snapshots improve our experience while we're on the road, or only after? Would we even want to travel so much if we could not capture and share images of our adventures? If not, does that mean photography is part of the reason we travel to begin with?

The cover of *The Tourist Gaze 3.0*, the third edition of John Urry's classic on photography and travel (coauthored with Danish geographer Jonas Larsen), shows a crowd of tourists in Times Square, all madly snapping photos, of course. He used to ask his students to consider how the world would be different if photography had never been invented. Travel, he notes in the book, was forever changed after the daguerreotype and competing technologies emerged in the 1830s: "1840 is one of those remarkable moments when the world seems to shift and new patterns of relationships become irreversibly established. . . . There is the peculiar combining together of the means of collective travel, the desire for travel and the techniques of photographic reproduction. From 1840 onwards tourism and pho- tography were assembled together and they remake each other in an irreversible and momentous double helix."[20]

The very existence of photographs—the idea that you could see startlingly realistic images of faraway sites rather than depending on drawings and words—was profound. It allowed people to see places as they really were, rather than in artists' interpretations or their own fantasies.

It also changed the way people react to places and continues to change them to this day. Twentieth-century American author Walker Percy noted in his essay "The Loss of the Creature" that the way we see the Grand Canyon is utterly different from how García López de Cárdenas and his party saw it when they were the first Europeans to reach there in the sixteenth century.

In the twentieth century, instead of confronting the canyon itself, an imaginary visitor encounters "the symbolic complex which has already been formed in the sightseer's mind."[21] And what does he do? Instead of even attempting to take in the Grand Canyon as it is, he "waives his right of seeing and knowing" and instead pulls out his camera, attempting to re-create the Grand Canyon as he already knows it: as a postcard.

Of course, we're not all this predictable. Though we do take our formulaic Grand Canyon picture—without the limitations of the 36-exposure Kodachrome roll or even the need to buy a camera other than your phone, you might as well—most of us also pause to appreciate its grandeur, point out something to our children, even squint our eyes and try to imagine what it looked like to López de Cárdenas, or to the Native Americans who were there before him.

But there is more to photography than that. I also take pictures to frame my subjects not just literally but figuratively, to make sense of them, to categorize them in the world. Perhaps you do, too. When I'm presented with frantically busy cityscapes or overwhelming nat- ural beauty, it helps me separate the layers, see the details. On a trip in Glacier National Park a few years ago, I was faced with the splendor of finger-shaped Bowman Lake, which from my perspective stretched eight miles into the distance—more dramatic, untouched nature in one shot than the entire eastern half of the United States combined.

So I poked around with my camera to discover the smaller elements that made up the scene. Smooth stones the colors of curry powder, airport tarmac, and raspberry ice cream covering the bottom of the shallow end of the lake. A young girl on a stand-up paddleboard rowing by, breaking the stillness and horizontality of the water. Then I zoomed in on the backdrop, consecutive mountains dipping their toes into the lake from alternating sides of the water. Some people might notice such details in isolation; I need my camera.

Even as my smartphone edges closer to the quality of my eight-year-old, nine-times-heavier Canon 7D, I continue to prefer looking into a viewfinder and closing one eye, cutting off all context. It forces me to consider lighting, something I tend not to notice as much as the more artistically inclined, and to choose which parts of the scene to include and exclude, looking for beauty in isolation. Or ugliness— the system works especially well in commonplace settings—say, public buses or trivial cityscapes—to isolate some quirky aspect of a wooden seat or to frame a pair of pajamas drying on a balcony.

Even though many of us strive for postcard quality in our photography, "Your picture looks nothing like a postcard" is actually the ultimate compliment. It means you've used your camera as a tool for seeing things differently.

It has been postulated that one reason we so love watching the view from a train or bus is that the rectangular windows replicate the viewfinder of a camera. In fact, travelers have used cameralike devices to interpret visual reality since long before cameras (and trains and buses) were invented. The Claude glass, a portable, tinted, convex mirror, became popular about half a century before the first daguerreotype. The mirror had the effect of transforming a landscape you'd see with a naked eye into something that looked more like a painting. The glasses were named for Claude Lorrain, a landscape painter whose muted tones the glass was supposed to reproduce. A team out of the University of Windsor described it this way:

The distorted perspective, altered colour saturation and com-
pressed tonal values of the reflection resulted in a loss of detail
(especially in the shadows), but an overall unification of form
and line. The Claude mirror essentially edited a natural scene,
making its scale and diversity manageable, throwing its picturesque qualities into relief.[22]

It was an eighteenth-century Instagram filter—producing what for
some was a fake reality, for others a way to interpret the world in a
way the eyes alone can't achieve.

Of course, there are two far more prosaic reasons we take pictures as we travel. If "Name a reason you take pictures when you
travel" were a Family Feud question, the number one answer would
undoubtedly be: for the memories. For pulling out years later when
your kids have grown up or when you're nostalgic for the days when
your back could handle a fifty-pound pack.

The second reason we really take pictures on trips probably
wouldn't make the survey: showing off. We use photos to tell a story
about ourselves not visible to the naked eye. These images of places
we've been (or fish we've caught or celebrities we've met) are displayed on walls at home, desks in offices, and Instagram feeds, but
there is no better example than the images people choose for their
dating profiles.

Perhaps *images*, in the plural, is inexact. At least in the category
I'm familiar with (women seeking men in New York City), there's
really only one such image: a picture of your windswept potential
partner perched above the Incan ruins of Machu Picchu.

It's so common that it's become a running joke among my friends.
The women are surely not attempting to make us laugh, much as
so many men cluelessly invite mockery with their shirtless self-
portraits. My interpretation: The women are keen to have swipers
believe they are adventurous, physically fit travelers—most people
get up there after tough multiday hikes—but not Eurocentric ones.
A shot in front of the Eiffel Tower (or skiing in the Alps), presumably, would be too much of a cliché.

Boasting of our travels via dating app or Facebook post or Instagram feed is not a manifestation of modern values. People have been traveling (in part) to show off since they started traveling at all. And though we're in the heyday of bragging via selfie, using images to boast of your worldliness is older than even a $2.65 Brownie.

Consider the postcard. It first caught on in the late nineteenth century, propelled by the massively successful Paris Exhibition of 1889. Visitors could purchase and mail a photo of a brand-new wonder called the Eiffel Tower to the saps back home who couldn't make it there themselves. Though of course the senders did not appear in the image, they could do the next best thing: jot a message in their own handwriting. They then affixed a French stamp that would be canceled and dated with a Paris postmark—*très chic*. Postcards remained popular even after people traveled with cameras—and even after email made communication instant. That was in large part because they allowed word and image of your adventures to reach friends and officemates before you even got home, serving as both proof of life and proof of a life better than theirs.

Only with digital cameras that allowed same-day transmission of worldliness for those willing to download photos and upload them to email or blog posts did postcards begin to fade, before ceding almost completely to the social media tools that scaled up travelers' audiences effortlessly. Show off to the boss, your crush, and Grandma, all in one tap of a smartphone (and without paying for a stamp)!

✳ ✳ ✳ ✳

But even before postcards, travelers found pictorial ways to flaunt their experiences. Grand Tourists, for example, could not simply return to England without evidence they had seen the Parthenon. They needed a souvenir as well, something "that would display to everybody where they had been and what they had seen," as Eric Zuelow wrote in his history of tourism. He continued:

> A small industry developed to feed this need. Paintings depicted important sites such as the Pantheon and the Coliseum in Rome. . . . Equally important, the paintings nearly all feature tourists *looking* at the sites/sights in question. These figures

visually consume the spectacle, while at the same time project-
ing the message to whomever looks on the canvas: The owner
of this painting was here; he bought the experience. Paintings
worked in much the same way as contemporary postcards
emblazoned with the words "Wish You Were Here!" Such cards
do not truly mean that the sender wishes that the recipient were
literally underfoot, but rather announce that "I am seeing these
places and you are not."[23]

Posting selfies on social media is only superficially different. I do
have a few friends who are skilled enough photographers or caption
writers that their posts from abroad largely mask what I presume
is their principal "look-where-I-am" motivation for posting. I am
among the guiltiest. The most common reaction when I posted photos from my Frugal Traveler trips was not, despite my bids at clever-
ness and photographic artistry, either "hahaha" or "how beautiful"
but rather "I want your job." And that felt good, especially when
I was at my wit's end trying to make deadline in a cramped and
uncomfortable guesthouse.

TO MAKE MEMORIES

We also travel to remember our travels. Of course, as you're packing your bags, you don't often think, "I can't wait to return home
and look back on this trip." But surely travel would be far less
appealing if upon your return everything that happened was erased
from your brain, leaving you only with a tan and a seemingly indigenous bracelet from a culture that was quite potentially fascinating
to have visited.

And it turns out that our desire to create memories affects the
way we travel in a way that, as with cameras or bucket lists, might
not be ideal.

Daniel Kahneman, the psychologist who shared a Nobel Prize in
2002 for his work in behavioral economics, seems like an unlikely
travel guru. But in a 2010 TED Talk about happiness, he used vacations as an example—along with colonoscopies.

He began by drawing a distinction between "the experiencing self," how you feel in your life as you live it, and "the remembering self," how you feel about your life when you reflect on it.

Humans focus more on the remembering self, he argued, using an example of two patients receiving colonoscopies. One experienced relatively constant pain throughout a short procedure; the second experienced a much longer procedure in which pain lessened toward the tail end. Though the first patient actually experienced less total pain, he remembered it as more painful, because the pain continued to the end. The second patient remembered the colonoscopy as less painful than the first, because it ended well.

Then he moved on to vacations:

> From the point of view of the experiencing self, if you have a vacation, and the second week is just as good as the first, then the two-week vacation is twice as good as the one-week vacation. That's not the way it works at all for the remembering self. For the remembering self, a two-week vacation is barely better than the one-week vacation because there are no new memories added.[24]

For the portion of us traveling for the memories, or even the after-trip glow, this suggests an easy fix: Tip the scales to make sure the end of your trip is the best part. Need to choose between an inconvenient layover going or coming home? Get it over with on your way there—you'll never remember it by the end. Or reserve a few days at the end of the trip for something you know you'll love—a spa day, an upscale restaurant, a city where a good friend will host you and make everything easier.

Kahneman's main takeaway is that the experiencing deserves more attention than we give it. Two weeks at the beach is no better than one? That's insane. He notes that the best trip he ever took was to Antarctica, even though it did little for his remembering self, claiming to have thought about it for maybe twenty-five minutes total since he got back.

I agree we need to focus less on planning the trips we want to *have taken* and more on those we want to *be taking.* Implementing this policy worldwide would reduce trips to see the *Mona Lisa* by half.

But let's recall that Kahneman's Nobel Prize was awarded for economics, not travel. Actively remembering a vacation—storytelling, gazing at photos—is not the only lasting benefit. Travel experiences are not erased just because they never become your screen saver. One supposes that on his Antarctic trip he also learned something, shared emotions with his wife, made new friends, caught up on reading—all benefits that last long after the trip is over. To me, this represents a third self: the growing self, which benefits from travel by making us smarter or more thoughtful or better people. (Nobel Foundation, I can be reached via sethkugel.com.)

There is plenty of evidence that travel can change us in ways that are imperceptible, perhaps even to ourselves. Two German researchers, Julia Zimmerman and Franz J. Neyer, collected personality questionnaires from a thousand German university students. Those who studied abroad, they found, measured higher in extroversion, openness, and emotional stability than those who didn't.

A series of studies by Jiyin Cao, Adam D. Galinsky, and William W. Maddux set out to test Mark Twain's most famous quote on travel:

> Travel is fatal to prejudice, bigotry and narrow-mindedness, and many of our people need it sorely on these accounts. Broad, wholesome, charitable views of men and things can not be acquired by vegetating in one little corner of the earth all one's lifetime.[25]

More specifically, they tested whether travel abroad increases "generalized trust," which they define as "belief in the benevolence of human nature . . . especially critical in an increasingly globalized economy, where interactions with unfamiliar others are inevitable."[26] All five experiments—which ranged from trust games to longitudinal studies—found that this trust was increased in those having a broad range of foreign experiences.

I doubt many travelers need convincing that this is true—we have our lives to prove it. Who we are is based in part on where we have been and what we did there. Evidence can surface in the oddest places—say, a Japanese curry restaurant in Manhattan's East Village where, early in 2017, I found myself with two friends, Puerto Rican and Dominican New Yorkers. We were talking about food—for that's what you talked about in New York in 2017—and got onto the subject of *tostones*, the disk-shaped, twice-fried green plantain slices that are the French fries of the Spanish Caribbean.

It's not a topic every non-Latino can enjoy. But in the summer of 1993, twenty-three-year-old me—then a third-grade teacher in the Bronx—accompanied the family of one of my students to spend the summer with her grandmother in the Dominican Republic, and by the end of six weeks had became the biggest *tostón*-lover and finest plantain-fryer suburban Boston has ever produced. I came home with a *tostonera*, a metal implement used to smash the plantain slices between trips to the frying pan, and I have been looking for 6/$1 green plantain sales at New York bodegas ever since.

A trip a quarter-century earlier had allowed me to enjoy my friends' company just a bit more than I would have otherwise. It didn't matter at all that I hadn't looked at the pictures of my trip in years.

WHY WE *DON'T* TRAVEL

So the reasons we travel—personal, historical, sociological, psychological, educational—are far more complicated than we think, and more so than I ever imagined when I scribbled a chapter named "Why We Travel" in the original outline for this book.

It also didn't strike me at the time that there was an implicit assumption in the title—that members of contemporary society all want to travel in the first place. That it is something we instinctively desire, like chocolate or tight abs.

Is it possible to dislike travel, to actually prefer "vegetating in one little corner of the earth all one's lifetime," as Twain rather dismissively put it?[27] If you are anything like me and regard travel as an irreplaceable element of a fulfilling life—and the fact you picked up this book seems to indicate you are—your first instinct may be "That is absolutely preposterous!"

If so, I'd guess you're probably not on a trip right now. Or, if you are, you're over your jet lag, your stomach is settled, you haven't gotten lost, and your travel companions are pleasant and agreeable twenty-four hours a day. As I said, you're probably not on a trip right now.

For it is a rare journey that does not involve some level of misery. Travel can be lonely, challenging, uncomfortable, and frustrating at times. Yet before we leave and after we get home, we tend to forget that, in part because the industry markets travel the same way McDonald's markets Big Macs—lettuce remarkably crisp, buns unsmushed, indigestion and calorie count never mentioned. Actually, it's not just the travel industry, but also your friends on social media. At this very moment, #waterfall has appeared 7,434,527 times on Instagram, #squattoilet just 686.

Yet people have different levels of tolerance for the discomforts of travel, and not always by choice. Severe allergies or hypersensitivity to gluten, for example, can make traveling a nightmare in places where language barriers can lead to disaster. Being in a wheelchair can make travel to many places almost as complicated for modern travelers as it was for eighteenth-century Londoners to travel to Edinburgh by stagecoach.

It also isn't free. Billions, of course, don't have the time or money to travel at all. Even for those who can, travel comes at the real expense of something else—nicer clothes, a better health plan, financial security. Even for those with plentiful discretionary income, travel also takes up free time when you could be doing something else.

What kind of person chooses not to travel? As it turns out, my high-school soccer teammate, grad school roommate, and guy I still talk to every Tuesday night at 9 p.m., Jon Chapman.

Jon is an exemplary human being who teaches science at a high school for recovering addicts in the Boston Public Schools and picks up others' litter obsessively. He is beloved among friends for his quick-witted, self-deprecating humor and respected for his extraordinary generosity (and handyman skills). His main detractors are those who want to get a word in edgewise when he's on a roll at a dinner party.

He also does not like to travel. I requested a formal interview—not on a Tuesday at nine—to find out why. His answers were way too reasonable.

"I'd rather spend on things that will be more long lasting, that I can use over and over again, like a new set of golf clubs," he told me. He did not mention it, but I know he also prioritizes charitable giving, donating a higher percentage of his salary to good causes than anyone else I know. But he has little of the wanderlust that many of us at least think we have. "I'm very happy here," he says of Boston. "I've never felt the need to escape anything—my parents, the climate, the culture." His ideal trip is an hour-long drive to play golf with his dad.

Travel seems like a gamble to him. "You've got to plan it out way in advance," he said. "And then well, geez, I hope I don't get strep throat right before the trip. What if you lose your luggage? What if you break your leg? It's not just the physical risk but the financial risk: spending a grand and not getting a grand's enjoyment from it. What if you have the flu in Disney World? You're paying $250 a night, and you're throwing up in your $250 a night toilet."

Jon is not an absolutist, however. He had a blast the couple of times he and the third high-school teammate on our Tuesday-night calls, Doug Mollenauer, joined me for Frugal Traveler adventures. "It's like a lottery win to go with a travel writer," he said, recalling an adventure we had searching for a Somali restaurant in a suburban Seattle mall. But the idea of planning his own vacation intimidates him. He doesn't want to act like a tourist, "in a place where a thousand people are all looking at the same mountain," but he's not sure how to pull it off.

Yet he feels the pressure to travel from his friends and colleagues—especially one he refers to as a travel evangelist. "She felt I was missing out by not traveling," he said, "that I would not realize my potential as a person until I engaged with preordained travel, in the same way that Christ had a plan for me, or Buddha or Mohammed would have the answers. 'I need to help Jon engage in this life-changing experience.' It's like there's a list of places you have to go and, implicitly, if you don't get there, you're diminished."

He told me he doubts other people's vacations are as great as they say. "It's the Emperor's New Clothes—everyone is saying the emperor's trip to Burning Man is so great, but then someone finally says, no, it wasn't—he was standing around in thousand-degree heat with dust in his eyes."

On the other hand, he insisted, staying at home for vacation is risk-free: "I can start having fun as soon as my day begins. I don't need to go anywhere."

✳ ✳ ✳ ✳

I spoke to Jon in 2014, when I began thinking about this book. Since then, he has married, bought a house, adopted two greyhounds named Smokie and Butter, and, with the exception of his honeymoon, has continued not to travel.

Jon may not travel much, but he's not provincial. He reads, he has a keen interest in the experiences of immigrant friends and acquaintances in Boston. He finds ways to travel without traveling. And those ways have multiplied. There are ever more technologically advanced ways to explore the world from home—all the way up to 360 video and virtual reality that can simulate, in ways that are only going to get better, actually being somewhere else.

WHY WE DON'T NEED TO TRAVEL

When the Grand Tourists crossed the English Channel for the first time, they had never seen a true-to-life image of the Seine or the Roman Coliseum or so much as a genuine Continental breakfast. Now we have phones, we have photography, we have video, we have virtual-reality video, we have . . . who knows what comes next. Even though you can now take a train from London to Paris in two and a half hours or fly there in just over sixty minutes (plus seventeen hours in airport security lines)—travel has, in some ways, grown less necessary.

Consider this: Sixty years ago, there was not a single Thai restaurant in the United States. Today, there are three Thai restaurants in Minot, North Dakota, population forty-six thousand. Their authenticity may or may not be suspect. But no American has to go nearly as far as Thailand to get Thai food that comes pretty close to the real thing. New York's best Thai has "authentic, hyperregional dishes" that can be "genuinely life-changing," according to the very trustworthy folks at *New York* magazine's *Grub Street* blog. Four happen to be within walking distance of my apartment—and under thirty minutes from the Empire State Building by subway.

Today you can also watch Thai movies, take Thai language lessons online with a native speaker in Thailand, and instantly see any attraction in the world on a screen.

You could argue that all these resources make your trip better. Aside from piquing curiosity, they give us the chance to preview sites and bone up (literally) on Thai cuisine and (figuratively) on the language. But they also make it less frustrating if we never do go. I have never been to Thailand. Do I want to go? Sure. But I can walk one block from my apartment to Kitchen 79 (no. 4 on *Grub Street*'s list) and have *miang khanaa*, an explosively limey dry-pork salad wrapped in round Chinese broccoli leaves, for $9. For about $1/200$ the price of the cheapest possible trip, it's a pretty good substitute.

Immigrant neighborhoods are not perfect substitutes by any means, although my neighborhood, Jackson Heights in Queens, is about as close as it gets: more than 60 percent foreign-born, best known for its Indian, Pakistani, Bangladeshi, Tibetan, Nepalese, Colombian, Ecuadorian, Peruvian, and Mexican populations (and restaurants), and that's just the beginning. Not everyone has a Jackson Heights nearby, but most Americans live within driving distance of immigrant communities, and vast numbers of us have friends from other countries—if we are not immigrants ourselves.

When Jon visited me in New York while I was reporting an article that took me to the less touristy corners of Manhattan's Chinatown, he started to tell me a story. "Back in the States . . . " he began, before catching himself. He had forgotten what country we were in. The same thing has happened to me: at a Mexican supermarket in Los Angeles; at the Queens International Night Market; in a Vietnamese farmers' market in New Orleans. (At the latter, it helped to arrive in the early morning when mist obscured the strip mall nearby.)

Heck, I can choose among about a half-dozen taco trucks in my neighborhood. When I was growing up in Newton, Massachusetts, in the 1980s, there were zero Mexican restaurants (according to my memory and the 1984 Yellow Pages, dug up by a friendly Newton librarian). Today, there are at least four, not counting Chipotle.

Yet I still want to go to Thailand, and Mexico, and I'm guessing you do, too—even you, Jon, if the circumstances were right.

That's because travel is awesome. But it can be even more awesome if we filter out some of the historical, societal, and commercial pressures to travel in a certain way to certain places, and just go where we truly want to go, and for the right reasons.

That can be complicated, since our very desire to travel, not to mention the development of an infrastructure that allows it, is also the result of some of the same forces. The idea is to separate the good from the bad.

Below is a recipe you might try for figuring out the right trip for you and to separate you from those on the more standard path, be it beaten or unbeaten.

1. Make a list of places you want to go, with very specific reasons for each. Consider whether that reason will make you enjoy the trip itself and benefit from it in the years that follow. (When you eventually go on the trip, remind yourself of those reasons every morning and use them to plan your day.)

2. If you are married or otherwise locked into a specific travel partner, make individual lists with reasons and compare. Kids can get involved, too. If you are free to travel alone or choose your companion(s), consider which potential travel partners will enhance your trip—say, through their language skills or tolerance of your bad habits—or detract from it, because of different standards of comfort or differ-

ent values. (For example, I've been surprised by travel partners who consider patronizing prostitutes a key component of foreign travel.)

3. Once you choose a destination, be sure the sources that led you to that choice are reliable and independent. Was there tourism industry money behind that blog you read? Do the friends who gave you the ideas have the same interests? Might they be embellishing their adventures?

4. Don't feel the need to be original. You won't be. Someone already went in search of the greatest cheese in Tajikistan. And you don't need to find the little-known most romantic inn in Provence. A well-known, medium-romantic inn will do just fine. (Not so sure the same is true of Tajik cheese.)

5. Don't obsess about "escaping" or "relaxing." Even difficult trips can bring you back refreshed, and even luxury beach getaways can end in disaster, or rain.

6. If stuck between two finalists, choose the destination that is the most different from your hometown or region. Country versus city; hot versus cold; a place where your values might be challenged. Studies show that you get more out of destinations that are different from what you're used to; snow can be as appealing for some as escaping snow is for others.

7. Review your proposed itinerary and consider eliminating half the destinations and doubling the time you stay in each place. Build in flexibility that will allow you to change plans and stay even longer in a place you like, or skip out of a place you don't. For some people, the best two-week tour of Spain starts with ten days in Madrid, no matter what your friends say about Barcelona.

Nuns in Rio de Janeiro.

Chapter 4
· · · · · · · · · · · · · ·

TECHNOLOGY
AND TRAVEL

Americans believe the Wright brothers flew the first air-
plane in Kitty Hawk, North Carolina, in 1903. Brazilians feverishly
object, arguing that Wilbur and Orville's use of headwinds, cata-
pults, and other cheats disqualified them. It was their own Alberto
Santos-Dumont's glorious 722-foot trajectory in Paris three years
later that made them "First in Flight," North Carolina license plates
notwithstanding. But both countries agree on two aviation-related
facts: The airplane transformed the way we travel, and the airline
industry makes it excruciatingly hard to get from the United States
to Brazil's paradisiacal northeastern beaches.

During the 2014 World Cup, the lack of direct flights created a
problem for thousands of American soccer fans (including me) when
the United States men's national team drew Ghana in Natal, an
800,000-person city on that beach-lined coast's easternmost nub,
which juts out toward West Africa in a lopsided, sandy grin.

New York to Natal is four thousand miles as the crow flies, about
the same as New York to Berlin. If only you could take a crow. The
"best" option for Americans like me who had finagled a game ticket
out of the mysterious FIFA lottery system was to fly via São Paulo,
fifteen hundred miles out of the way. Depending on your connection, this could cost you fifteen to twenty hours and around $1,400.
It was so inconvenient that flying back and forth across the Atlantic
via Lisbon was a viable alternative.

Viable, but horrible. So I stopped looking for a flight online and got out my *National Geographic Atlas* to see if there was a better way. My trusty atlas revealed there was: I could fly to Guyana, then make my way overland through Suriname and French Guiana— three miniature, coast-hugging countries (really two and a French province) that form a narrow buffer between the blue of the Caribbean Sea and the green of the Brazilian Amazon. From there, I would need to cut through the state of Amapá, and get across the gaping mouth of the Amazon to the sizable city of Belém. Then I could fly, or bus it down the coast, to Natal.

Hundreds of thousands of New Yorkers of Guyanese descent had created a need for flights from JFK Airport to Georgetown, Guyana's capital. The one-way, five-and-a-half-hour trip would cost $334. I was able to book Belém-to-Natal for fifteen thousand Delta SkyMiles even on the eve of the tournament—most people were coming from the opposite direction.

It was the overland part that was the problem. Another double-edged miracle for travel, Google Maps, asked forgiveness: "Sorry, we could not calculate driving directions," it told me. No wonder—all three international borders were formed by rivers without bridges, or without working ones at least. And I needed to know not only the route but also how long it would take via public transportation, if that was even possible. I wasn't a gap-year backpacker who could laugh off delays, I had a game to catch.

In just a few nights, deep dives into travel forums and some smart Googling allowed me to patch together plans from a handful of travelers who had done stretches of the trip before and posted about it in disparate corners of the web. Turns out you can get across the three countries and all the way to the French–Brazilian border using unscheduled but regular minibuses, shared taxis, and the motorized canoe-shaped boats called pirogues. From the Brazilian border town of Oiapoque, it was a six-hour shared 4x4 to Macapá, an overnight ferry across to Belém, and then that miles flight to Natal.

It looked to be about a week without stops, so I gave myself sixteen days to allow time to see the sights—whatever they were. The total cost would be less than a one-way flight from New York to Natal.

That left many details to be figured out along the way, and much opportunity for things to go wrong, but that was part of the fun. As was the strange sequence of visiting a former British colony full of Hindus (Guyana), a former Dutch colony with a large population of Javanese (Suriname), and a former penal colony that did business in euros (French Guiana). I had roti and boiled-bark mauby in the first, Indonesian chicken soup in the second, baguettes in the third. The total population of the Guianas is not even 1.6 million but by some measures is more diverse than the rest of Latin America combined.

* * * *

Twenty years ago, my trip would have required a travel agent or months of advance planning, and possibly the extensive use of post-age stamps. Eighty-five years ago, even that wouldn't have helped. I couldn't have even made it to Europe and back for that kind of money. An off-season third-class round-trip ticket—the cheapest of the cheap—on a Compagnie Générale Transatlantique steamship from Manhattan's Pier 57 cost $135 in 1933, equivalent to $2,500 today. Complimentary seasickness was provided; Dramamine wasn't invented until 1949.

I also couldn't have done it in two weeks. Back then, getting from New York to Paris meant donning a suit and tie (a fur for the lady?) and lugging (wheel-free) suitcases up the gangplank of a Manhattan pier for a casual week at sea to Le Havre, and onward by train. In the time it took me to travel through four countries and take in a World Cup game, a traveler would barely have had time to disembark for a sip of Calvados before catching the return ship to New York. Hardly a Norman conquest.

Those were good days to travel if you were rich and idle, but few beyond the leisure class would want to turn back the clock. Commercial air went mainstream in the 1950s but was still wildly expensive. The 1957 Frommer's guide showed the cheapest round-trip fares to Europe at more than $400—equivalent to around $3,000 today. Even in 1965, *Time* magazine reported that only two out of ten Americans had ever been on a plane. Among the reasons: International and interstate prices and routes were regulated by the federal government, guaranteeing profits and thus forcing airlines to compete on something other than price, which led to onboard luxuries like fine dining and ample legroom, conditions that (rich) people look back on nostalgically.

It was legislation, rather than technology, that brought air travel to the middle class, when President Jimmy Carter signed the Airline Deregulation Act in 1978. Competition would do away with coach-class comfort by the early 2000s, but (when adjusted for inflation) prices had fallen almost by half. They have remained more or less stable ever since, despite a steady rise in oil prices in the first fifteen years of this century.

✳   ✳   ✳   ✳

Technology has made not just the actual traveling easier, faster, and cheaper, but travel planning as well. Kayak, Expedia, and other online travel agencies (OTAs) are imperfect, but booking through them is a whole lot simpler than visiting your travel agent, or calling the 800 number of airlines and hotel reservation desks. Many people probably can't remember the last time they made a reservation that required changing out of their pajamas, or even using their vocal cords.

And the list of feasible destinations has exploded. You can go practically anywhere these days, and still plan it yourself. Have you ever thought: "Boy, I'd love to go to Kyrgyzstan, but are tourists allowed? What is there to do? Where would I stay?"

If so, and if those thoughts happened in, say, 1990, your answers might have come by combing bookstores for an obscure guide-book, or going to a travel agent specializing in the recently defunct Soviet Union. But if it was, say, last week, within four seconds Google would have led you to Wikitravel's crowdsourced overview of the country's "incredible natural beauty and proud nomadic tradi-tions," the former quickly verified by clicking on "Images." It would then take fifteen seconds to verify that Americans don't need a visa; another ten seconds to have your computer belting out the correct pronunciation, *KEER-guh-stahn*. Five minutes more would be plenty to ascertain that the average price of a ticket from Chicago to Bishkek, the capital, was between $1,000 and $1,300 on Turk-ish Airlines with a stop in Istanbul. Then on to TripAdvisor, where, as of this writing, Bishkek has fifty hotel listings. There's plenty to read about most of them. The Park, for example, offers eighty-seven user reviews in English. You could even automatically translate the thirty-one Russian reviews, although results like "Work as a restaurant with a total breakfast and dinner individually flawless" might not be much help.

✳ ✳ ✳ ✳

Airplanes and the internet aren't the only reasons human beings took fifty times more international trips in 2016 than in 1950.

Inoculations, prophylactics, and eradication of many tropical diseases made far more of the world accessible for those not as willing to confront substantial risk of death as Mary Kingsley was. There is also some semblance of modern medicine in most corners of the world; even if those shiny hospitals in poor African and Latin American capitals are unjustly affordable only to elites, those elites include visitors like you. Whether you feel guilty about that is up to you, but I doubt you'll take your compound leg fracture to the public clinic to make a point. (Just by flying around the world, you've self-declared your elite status, so get over it.)

A century ago, some countries had literally zero miles of paved roads for newfangled touring cars. Millions of miles of blacktop have been laid since then, making countless potential travel destinations accessible.

Beyond asphalt, travel can still be dicey, but not insurmountably so. That shared 4x4 from the French Guianan border to the Brazilian city of Macapá cost me $136 for one of four berths, but it was safer and more reliable than the bus, which during rainy season (and I was there during rainy season) often can't make it through the mud. When there's tourist money to be had, things get even easier.

The trip to Machu Picchu is a pretty good indication of how far technology has taken us. For centuries, the fifteenth-century Incan citadel had been largely forgotten. Its (disputed) 1911 rediscovery by Hiram Bingham was big news but made the papers only after reporters rushed to interview Bingham on the deck of a United Fruit Company steamship, months after he left Peru. At the time, yellow fever and malaria were rampant. By the time a *New York Times* writer made the trip in 1950, there was a vaccine for yellow fever and chloroquine to prevent malaria.

Yet it still took him a while. Milton Bracker spent nearly a day on airplanes and hours more on a rather perilous high-altitude mule ride: "This correspondent is very partial to a brown mule known only as No. 6," he wrote. "It not only got him up and down securely—while another rider was thrown and broke both a collarbone and some ribs—but gave him a wonderful and Gary Cooperish feeling."[1]

Today, no mule is necessary. You can get there in less than a day—via plane, train, and bus. (You can also channel Bingham and hike the Inca Trail, suffering blinding altitude headaches as you chew fruitlessly on coca leaves, which is the way I chose to do it. But that was my choice.)

You can also use a translation app to communicate with ER doctors in a Beijing hospital, instantly book hotels from anywhere in the world with wifi, and FaceTime your kids during business trips, which sure beats bringing home a teddy bear in lederhosen.

But the downside is also clear. Before my first visit to the Dominican Republic as a teacher in 1993, I scoured New York City bookstores but couldn't find a single brand-name guidebook devoted to the country. I finally scrounged up the scrappy but short-on-detail *Hippocrene Insiders' Guide to Dominican Republic*. Though fine by me at the time, by today's standards it was at best a skeletal overview. For example, on the one page devoted to the northwestern port town of Monte Cristi, I learned I would find the "largest salt making facility in the country" and "informal beach restaurants playing merengue." There was mention of two hotels, one with air conditioning—but no addresses or prices. It was enough to get me on a bus.

The highlight of my time in Monte Cristi was meeting a Dominican guy named José who lived in Atlanta but was back home visiting friends. He recommended we go with his cousins to the most beautiful beach on the island, a place called El Morro. The *Hippocrene* guide mentioned it just once in a throwaway phrase I noticed later, calling it "a good but shadeless sandy beach." But José was right. It was a total score: a near-empty hidden crescent of yellow sand tucked away behind a cliff that was itself tucked away on the outskirts of a sleepy town movie set in the making.

Today all the big-name guidebooks have volumes dedicated solely to the Dominican Republic. And that's nothing compared to the fire hose of online information. It takes five seconds to learn about El Morro beach on TripAdvisor, the No. 2 of four "Things to do" in the area. Reviews are mixed—it's beautiful but hard to access; take sturdy shoes; the currents are treacherous for children. That's quite handy advice, especially if there's no English-speaking Dominican American from Atlanta around to take you there.

But if I had known all that before I met José—and browsed photos to boot—I doubt I'd have had the same reaction when I first clambered down the rocky path to the sand. The isolated beach in the distant northwest reaches of the country, a region too arid for tourists seeking palm trees, blew me away. (So did the area's goat meat, which gets an herby kick because the animals graze on wild oregano that thrives in dry heat.) I have been back to Monte Cristi twice, and each time the memory of discovering El Morro surges back. Had I known it was not even the highest-ranked attraction in Monte Cristi, I doubt I would have been quite as wowed in 1993, or 2006, or 2010.

✳ ✳ ✳ ✳

You surely know by now that I think excessive research and relying heavily on anonymous user reviews can bleed surprise, adventure, and wonder from any trip.

Yet the existence of and easy access to online resources is obviously a great thing. It would be absurd to maintain a multivolume *Playboy* collection, er, I mean encyclopedia set, on your shelves these days.

The problem is not technology itself, but the extent to which most travelers decide to use it—guzzling from the hose when selective sips will do.

We face these dilemmas in our daily life as well, of course. In my case, the answers are very different in theory than in practice. In theory, I think walking down the sidewalk with your head buried in your phone is despicable and represents withdrawal from civilized society; in practice, however, I know that marching into a utility pole while posting a picture of a chocolate-chip cookie to Instagram can be painful.

That said, I've walked home from the subway thousands of times and know the route, so why shouldn't I finish up an article I was reading on the train before I get to my apartment? As long as I keep half an eye out for teenagers precariously balancing Frappuccinos as they come out of Starbucks, that is, and I say that from experience.

When these habits persist while you're traveling—wandering through Cape Town, or along the Inca Trail, or even during a week-end on the Jersey Shore—then you're depriving yourself of discovery.

Leaving your phone at home was an easy option in the pre-smartphone era, but it's impractical these days, considering the things you'd have to pack to make up for it: a camera, a flashlight, a tip calculator, an alarm clock, a phrase book. And once the phone is in your pocket or bag, well, it's easy to fall into old habits.

In their 2013 book *The App Generation* Howard Gardner and Katie Davis examine children's uses of apps. But the way Gardner spoke in a 2014 presentation in Boston on the same topic, he might as well have been talking about travelers, not children: "Living in a world that is replete with apps, and where so many things can be done quickly, efficiently, handily—is that good or is that bad? It's good if apps are enabling, that is, if they open up vistas you haven't had before, allow you to ask questions you haven't asked before and allow you to explore new places [where you haven't been] before, but it's not so good if you became dependent on apps."[2]

For travelers who seek to open up vistas, to ask questions, to explore—which I think is most of us—it is worth considering which apps help us travel and which apps make us dependent on the solutions, directions, answers, and opinions we find in them.

These days, the opinions part comes largely in the form of user reviews. Since websites that funnel other people's opinions to us have so fundamentally changed not just how we plan our trips, I'm going to devote some time to their rise and current outsize presence in travelers' decision-making processes.

User reviews have influenced travel for decades, albeit under different guises. Arthur Frommer solicited tips from readers, and many obliged, including my mother, who sent him a letter after feeling unsafe at a hotel in Madrid in 1964. The hotel was removed from the next edition.

The Zagat Survey took things further in 1979, when it began publishing its beloved series of restaurant guides that clipped together mailed-in reader reviews into single coherent mash-ups like this one:

A "perennial" "shining star," Nobu Matsuhisa's "magical" TriBeCa "posh spot" is the "sine qua non" for "spectacular" Japanese–Peruvian fare that "leaves you in a state of bliss" boosted by "top-class service" and David Rockwell's "chic, modern" surrounds.[3]

The "easily satirized" if "once wildly popular" format made it the "go-to guide of the 1990s," though it now seems "quaint and outdated," given the rise of "newfangled sites" that offer a "torrent of detailed customer evaluations," which, though "sometimes long-winded and banal," drown out Zagat's "trickle of curated quotes."

But in the Arthur Frommer and Zagat guides, public opinion not only went through a selection and editing process. You also had to pay to access it. Now, for better or for worse (actually for better *and* for worse), the user-review world is both free and a free-for-all, with near-infinite assessments of just about every hotel, restaurant, tour company, suitcase, and travel pillow on earth.

TripAdvisor is the all-powerful king of the genre, and has been for a while. In late 2012, I headed to Florida for a story called "Going Beyond Disney in Orlando." (It was largely a ploy to eat fried plantains at restaurants run by the fast-growing Puerto Rican population.) My hotel was moderately priced, generically acceptable, and resort-oriented, filled with middle-class families headed to Disney. Once I checked out, I introduced myself to the manager and revealed I was a travel writer for the *New York Times*. He politely answered a few questions. Expecting the standard "When will the story be out?" query, I preemptively told him he should check nytimes.com/travel in a month. He thanked me rather offhandedly and then got deadly serious: "Please leave us a review on TripAdvisor."

Though most hotels still care more about a mention in the *Times* than a single TripAdvisor review, I'd bet some would trade a rave from me for a dozen five-star reviews without a second thought. User reviews are now the go-to source for opinions and shape travelers' purchasing decisions not just before but during their trips. That, in my opinion, is a questionable development. (I do admit that, as a travel writer with a high opinion of my own opinion, I'm biased. But don't worry, I'll eventually get to the number of reasons why user reviews are great, and how to take advantage of them.)

The fundamental problem with user reviews is that those reading them don't know the tastes, the standards, or the sincerity of those writing them. Do we trust the wisdom of humanity in general? Or, if instead of trusting individuals you turn to overall scores and rankings, are you so average that you believe the aggregate of thousands of human opinions will match your own? Consider my favorite Italian restaurant in Manhattan, one originally recommended to me by several food-writer friends: the reasonably priced Porsena, situated on a cozy East Village side street. It has an average rating of 4.0 on Google. Meanwhile, a standard Subway on soulless West 29th Street gets a 4.1. And it's not just Google. On TripAdvisor, the McDonald's in Terminal 1 of the Dubai International Airport ranks in the top 10 percent of the city's 8,500 restaurants.

If someone you knew raved about McDonald's and Subway, would you ask them to help you choose a romantic date spot? Why do we trust people online when we would likely ignore them in real life?

Consider some opinions collected by the British newspaper the *Telegraph* from one-star TripAdvisor reviews:[4]

The Grand Canyon: "Went there from Vegas for a few hours. . . . Nothing special."

The Taj Mahal: "Do not visit—you are better off watching it
on the 'net."

The Louvre: "Quite frankly one of the worst museums I've ever
visited—never again!"

Those are extreme examples, but they prove a point that lies at the
core of why planning based on strangers' opinions is so risky: We
simply aren't all alike.

A listen-to-the-experts argument would go something like this: We
should not trust reviews by relatively inexperienced travelers whose
first priority is having fun but who moonlight in opining to TripAdvisor's or Google's all-encompassing readerships. Instead, we should
rely on calibrated, deeply researched, unbiased reviews by people who
have stayed in countless hotel rooms and visited endless attractions
for the sole purpose of evaluating them for a specific audience.

Alas, that's not always how travel writing works. But there is
clearly an advantage to trusting a guidebook brand, TV personality,
glossy magazine, or, ahem, travel columnist, on experience alone.

✳   ✳   ✳   ✳

I had always dreamed of going to Indonesia—at least, ever
since I had made a wall-size map of the massive archipelago in third
grade, using an opaque projector and a roll of butcher paper and
fitting in as many of the more than nine hundred inhabited islands
as I could. After many failed pitches, I finally convinced an editor
to let me go in 2015. One sweetener I had added to the pitch was a
Bali-on-the-cheap story, written from the country's most-dreamed-
of island, fetishized by everyone from young Australians in search
of cheap booze to older spiritual types looking to re-create the latter
third of Elizabeth Gilbert's *Eat, Pray, Love*.

I stayed at a guesthouse in Kemenuh, which locals called
a "village," but to me it felt more like a random patch of urban
sprawl around Denpasar, Bali's capital. My bare-bones single in
an elegant, templelike complex was so cheap—$9 a night—that I
decided to hire a driver for a day, an unspeakable luxury for the
Frugal Traveler.

I asked the driver, Jay, to get me out of metropolitan Denpasar to a more traditional village. I was not expecting tattooed, pierced tribesmen in thatched huts—just a glimpse of a more rural lifestyle, preferably not in an area overrun with travelers. I had been a bit traumatized a few days earlier by the *Eat, Pray, Love* setting of Ubud, where rice paddies are traversed by well-maintained bike paths dotted with organic cafés, yoga studios, and a tourist-packed Monkey Forest.

Jay said he knew just the place: Penglipuran, twenty miles outside the city limits. But when we arrived, it became clear I had not accurately communicated my desires. To enter the village, we had to park in a large parking lot and pay a $1.30 admission fee for a slip of paper with a number on it, indicating which house I had been assigned to visit.

Penglipuran turned out to be the oddest combination of real life and tourist attraction I have ever seen. Structurally, it was indeed a preserved traditional village—gardens, temples, and a bamboo forest beyond. Real families lived in the houses. But it was also a full-blown tourist attraction complete with maps, souvenirs, and snacks. For all I know, it was well meaning and benefited those living in it, but it felt like a creepy human zoo.

That night, I looked up what TripAdvisor reviewers had to say.

And I was astonished. Most write-ups played along with the fiction that it was a real village, just as Jay had. Here's one of the top reviews that appeared:

This is perhaps THE MOST BEAUTIFUL VILLAGE we have ever visited during all our travels around the world to 118 countries!

After a drive from Ubud during a private tour of Bali, our guide/driver took us to this traditional Balinese village. We drove up into the hills and through stands of tall bamboo forests. Awaiting us was this Shangri-La. A fairy tale village of colorful neat homes, each with tiled roofs and gates carved intricately from black lava. Located in each yard in the northeast corner of each home was an equally beautifully designed private temple.

The quiet, immaculately clean lanes and paths were made from pavers and small stones arranged in patterns of flowers and animals. Colorful and lush plants lined the lanes and filled the yards.

After the heat and chaos of Ubud, the atmosphere here was cool, serene and fresh. The village and its friendly, unpretentious people exhibited a quiet peacefulness not found in other places in Bali. It was an almost spiritual experience. I wish we could have stayed here for a longer period of time rather than an hour's visit.

There is so much more of Bali to explore than its beaches. This is Bali at its best. If you miss this place, you have NOT experienced the REAL Bali.[5]

The real Bali? That's preposterous.

Though Penglipuran wasn't for me, I can imagine visitors who know what they're in for finding a lot to like there. But not by pretending that the families who live and work there have maintained the ancient layout of their homes and exhibit a "quiet peacefulness" by choice, rather than (at least in part) to make a buck. "Sort of like Colonial Williamsburg, except families actually live there"—now that would have been a helpful review.

In my opinion, that is. For the Bali experience I wanted, that is. In the context of my prior travels, that is. But the typical visitor arrives in Bali with an agenda different from mine. To begin with, I had come from halfway around the world, whereas the large majority of Bali visitors—and thus potential TripAdvisor reviewers—are Asians, including many Indonesians making the short and easy hop from Jakarta. Another major chunk consists of young Australians, who fly six hours direct from Melbourne to party on the beaches of Kuta. For me, depending on TripAdvisor reviews from the average Bali-goer would have been like a Ukrainian anthropologist going to Mexico and depending on the reviews of American spring breakers.

TripAdvisor is also a victim of its own success. It's a many-headed monster, supporting twenty-eight languages and attracting international travelers of every stripe. Thus, almost by definition, most TripAdvisor reviews are written by people unlike you. It is true that on TripAdvisor (and other similarly gargantuan companies like Amazon) you can filter the reviews by type of traveler (solo, couple, family), time of year, and language, so perhaps filtering out Indonesian reviews would reduce the influence of those on short domestic trips. And TripAdvisor also displays how active reviewers are—presumably those who write the most reviews are the savviest travelers, undercutting the argument for "professional" guidebook writers and journalists. You can also see where they are from, a good way to eliminate Australians on drunken beach weekends. That said, filtering is not foolproof. I regret to report that the author of the Penglipuran review is an elite Level 6 Contributor from the Midwest.

Another issue with many generalist review sites is that there's no obvious way to filter for reviewers' standards. I'm especially wary when I read reviews of budget accommodations like, say, Motel 6. If a reviewer complains of a mediocre mattress and cranky shower, how am I supposed to know their standards, what they're measuring against? If written by a couple accustomed to five-star accommodations who had had car trouble and made an unexpected stop, the fact they had nothing worse to say might make this the most luxurious Motel 6 in America. A glowing review of the $1,400-a-night Junior Suite at The Plaza in New York by a frequent Motel 6 customer who just won big on *Wheel of Fortune*, however, wouldn't hold much water.

There is one group of travelers who will never find their kind represented in TripAdvisor reviews: those who never leave reviews. I'm not sure how reviewers differ from nonreviewers, but I'm betting they do.

❋ ❋ ❋ ❋

And what of fake reviews, accusations of which have plagued TripAdvisor, Yelp, and other companies almost since they launched? The companies argue that their human and algorithmic detection systems catch and remove most blatantly fake opinions, and that is likely true. But even a few malicious reviews slipping through the cracks can ruin new businesses.

Fake sugary-sweet ones, on the other hand, can bestow an undeserved sterling reputation on a business, even one that doesn't exist. An Italian magazine created a fictional restaurant that became TripAdvisor's No. 1 ranked eatery in the town of Moniga del Garda, proving, at the very least, that savvy restaurateurs could game the system for a while before being caught.

Successful fakery is much harder once businesses are well established and have received hundreds or thousands of reviews. And not all sites are equally vulnerable: Booking.com won't allow you to leave a review unless you've booked and paid for a stay, making fraudulent entries quite expensive.

Sometimes the lies seem harmless, such as when new business owners ask their friends for their potentially honest, though almost certainly biased, opinions. A friend who had recently launched a product sent me (and presumably many others) the following email:

BOOM! My cologne is up and selling on Amazon, bizzatch! Please buy one and leave a great review. (I will pay you back.)

A couple of notes: First, I did it. Second, most of my friends do not address me as "bizzatch." Third, and most important, Amazon is not a travel site. But user reviews hold similar sway there, and members of the travel industry certainly use similar ploys. Jay, the driver from Bali, courted me on WhatsApp for a year with harmless chitchat before asking me to leave a positive review. "I need your help one more time to click [a link to his TripAdvisor page]. To write something good for me,,, please,,,," he wrote. Once again, kind words in the *Times* were not enough. And this time, I didn't do it.

Sometimes the whole thing turns nasty. A motel owner not far from Daytona Beach once regaled me with war stories from his TripAdvisor battle with another local motel: His friends left positive reviews for his place and trashed his rival's; his rival's friends did precisely the inverse. Perhaps TripAdvisor's algorithm spotted them all and promptly removed them. And by "perhaps" I mean "I highly doubt it."

✳ ✳ ✳ ✳

Here's another, more subtle problem with user reviews that is particularly relevant to hotels. When you read a review, you don't know how much the person paid per night relative to the price you will be paying. I once wrote about the Greenporter, a once-aging motel that had been gussied-up to chicness on the North Fork of Long Island. I paid $133 a night off-season. To me that seemed like a good deal for a romantic weekend getaway. (Or a platonic getaway with my friend Jeanny; sometimes I used stunt doubles to serve as faux girlfriends when no real one existed.) It easily met my $133 expectations. But the user reviews were rife with complaints: According to guests, management had refused a request to change rooms, rugs were not utterly spotless, there was no fresh fruit at the free breakfast. Those complaints sound valid for someone paying regular rates of $239 or $289, but at $133 they were irrelevant.

✳ ✳ ✳ ✳

So far, I've just been ranting. But since user reviews have a huge impact on businesses both inside and outside the travel industry, they are often studied by academics, especially at business schools. An article in the *Journal of Consumer Research* by three professors at the University of Colorado breaks down some of the major findings, which I've paraphrased below:[6]

- ◆ Customers are more motivated to review a product when they want to rave or complain about it. Users who find the product mediocre, acceptable, or just "sorta OK" are thus underrepresented.
- ◆ Cultures vary in their willingness to be extreme. My interpretation: When Americans read that somewhere is the "worst place ever," they tend to understand it is not actually as bad as a World War I foxhole or a Syrian city under ISIS rule. But people in some cultures are more literal or even

too polite. Thus, an American may read a review by, say, an Englishman who found a hotel room "a bit musty" and think, "no big deal," only to find that, in American terms, it is actually "the mustiest place ever."

◆ User reviews can be influenced by earlier reviews of the same product, leading to herding behaviors. Someone who reads a positive review somewhere might feel subconscious pressure to leave another positive review.

◆ There is evidence that reviews are manipulated by business owners and their competitors (so I wasn't making that up).

The professors then delve into their own study, which compared Amazon user-review averages to *Consumer Reports* scores for the same products and asked whether average consumers and professional testers would come to different conclusions. The answer was yes—there was "poor correlation" between amateur and professional reviewers. Of course, whether you trust users or *Consumer Reports* is up to you, but I'd go for the professionals, who most likely tested the products more objectively, rigorously, and scientifically.

The parallel with travel is only partial. *Consumer Reports* largely tests physical products, whereas travel writers evaluate experiences, and not necessarily rigorously or scientifically (though many of us try our hardest). And, as I'll get into in more detail later, there are plenty of reasons to distrust the objectivity of certain publications, especially those that accept complimentary services and whose unanonymous reviewers are thus coddled by business owners.

More applicable is the authors' conclusion that many consumers interpret review sites poorly. For example, they "place enormous weight on the average user rating as an indicator of objective quality compared to other cues." An "Exceptional" 9.8 average score over 1,500 reviews for a big hotel on Booking.com is vastly more reliable mathematically than the same 9.8 average score on the same site for a rental apartment with only fifteen reviews, but many consumers either don't notice that or don't look at the sample size.

The blog *fivethirtyeight* took a clever approach to the same issue, comparing Yelp's user reviews to the (presumable) gastronomes who award Michelin stars to restaurants. It compared restaurants that had just lost a star with those that retained or gained stars, under the assumption that these restaurants were in similar leagues but the star-losers had been evaluated poorly by the Michelin folks.

Yelp came out looking quite good: Restaurants that had lost Michelin stars averaged 3.83 Yelp stars, barely better than the city average, whereas each additional Michelin star raised its average two-tenths of a Yelp star. In other words, Yelp reviewers agreed with the Michelin reviewers' decisions.

But there was an odd footnote: Yelp reviewers favored more expensive restaurants significantly more than Michelin reviewers did—the opposite of what I would have expected, since Yelpers pay for their meals and Michelin writers are on expense accounts. It's unclear why, though *fivethirtyeight* creator Nate Silver posited that Michelin reviewers focused exclusively on the food, whereas Yelp reviewers were impressed by the elegant atmosphere and top-notch service regardless of food quality. Which scores are more accurate? It depends on what you look for in a restaurant.

If approached differently, however, user reviews can be a useful tool for far more than evaluating the atmosphere of restaurants. The more than 600 million reviews of more than 7.5 million businesses on TripAdvisor alone, and countless more from other companies, is an extraordinary resource. So let's talk about ways to harness their power.

Extract the Facts

Forget (for now) about the god-awful din of contradictory and sometimes downright insane opinions out there. TripAdvisor, Yelp, and others are also extraordinary treasure troves of verifiable facts. Let's say I am looking for an affordable place to stay in London, and I apply a "£75 or less" filter to the site I'm using. Scrolling through the first dozen reviews for one place, I ignore occasional mattress and shower complaints (recall Motel 6) and the riffs on rude reception clerks (not infrequently a projection of a rude client). But then in review no. 13, I read: "The hotel is a more than 20-minute walk from the Tube." This gets my attention, and I check a map to verify. If true, I'm moving on to the next place—in London, being near public transportation is too vital. For a resort, a review that reads, "the beach is rocky, be sure to get up early to snatch a sandy spot," might send me into a Google Images search to check just *how* rocky. For a bar, a note such as "Friday night's a zoo and there's never more than one bartender on duty" may not be instantly verifiable, but on TripAdvisor and some other sites, you can search by keyword, so I'd use "Friday" to look for similar complaints. And then go on Thursday instead.

Facts found in user reviews can also be used to stave off problems before they arise. If a lone reviewer notes that "The wifi sucks"—an opinion—maybe she was trying to download feature films. If someone else writes: "The wifi does not reach the third floor," well, that's (at least provisionally) a fact—one you might double-check with a call or email to the hotel. Or just be safe and request a room on one of the first two floors.

Look for Facts in Strange Places

Let's say you're planning a trip to Martinique and are fishing around for restaurants when you come across the following TripAdvisor entry:

La Mandoline, No. 2 of 607 restaurants in Martinique

Most people would see that line as an opinion, albeit a collective one: La Mandoline is the second-best restaurant on the French Caribbean island of Martinique. But it also contains a quite surprising fact: There are 607 restaurants in Martinique. Say what? Where are these restaurants? You might open up TripAdvisor's map and look for hidden corners of the island far from your hotel (though not *that* far, since you can drive across the island in a couple of hours), perhaps sparking an adventure.

To me, this, not the reviews, is the most useful aspect of TripAdvisor. It's the biggest travel resource list ever compiled in the history of the universe. I'm always looking for surprises, those special everyday spots that say more about a place than its celebrated Wher-ever Museum of Art (WheMA). So I'll skip the Top 10 or Top 20 "Things to do" or "Restaurants" and dive into the middle of the list. Just now I searched Philadelphia and, on a random, middling "Things to do" page, found myself intrigued by places I had never heard of: the Mummers Museum, the Physick House, and a place called the Woodford Mansion, which had a perfect score after nine reviews. (Small sample size, I know, I know.) I'm not sure I'd like any of those places—I don't even know what a "mummer" is—but it's easy enough to find their websites and learn more.

Even better than the middle of the list is the end. You'd expect to find the worst attractions in town (No. 998 of 998 "Things to do" in Ottawa: Used Kitty Litter Depository) or the most disgusting places to stay (No. 546 of 546 Seattle B&Bs and Inns: the Clogged Toi-let Lodge). There might be some of that. But you might also find a quirky eatery no one has yet thought to review, a unique new guided tour, or an out-of-the-way guesthouse that just opened and has great specials.

Use Opinions Wisely

So you could use TripAdvisor as a facts repository. But as long as the opinions are there too, how do you make the most of them?

First, don't take *exact* average ratings too seriously. It's silly to think that a hotel with 4.2 stars will suit you better than a hotel with 4.1 stars. Delve into specific opinions.

You might even grab a saltshaker and dive into the unhinged world of one-star reviews. (You'll need to take them with more than a few grains of salt.) What did people hate? If there's a distinct pat-tern, decide whether it matters to you. Horrible breakfast is fine if you're in a place with a famous bakery next door (or you don't plan to get up before noon); "no English-speaking staff" is fine if you speak the local language. A night clerk known to sexually harass solo travelers? Now that might warrant your attention.

Second, consider that TripAdvisor might not be the best resource for you, personally. One way to do that is to reverse-engineer your way to the site that best suits you. After your next trip, rate the places you stayed and ate and then check them on TripAdvisor, Yelp, Booking, Google, OpenTable, Urbanspoon, Foursquare, and more if you can stand it. Which source best matches your own opinions? That should be your go-to from then on. While you're at it, check non-crowdsourced sites, such as LonelyPlanet.com or Frommers .com, or even mentions in the *New York Times* (or the the *Guardian* or *Travel + Leisure*), if you can find them. If what one publication wrote about your destination jibes with what you thought, favor it as a resource.

Next, use the filters. Let me put that differently: USE THE FILTERS, DAMMIT! I love Trip.com's "Tribes" filter—you can see picks for history lovers, vegetarians, budget travelers, art and design buffs. If a review app allows you to filter out business travelers, you really should—business travelers have totally different criteria.

And then get creative. Say you're checking TripAdvisor for a genuine French restaurant in New York. You could filter for French-language reviews and read (in translation) what native speakers had to say. Should you be feeling extra snobby, you could glance at where reviewers are from and skip them if they're from Québec or Tahiti or Belgium.

Finally, favor recent reviews over older ones—tour guides leave, chefs change, loud construction projects begin across the street— and give more merit to frequent reviewers over infrequent contributors, who may have a bone to pick or be a friend of the owner.

Make User Reviews Your Last Resource, Not Your First

Though it's easier to access the opinions of strangers, it is very much worth trying your friends, or friends of friends, first. This can be done face-to-face or through social media. Depending on how widely those in your social media circles travel, a simple "Who has restaurant recommendations in San Francisco?" could circumvent user reviews altogether. I trust my friends' tastes; that's why they're my friends. It's also more fun to go to a place your friends recommended—and send them a photo while you're there. Maybe they'll even give you a name, like Ted, their favorite server who also happens to be their cousin's roommate. That doesn't work with user reviews. ("Oh, hey Ted! Vibeke472 of Copenhagen says Hi!")

This may not work if your destination is Naypyidaw, Myanmar. That's where sites for travelers with shared interests—Chowhound, for example, for the food-obsessed—come in handy. If you have no connections or resources at all, then ask for advice during your trip. Tips from the person sitting next to you on the plane have a surprising success rate, in my experience.

If you have any reason to question the opinions you get, then the perfect use for TripAdvisor or its competitors is as a brief check for reassurance that advice from known human sources isn't totally off the wall.

Complain

Finally, one of the best tools user reviews have given us is the complaint. There's no longer any need to demand to speak to the manager, or to curse your way out of there while vowing to write a letter or email to a generic address and hope someone reads it (which you'll never do anyway). But now there's no excuse, because most businesses pay careful attention to reviews and quite often respond. It works far better, by the way, to address the specific problem(s) and provide details in a respectful tone. Not only will this help the management solve them, but it is much more likely to be taken seriously by future readers of your review than a rant.

ONLINE TRAVEL AGENCIES

It used to be that user-review sources stood on their own and could claim that informing travelers was their sole mission. Their services were free, and it was common for travelers to look for information there and then book somewhere else, either directly with the business or through an online travel agency (OTA) like Kayak.

But today these companies have either become OTAs themselves or have partnered with another OTA and receive a portion of the revenue when bookings come via their site. Until 2013, TripAdvisor's main revenue source was from businesses themselves, who paid if they wanted their website and phone number listed on the site; now you can often book without leaving TripAdvisor.com or the app. Yelp, which has also long offered a similar "enhanced listing," now makes a portion of its revenue when you order delivery or reserve a table through one of its services. And OTAs have either started their own user-review systems or entered into agreements with TripAdvisor, Yelp, and the like to embed theirs.

The sites and apps you use to book travel are also now part of humongous corporations with demanding shareholders. Booking Holdings (formerly called Priceline Group), for example, owns Priceline, Booking.com, Kayak, Agoda.com, and OpenTable, and is worth more than $87 billion, according to Forbes; TripAdvisor is a relative pipsqueak at about $6.2 billion—but still enough to make you realize they are not out there for altruistic reasons. Travelers who book a $250 hotel room on an OTA often don't realize that $40 or $50 or so of that is going to the OTA, or perhaps being divided between the OTA and the company that led you to it. That's a huge commission, but most hotels, airlines, and tour companies know that OTAs are used by so many travelers that opting out would make them nearly invisible, so they've given in.

There are exceptions, like Southwest Airlines, which has managed to stay off Expedia, Kayak, and the like and survive. (I usually forget to check southwest.com when I fly, but others obviously remember or they'd be out of business.) Many small inns and guesthouses opt out, as well. You won't see two of my favorite lodgings of all time—Bowen Farm Bed & Breakfast, in Stanton, Kentucky, or Friendly Bike Guest House in Portland, Oregon—on either Booking or Expedia. They're good enough to survive largely via word of mouth, good old-fashioned press, and guidebook listings—so if you always use OTAs, you'll have a tough time finding them. (Bowen was recommended to me by a friend in Lexington, Kentucky, and I found Friendly Bike in an article in the *Guardian* unearthed by a specific Google search.)

You may be wondering why hotels and airlines don't undercut the

OTAs by offering special prices on their own sites. After all, they could cut direct purchasers a 10 percent discount and still come out ahead. The answer is *rate parity*, an agreement between OTAs and travel providers to ensure rates don't vary across publicly available platforms. The hotels hate these agreements, but they have to participate or, again, face becoming invisible. Though several European countries have outlawed the practice, it's still going strong in most of the world. The most important lesson is to remember that the companies you use to book travel are not simple middlemen, but instead are deeply engaged in the effort to get you to spend—not necessarily by any means necessary, but by a lot of means that you're not aware of.

For example, have you ever wondered how the OTAs decide which listings to show you first?

In August 2016, I decided to look into whether business interests held sway over traveler interests when search results were displayed on popular OTAs. At the time, I was a loyal customer of Booking .com, largely because they had the most exhaustive listings, often unearthing small, locally owned hotels that were nowhere to be seen on competing OTAs. They also had that more fraud-proof review system. Plus, they called me a "Genius"—a user status that often meant a 10 percent discount. I considered myself a savvy user of the site.

I was not.

I had never noticed, for example, that many Booking.com listings had mysterious little yellow thumbs-up signs next to them, with no apparent explanation. Unless, it turns out, you know to hover over the symbol with your cursor. In 2016, those came with the following explanation:

> This property has agreed to be part of our Preferred Properties Program, which groups together properties that stand out because of their excellent services and quality/price ratio with competitive prices. Participation in the program requires meeting a specific set of criteria and takes feedback from previous guests into account.[7]

A Booking spokesperson explained to me at the time that about 30 percent of its properties were part of the program, and that the Preferred Properties almost always appear before un-Preferred ones on the site's default "Our Picks First" search results.

As well they should, you might be thinking. After all, these hotels have met "a specific set of criteria"! And the main criterion is (drum roll please) . . .

They pay Booking more.

The Booking spokesperson told me that another requirement for being listed in the Preferred Properties section was at least an average 7 or a 7.5 user rating. That was untrue: I had been searching New York City and noticed that the Hotel Pennsylvania frequently showed up toward the very top of my search results, with an average of 6.0. That score sounded right: The hotel, located near Madison Square Garden, is widely known as the kind of place you get if you are looking for a midtown hotel and can't afford a mediocre one. A 6.0 score got it a euphemistic "Pleasant" Booking rating, one category below "Good." It's so pleasant, it was the 381st-ranked hotel of 383 in New York City when I looked. The Booking spokesperson had no explanation for the discrepancy, but I did: The description of the Preferred Properties Program was blatantly dishonest. The wording has since changed: Now properties "may pay Booking.com a little more to be in this program," though "may" may be "a little" dishonest. The Hotel Pennsylvania, whose average reviews score has now fallen to 5.7, is still in the program.

The Booking problem was the worst I found, though I'm sure I missed some beauties. Expedia's similar program—higher commission for a nudge up in visibility—didn't seem quite as awful: A representative explained to me that hotels used it only on specific days with low occupancy, and that it was only one piece of the ranking algorithm, unlike Booking, where just about all "Preferred Properties" leapt to the top of the rankings.

I was happy to detect nothing untoward about the way TripAdvisor listed its results. And, unlike any competitor I could find, they even list the hotels you cannot book through them or their partners, a legacy of their original objective of collecting user reviews on

every place under the sun. I was happy to see the Bowen Farm Bed
& Breakfast and the Friendly Bike Guest House listed—and well-
reviewed—on there.

I was less happy to see the way TripAdvisor actively and effectively discourages you from staying at them, instead nudging you
toward places that will give them a commission. This makes sense,
of course, if you think of TripAdvisor as a for-profit business. But
not enough of us do. Christopher Frick of the Friendly Bike Guest
House first pointed this out to me. I tested it out later, and indeed, if
you try to book his place in TripAdvisor, the site informs you:

> We can't find prices for this hotel.
> Our online travel partners don't provide prices for this
> accommodation, but we can search other options in Portland.[8]

Below that, there's a big yellow button labeled "Show Prices."

I had two choices. Either Google "Friendly Bike Guest House,"
navigate there, type in my dates again, and reserve through their
site. Or, easier, click the yellow button. But when I did that, I was
shown mostly big hotels downtown, the absolute opposite of what I
was looking for.

Kudos to TripAdvisor for at least listing the place, unlike the OTAs
that ignore its existence. But it is another example of companies we
sometimes consider neutral pushing travelers toward decisions meant
to maximize profit, not do what is best for the traveler.

The same is true of the "Things to do" function. Back in the day,
TripAdvisor's "Things to do" got you a ranked list of the "best"
activities in a city or region. It was pretty simple, and seemingly an
afterthought to a site more focused on lodging and, later, restaurants. In 2014, though, TripAdvisor bought Viator, a booking site
for tours and activities. Soon afterward, the "Things to do" pages
were dramatically transformed. They were now hawking tours
and services they stood to make a profit from, with organic search
results relegated far down the page. As of this writing, it's a little
more balanced, but still clearly prioritizes profit over information.
Just about every attraction has some way to spend money: The list-

ing for Central Park boasts 111 booking items. Most sane people, of course, do not pay for a tour of Central Park; they use their own two feet, or, as the first four reviews suggested, rented bikes cheaply by the hour, no reservation necessary. Alas, those reviews were buried far down the page.

Because they can't compete publicly on price, the OTAs and company websites are engaged in a whole range of shenanigans to try to get you to buy from them and not from the competition. So a hotel chain will offer free perks if you buy direct on their website; an OTA may offer loyalty points or other discounts; I've already mentioned my Genius status on Booking. One site, getaroom.com, actually gives discounts only if you call them up. I often wonder whether hotels treat customers differently depending on where they booked. It would certainly make sense. If I heard that a couple reserved my hotel through Booking, I'd be quite keen to see them treated well, since I know Booking will be pursuing them after their stay to get them to write a review.

Perhaps these seem like minor details. But it's important to remember that the relationship between OTAs and hotels (and airlines and tour operators and . . .) is now extraordinarily complicated and difficult to decipher.

That's not what they say, of course. When I ask as a reporter, they always give me more or less the same spiel: Their mission is to lead you, the customer, to make the best travel choices—that they happen to make money at the same time is secondary.

"If we help you as a consumer find the right hotel and help you book it at the right price with the right partner, you don't care that it's a commercial relationship," Adam Medros, then senior vice president at TripAdvisor, told me in a 2014 interview. Well, that depends on your definition of "the right hotel." If it means "a hotel that will satisfy you," OK. If it means "the best hotel out there for your needs," I'm not so sure at all, especially if you've picked one of Booking's Preferred Properties lodgings.

So . . . to use OTAs or not? They invest oodles of money into designing their websites to push you toward buying, but then again, who doesn't? It's often harder to make changes to a reservation through them than if you book direct with an airline or hotel. But they are incredibly convenient and easy to use and combine user reviews, easy filters, and quick booking all in one place—not to mention the discounts for "Geniuses" like me.

I tend to deal with the dilemma on a case-by-case basis: If I'm in a hurry and just want a good-enough place to sleep, I'll go on one of the OTAs. But if I'm looking for a really special place, I'll look elsewhere. I'll go to local bed-and-breakfast listing sites; I'll look at official tourism sites, which often have complete, free listings of all local lodgings; I'll Google articles about the region. In smaller towns, I'll often go to TripAdvisor and scroll straight down the list to the bottom, digging for hidden treasures. Then, I'll look up the place online and call them. Not only does that give you a real sense of the service there, but it could save you some bucks. "I was thinking of booking you through Travelocity," I'll say. "Do you have any discount for booking direct?" If they're smart, they'll knock 10 percent off, knowing they'll lose 20 percent or more if I book through an OTA, and we'll both come out ahead. Weirdly, the opposite can also be true if you show up and try to book on the spot: Sometimes the rate the hotel (or motel or inn) offers you is actually higher than the OTA's price, and they refuse to budge. On several occasions, I've broken out my phone and reserved via OTA while sitting in the lobby of the hotel.

Using OTAs has become so automatic that we kind of forget there's any other way to do it. A deep dive into hundreds of choices with thousands of reviews can eat up your evening, or your week, if you let it. Sometimes, when I use an old-fashioned way of finding a hotel—say, from a friend's recommendation, or a travel agent—I'm delighted at how much time I save.

Despite all my whining, there is a huge upside for travelers in the mere existence of OTAs. They have a massive democratization effect, bringing tens of thousands of small businesses with next to no budget for marketing to every traveler with an internet connection. And that commission? OTAs will argue that it is not extortion, but a very reasonable marketing fee.

Major hotel chains spend huge amounts on marketing. In late 2015, Sheraton launched a $100 million campaign to "revive the tired brand," as Skift put it. That's about $222,000 per hotel in one campaign alone. Compare that to the Cleverdale Guest House in Barbados, where I stayed in 2010. As of 2018, they are doing well on Booking, with an 8.7 rating (a noneuphemistic "Fabulous") and very few available dates. Assuming they pay a 20 percent commission every time they get a reservation through Booking (and competitors), the most they would pay in commissions, if they filled every room year-round through OTAs, would likely be under $25,000. That isn't small change for what is in effect a year-long, worldwide marketing campaign, but it's not bad, at least compared to Sheraton's costs.

Plus, how else would anyone find a place like the just-off-the-beachfront Cleverdale in Barbados? I did, by sheer luck, back in 2010. They were not yet on Booking.com, but a couple I met over piles of fried marlin at a Friday-night fish-fry recommended it when I mentioned I was unhappy with my hotel. It has appeared in some blogs, and it's on Airbnb as well, though in a sense that's just a different sort of OTA. But OTAs are the most direct route.

As of this writing, if you search Booking.com by average review score, Cleverdale appears 23rd on the list in all of Barbados, on page two of search results. If you just leave it to the default ranking— "Our Top Picks First"—it falls to 100th of 226. The first twenty-one are members of the "Preferred Properties Program." Beyond that, it's a mystery why it drops so far: I presume the Cleverdale has some other algorithmic formula going against it.

I should note that I haven't stopped using Booking, but the first thing I do when I search is reorder the default search results by review score.

FOOD SEARCH

Famished after a two-leg cross-country flight rife with delays and scarce on nutrition, I tapped Google Maps on my phone and scanned the area around my LAX airport hotel in hopes of an ill-advised late-night nosh at a nearby hole-in-the-wall.

McDonald's and Denny's appeared instantly, next to little white circles with orange fork-and-knife symbols inside. Not a good start. I then typed in "restaurants," which turned up a handful of red circles with similarly embedded forks and knives. Among the choices that were utterly unappealing to me were a Carl's Jr. and a hotel cocktail bar. Mariscos Moni ("Simple shack for seafood and Mexican grub") sounded promising, but it was closed.

OK, I wasn't in a foodie redoubt like Koreatown or Silver Lake, but still, was this the best Los Angeles could do? I zoomed in to look street by street. If there were no good restaurants, what was there? Answer: good restaurants. Smaller red dots began appearing. Thai. Somali. A Greek spot. And then Melo Burger, an "Old-school, 24/7 burger stand." Bingo. A delicious dinner awaited.

But I was left wondering: If our smartphones are supposed to know us, why had Denny's, McDonald's, and Carl's Jr., precisely what I wasn't looking for, popped up first?

I talked to a bunch of people, and the answer is: It's complicated.

First things first: A Google spokesman assured me the big chains' presence "has nothing to do with any sort of commercial relationship." That, of course, doesn't account for ads that may appear—or Google's "promoted pins"—but those are all clearly marked.

So what could account for Google's extremely bad taste in restaurants near LAX—at least to users who prefer highly rated local spots to mediocre national chains? Google's algorithm is secret, and too complicated for me to understand anyway, but the company states publicly that "relevance, distance, and prominence" play key roles. Prominence seems to have been the culprit in my case. "Well-known store brands that are familiar to many people are also likely to be prominent in local search results," explains a Google page for businesses titled "Improve your local ranking on Google."[9]

You might be thinking: "Why would an experienced traveler use Google Maps when there are so many great apps and sites out there that specialize in unearthing cool restaurants based on user reviews that you, a travel writer, must have on your phone?" (I do.) My excuse: I was exhausted. I wasn't writing a story. I just wanted to eat and go to bed. And when we want something fast these days, face it: We all Google.

Later, I went and looked at what would have popped up had I done the same search for restaurants on Yelp, TripAdvisor, and Mapquest (the new Mapquest, by the way, which is great). The top ten restaurants listed were wildly different on each app. There was next to no overlap, except for Aliki's Greek Taverna, which showed up everywhere. I thought that might be because they each had different sets of my personal data, so I logged myself out—and got the same results.

Assuming the spokespeople for all those companies were being honest when they told me there is no commercial interference in search results, then what? The algorithms, of course. We can't know what's going on in there, but here's one clue: Yelp told me they work hard to develop a community presence, so a large percentage of their reviews are being written by local residents. TripAdvisor reviews are, of course, largely written by travelers. Which is better? That's up to you. Local reviews seem appealing to me as an adventurous eater, but an American in Taiwan, or a Taiwanese in America, might prefer to read reviews in their own language written by travelers like them, rather than local (and often machine-translated) evaluations.

And if businesses cannot directly influence their rank, they can pay to be more visible—or, in Yelp's case, less invisible. Unless a business ponies up for an "enhanced profile," Yelp places competitors' ads above the photos and reviews of its place. None of us are impervious to ads, whether we claim to be or not. So there's a decent chance that even if the No. 1 Greek restaurant in Chicago is the perfect place for you, Yelp will nudge you toward the competition.

How to choose the source that's right for you? Again, reverse engineering. With restaurant apps, you don't even need to travel—just search your city, or a city you know well, and see what Mapquest, Google, Yelp, TripAdvisor, and others like Urbanspoon and Foursquare, have to say. Whichever matches up best with your taste is your future go-to.

When I did just that for Times Square, I was again shocked at how different the results were for restaurants. Google's twelve or so highlighted restaurants include Barbetta, a highly rated classic, but also Utsav, an Indian place with mediocre reviews, and the Olive Garden (sigh). TripAdvisor lists five independent Italian places in the top eight. Then I logged into my account, and it added Olive Garden and Sbarro. Come on! Nothing against Olive Garden in a suburban mall, but in New York City? My first thought: Could TripAdvisor know me worse? Then I realized I was logged in via Facebook and it was prioritizing restaurants my Facebook friends had reviewed. My former friends, I should add.

THE "SHARING" ECONOMY

The internet has done far more than just catalog, promote, and facilitate the purchase of traditional travel services. It has allowed for the creation of a parallel world of person-to-person travel services, rendering large sectors of the formal travel industry—really all but the airlines—largely unnecessary for travelers who want to avoid them. It's part of what we've come to call the sharing economy.

So now you get a ride from someone you don't know to the apartment of a stranger who's rented you her spare bedroom, then rent a bike from another random person before you take a cooking class in some guy's house and top it off with a date who looks nothing like their profile pictures.

Deception in online dating has been around since long before I broke up with my girlfriend and created a profile in Yahoo! Personals in 2000. But it wasn't until 2004 that Couchsurfing began its community of people offering—much less deceptively in most cases—free places to crash. Things really got rolling (though became less idealistic) when Airbnb began offering paid places to crash in 2008. Since then, everyone's just been copying them. The world has since seen Airbnb for bikes (Spinlister); Airbnb for cars (Turo, Drivy, GetAround, etc.); Airbnb for canines (DogVacay); Airbnb for weddings (WedShed); Airbnb for event space (HireSpace). There's even a site that claims to be "Airbnb for Airbnb," finding people a place to stay while others are renting their house through Airbnb. And, of course, Uber and its brethren.

There's a lot to love about how these services offer an escape from stuffy and traditional travel companies, often at far better prices. But the pure intentions and organic ideals of peer-to-peer exchange have been marred by astonishing rounds of financing and slick marketing campaigns by monopoly-seeking behemoths like Airbnb and Uber. In other cases, travel-industry stalwarts who want in on the action have snapped up start-ups. In addition to its purchase of Viator (Airbnb for tour guides) for $200 million in 2014 TripAdvisor bought a minority share in EatWith (Airbnb for home-cooked meals) and integrated it into its restaurant pages in late 2016.

It is as regrettable as it was inevitable that some of these companies strayed from their original purpose and started behaving more like the industry they had so much potential to replace. Much as I love the service Airbnb markets—staying in someone else's home instead of an anonymous hotel, wow!—that's not always the service it provides. More and more listings on Airbnb are purely commercial enterprises. Airbnb doesn't deny this, but they certainly don't promote it, either. Etiquette calls for each listing to be accompanied by a friendly profile pic and first name, with the implication that this is the person whose home you're "experiencing" while they're away. And while some "hosts" openly admit that they are actually managing a slew of apartments, others still pretend to be a friendly homeowner. And no wonder, their reviews depend on it. A study commissioned by opponents of Airbnb found that 30 percent of its New York City rentals were "classified as Commercial based on the number of units controlled by the host and the length of time the listing is available." But the listing is still under Rick, who's wearing a T-shirt and goofy hat in his profile pic.

"Book rooms with locals, rather than hotels," went the pre-2010 Airbnb branding, and back then it was real. But a 2016 promotional video called *What is Airbnb?* featuring actual guests and hosts is almost shockingly dishonest. "Airbnb is a community of people who share their space for travelers from all over the world," says one host. "When you travel with Airbnb, you travel with real people, in real neighborhoods," says another. "Your host will take very good care of you," says a third.

It accurately describes some of my Airbnb experiences. But the other kinds of owners are conspicuously absent. Where's the guy with ten apartments who hires a staff to take care of them? "Airbnb is great, because I'm making far more money than if I rented my investment properties out by the month or year!" he would say. Or perhaps, "I do everything I can to make my places seem like real homes, even though I've never lived in them. Actually, I don't even live in the country!"

Before the 2016 Olympics, I rented an apartment in a residential neighborhood of Rio. Online, it looked lived-in. But when I arrived, I realized I had been duped. The place looked as though the owner had bought some customized kit ("Young Francophile," perhaps, from the clichéd French posters) to create fake homeyness. The closets and shelves were devoid of any sign of personal items and the kitchen didn't even have a stove. The place was just fine, but it's a long way from what Airbnb used to stand for.

You do still get to live in a neighborhood, if you choose well. I loved spending two weeks in an apartment in Príncipe Real, an elegant and vaguely hip area of Lisbon, via Airbnb, even if it, too, was not an actual lived-in place. But so many of the neighborhood's apartments were rental properties (through Airbnb and other services) that I sometimes heard more English than Portuguese spoken in the streets and saw more *Lonely Planets* than newspapers being read in the plazas.

This transformation is sad for cities, and sad for less savvy travelers who are expecting a real home and walk into a soulless (if often stylish) investment property. That Airbnb allows this is too bad, though, as they gear up for a likely IPO, probably inevitable.

Maybe it's just the voyeur in me, but I love when I walk into an Airbnb apartment and know instantly I'm in someone's home—the place they live most of the year. It shows in the decor, but it's also obvious in the battered kitchen utensils, worn books on the shelves, and contents of dresser drawers—though those are usually locked up (not that I have tried to open them).

One way to up your chances of staying in a real, lived-in house where the owner is present is to rent only a bedroom. But not always: I've even stayed in subdivided apartments with separate codes on each of the bedroom doors.

Smart users can avoid such pitfalls. On Airbnb, check the owner profile and see whether they rent multiple properties. Ask up front whether it's a real home. In fact, for all services that claim to be part of the sharing economy, contact the provider directly and scan the reviews for signs you're being connected with a person and not a company. It's worth it, because at their best, these services are still providing a streamlined route into a richer, more personal travel experience. Sometimes when you least expect it. Like the time I thought I was just renting a car and ended up being thanked for liberating a nearby village during World War II.

It was in Besançon, France, where I had gone in 2015 in search of a less-touristed corner of the most-touristed country in the world. Besançon is a cobblestoned medieval charmer, home to 117,000, and was then capital of a region—Franche-Comté—famed for its Comté cheese and no slacker in the fondue business, either. Yet its hotels had received an average of seven American visitors a day in 2014. (In 2016, Franche-Comté was absorbed into Bourgogne-Franche-Comté, with its capital in much larger and more mustardy Dijon.)

The area was full of wineries and fromageries, not to mention the intriguing-sounding museum I mentioned earlier, the Musée des Maisons Comtoises (the Museum of Comtois Homes), in which houses dating back to the 1600s had been transported from their original settings across the region to an expanse of rolling countryside fifteen kilometers outside of the city. It's like Penglipuran, without the people and the inaccurate TripAdvisor reviews.

I would need a car to get around, but the cheapest available from an agency was more than fifty euros a day, about $47 at the time. On the Frugal Traveler budget, that was out of the question. So, for the first time, I tried Drivy, the French-based car-sharing company. I found a 2009 Renault Clio available for about thirty euros and hopped on Besançon's brand-new light-rail system to pick it up. (Fondue and a light rail? Too good to be true.) The owner had left the keys with her mother, Noëlle, who was the epitome of the American stereotype of an eighty-four-year-old French woman—dressed with elegant ease in a cowl-neck sweater and spiffy blue coat, fashionable sunglasses, coiffed gray hair, and meticulous lipstick. When I said in stumbling French that I was from the United States, her face lit up—a reaction unimaginable in Paris.

Noëlle had her reasons. Back in November 1944, months after Dijon and Besançon had been liberated by the Americans, her nearby village was still in German hands. Her seventeen-year-old cousin had been killed fighting for the Resistance, and she had spent three days in a basement taking shelter from Allied bombing before the GIs finally arrived.

Among the Americans to march into her village was a tall, strapping soldier named Bill. "*Bay, ee, deux L,*" she spelled it, dreamily, her unabashed, undiluted crush now seven decades old.

Soon after the liberation, she went to Dijon to "*faire la fête*"— i.e., party. She would have been fourteen. "The big soldiers, they smoked, they gave out chewing gum, there was jazz music in the streets," she recalled. I was delighted and she was delighted with my delight, admitting sheepishly that her family was sick of hearing her stories of the war.

She gave me the keys and I thanked her. Knowing full well she was being clever, she replied, "It's nothing, compared to liberating my country."

It was maybe a five-minute interchange, but the kind that leaves you inspired all day and sticks with you long afterward. The American liberation of France, which to me had been a story told in black-and-white newsreels, now bears the full-color face of Noëlle. Hopping online that night to read up about the period, I learned about a darker side: accusations of sexual assaults by some of those same soldiers. The newsreels, not surprisingly, had been gauzy versions of history, but the story of Bill and Noëlle, and the articles it led me to, had been the best kind of history lesson.

When I returned the car twenty-four hours later, Noëlle wasn't home. Her daughter was, though, and in inherited deadpan told me her mom was thinking about packing her bags and heading back to the United States with me.

Need I compare this experience to what would have awaited me at the Besançon Hertz or Europcar counter? Best-case scenario: a short line, a car in an unembarrassing color, and minimal haranguing about additional insurance options. In the unlikely event World War II stories had been available, they would certainly have resulted in additional fees.

Things do go wrong with even the best peer-to-peer services, as they are often not subject to laws governing the industry with which they are competing. The Airbnb apartment I rented at the last minute before that US–Ghana World Cup game in Natal, Brazil, was barren, save a mattress and sheets. When my brother had a Costa Rica reservation canceled at the last minute, Airbnb was slow to respond. We both dealt with it. But there are occasional tragedies— Louis Stone's death from a falling tree limb at an Airbnb property in Texas, chronicled in 2015 in *Medium*, is probably the best known.[10] And a study by Harvard Business School professors concluded that Airbnb hosts are more likely to reject black guests, something hotels with automatic booking systems could never get away with.[11]

There is an inherent conflict here: Informal exchange is by its nature unregulated; the more regulation, the more the service resembles the industry the traveler is trying to avoid.

Not all companies have gone supercorporate. Couchsurfing kept itself small and unchanged even as it became a for-profit company in 2011, avoiding the stratospheric funding rounds of Airbnb and the like. Founded in 2004, its origin story is a lesson in harnessing technology to improve travel: Casey Fenton was planning a budget trip to Iceland in 1999 when he decided to use the cutting-edge communication tool of the pre–social-networking era: email. He sent messages to more than fifteen hundred Reykjavik students, pleading for a couch to crash on. As *Entrepreneur* magazine put it:

The result was a new network of friends who offered to show him the "real" Reykjavik. After spending a weekend immersed in the culture of the area, Fenton walked away with disdain for the typical sanitized tourist experience—and an idea for a new nonprofit.[12]

The site was a great success, with millions signing up to host travelers and be hosted with no money exchanged. (The "cost" involves being a good community member, and maybe bringing a present, offering to cook, that sort of thing.) I signed up when I became Frugal Traveler in 2010 and started by hosting a few folks in my apartment—the quickest way to build up a good reputation in the community. It worked: A German couple and two French women came through, leaving nice reviews. And, thanks to them, along came two nineteen-year-old Mexican women, Karen and Breana, who deemed it safe to stay in the New York City home of an unattached forty-year-old man whose full name they did not know. I guess they saw the reviews from the previous guests and concluded that I did not have spy cams installed in the shower.

As I imagine many hosts do, I went out of my way to make them comfortable and give them privacy in the living room. (I do not have a guest bedroom.) They turned out to be inspiring travelers, not interested in a typical first-time-in-New-York experience. "The first thing we do when we get to a city is walk around aimlessly," Breana told me, showing no desire to make a *Sex and the City* pilgrimage for a cupcake at Magnolia Bakery or to get in line at the Empire State Building.

They sounded quite a bit like Casey Fenton in 1999, and like many of the people I met through Couchsurfing. The site was never perfect—whereas cute female Mexican backpackers rarely lacked a place to stay, forty-something American men have to try a bit harder. There is always the risk of assault or worse, and there have been a few incidents.

Couchsurfing increased its fees and raised a few million dollars in funding, but it hasn't shown too many other signs of a sellout and has largely stayed out of the news.

Plenty of other companies are still in purer stages of peer-to-peer sharing, and there are plenty of great experiences they can guide you toward—home-cooked meals, classes, private tour, even trips on yachts and private jets.

Ten years ago, I doubt very much that there was any way to find out about, much less reserve online, a village lunch with "Ben," fifteen minutes by *tuk-tuk* from Siem Reap, Cambodia. Thanks to withlocals.com, it's twenty euros plus tip, which sounds quite cheap from where I sit in New York, though (even minus the company's commission) it's probably pretty good money in Cambodia. Is lunch with Ben a genuinely local experience, or is it secretly part of a devious, profit-making scheme? If the latter, they have done an excellent job of faking it, starting with Ben's bumpy English: "Learn to make Cambodian tasty culinary food with the village chef at the truly Countryside."

COMMUNICATIONS

A couple of years ago, a Thursday night date with an out-of-town ex turned unexpectedly romantic. I suggested a weekend away in the mountains. She accepted, leaving me with less than twenty-four hours to plan. So I Googled bed-and-breakfasts in the area, looked up their reviews on TripAdvisor, made a list, and called around to try to get a bargain. The whole process took under an hour; I ended up paying $150 for what was listed as a $400 room in a place that either wowed her or brought out her best fake wowed look. Six months later, we were married.

Just kidding. She broke my heart, but I'm pretty sure that was in spite of, not because of, the lush pillows and decadent French toast at breakfast.

Imagine if I had been in that situation a few decades earlier. I'd have had to get to a bookstore to look up B&Bs, then ring them up to look for vacancies and ask for a discount as I racked up toll charges that chipped away at any discount I might get, what with each call costing a buck or two. (Adjusting for inflation, that's two bucks or three.) Or perhaps I could have called a travel agent and begged for last-minute help, but that would have been a crapshoot.

Modern communications have done much more than facilitate spontaneous adventures or save us trips to bookstores and quarter-a-minute long-distance fees.

It might help to recall how travel communications went, back in the late twentieth century, which some of you will remember.

To book a trip, you would choose among a number of methods: a package tour, a travel agent who could make magical reservations by typing green capital letters onto a black computer screen; or making them yourself, which involved some combination of phone calls and old-fashioned letter-writing, which, if you were lucky, your secretary typed.

Planning foreign trips on your own was even more hit-or-miss. You also had to hope that whoever received the letter could read and write English, or compose a letter in a foreign language long before Google Translate, or Google, for that matter. (A phrase book could help—"*Ada kamar untuk dua orang dengan AC untuk satu minggu?*" plus some dates might have gotten you a room for two with air-conditioning in Jakarta—though you'd be on your own to figure out the response.)

All this planning worked well enough for honeymoons and long-planned family vacations, but most independent travelers just winged it. My mother, traveling in Europe in the 1960s, would head straight from the train station to the tourist information office in any new city to find out what there was to do. I did exactly the same thing in 1991, according to the journal I kept during my semester abroad in France. That, along with hostel listings in my *Let's Go* guide or pensions in her Frommer's *Europe on 5 Dollars a Day*, got us places to sleep and maybe some ideas about what to do.

Beyond that, we mostly relied on people we encountered. I note in my journal that my travel buddy Dave and I met an Australian woman named Stella on a visit to Dachau and ended up having coffee with her in Munich. There she tipped us off to a German student party that cost us 10 deutsche marks (under $7) to get in and included what I documented as "free, quality beer and tons of pretzels with chive dip for all," and a university cafeteria where a pasta-and-salad lunch went for 5 deutsche marks, about three bucks and change.

How we stay connected with home has also changed. A lot. It used to be understood that if you were out of the country, you would be out of touch, at least on a day-to-day basis. You'd send postcards as soon as possible after you arrived somewhere so they might possibly get home before you did, or, for longer trips, you'd pen letters on flimsy blue aerograms. If you had a preplanned itinerary, you could do what my parents did and leave it with loved ones so you could (theoretically) be reached in case of (dire) emergency. Many travelers without set itineraries depended on American Express offices for collecting mail from back home.

For those who don't remember such times, imagine being in the Warsaw train station when your departure to Krakow is delayed by twenty minutes. Now get this: There is NO WAY to see, "like," or comment on your friend's baby's first birthday party that ended an hour earlier.

Keeping up with the news was also difficult—gloriously so, for most people—especially if you were in a place where newspapers and TV news came in an unfamiliar language. The local English-language paper or an expensive copy of the *International Herald Tribune* or *USA Today* might do the trick. But whereas today Americans abroad can keep up with the twenty-four-hour news cycle, travelers in "the old days" were mostly restricted to a zero-hour news cycle.

For fifteen-year-old me on my summer exchange program in Kenya, that meant losing track of the Boston Red Sox for weeks at a time. On July 25, 1985, we finally left our homestays near Lake Victoria and began the more touristy portion of our trip by heading to Crescent Island, a walkable game reserve on Lake Naivasha. After three weeks with no running water, no electricity, and water metallic from purification tablets, I catalogued a few firsts in stops along the way—flush toilets, cherry Fanta, bacon. But no baseball standings. Here's how that played out in my journal:

We left at 11 for Crescent Island after a pretty good breakfast of toast and eggs. We hung around this rich hotel for a while, seeing how the people who come and don't see Kenya see Kenya. We went into the gift shop in search of newspapers. I had a dream last night that the Red Sox were only a game out of first and I wanted to see if I was a prophet. They didn't have any.

I don't care so much about the baseball standings these days, but after digging up that journal entry, I was suddenly curious how the Red Sox were doing on July 25, 1985. It took me all of thirty seconds to find out: after a 5–3 win against Seattle, the Red Sox were in fourth place, seven and a half games behind the first-place Blue Jays.

I was not a prophet.

The terms cybercafé and internet café first appeared in mainstream-media accounts in 1994, mostly in stories about London's first one ever. The innovation spread slowly around the world, bringing the possibility of communicating by email when you were abroad, though even the tech-savviest youngster could not send an email to her parents if they didn't yet have an email address. Those were the days when someone with an aol.com account was still kind of cool (though I switched from skugel@aol.com to sethk@prodigy.net in 1995 #trailblazer).

But it wasn't until this century that travelers (especially those with worried parents) could be expected to check in regularly from almost everywhere. Even Tirunelveli, India. That's a Tamil city in southern India that by New Year's Eve 2000 had fifteen cybercafés for its four hundred thousand inhabitants. They were not so much for young travelers to check in with their parents, but more for Indian parents to check in with their traveling youngsters. Indian "parents who realize their children abroad are just a mouse click away stroll in routinely," reported *India Today*.[13]

It was also becoming cheaper to call—but not that cheap. When Skype was invented less than four years later, it seemed like a miracle to be able to talk—and actually see—friends and family from anywhere in the world, for free. That is, if you could find a fast enough connection.

But Skyping home meant catching up with only one person at a time—or at most 1.8 people, since parents of that era did not know how to operate webcams efficiently. Social media would exponentially expand that audience a few years later when people began posting their whereabouts, pictures of their whereabouts, or pictures of their sandy toes with their whereabouts in the distance.

Today it's pretty much possible to stream your entire trip live from anywhere in the world with good cell coverage, though (I hope) that is not yet happening. But showing representative ten-to-fifteen-second clips on Snapchat or on Instagram Stories quite nearly live is de rigueur in some crowds.

Though that's both fun and, for anyone who ever wrote an aerogram, absolutely amazing, it also has a profound impact on travel experiences. In 1990, we needed a pay phone and a quarter to call home from the hardware store. In 2018, we can live-stream ourselves milking a yak on the Mongolian steppe to our parents and anyone else who cares.

Is that bad? Yes. Why? (Those who don't need to be convinced can skip ahead.)

OK, first, friends can comment on your adventures in real time—meaning the quality of your trip is affirmed as much by how people react back home as by what is happening around you. At its most extreme, travelers are not so much taking in the world as churning out a curated photo exhibit or video show. As the host of a video show, believe me, it's not possible to be fully present on your travels when you're focused on your audience back home.

Even for those who aren't serial posters, social media and messaging apps can become an effective excuse for not forcing yourself to be social wherever you are. Solo travelers in restaurants, bars, trains, and buses buried in their phones remove themselves from at least five million social interactions per hour. (That's just a wild guess, but it's around there.) A device that connects you to somewhere else cuts you off from your surroundings. Buses are boring? OK, so substitute your phone for a book, or a knitting project, or a

Sudoku puzzle, and you've got a conversation starter. Doing nothing is also an excellent conversation starter. Here's a good line: "This bus is so boring, I wish I had brought a book."

The problem with social media—as with user reviews, as with OTAs, as with peer-to-peer services—is not the technology itself but the way it's used. Occasional posts are OK. But constant, show-offy "I am here so this is the center of the universe" missives can quickly turn into a cringeworthy train wreck. If you've never lowered your opinion of someone because of their annoying vacation-posting habits, you're kinder than I am.

One unmitigated boon of modern communications is the way you can now coordinate with pals made on the road without concocting an elaborate meeting plan or learning Morse code. I have no idea how my friend Dave and I reconnected with that Australian when we went to Munich in 1991. Neither of us had email yet, and it was about eight years before cell phones went mainstream. Did we set up the meeting place in advance and hope no one would cancel? Did we figure out a way to use a German pay phone and catch her at home?

Between then and now, keeping in touch locally while abroad meant springing for a local SIM card or incurring roaming charges. But now, WhatsApp and Snapchat and Signal and WeChat, and whatever free messaging service is in vogue locally, are totally free. Travelers who don't have international data plans on their phones still have to find wifi to get these messages—but that won't be true for long.

It's hard to remember life when our contact information was physically tied to a place—our home or office—whereas now our numbers and social media accounts and email addresses follow us everywhere. Running late or have an emergency back then? The other party was out of luck, unless they called the restaurant or bar and described you to the person who picked up. This system had but one advantage: the genre of joke exploited most famously by *Simpsons* writers.

MOE [ANSWERING THE PHONE]: Moe's Tavern.
BART: Hello, is Al there?

MOE: Al?

BART: Yeah, Al. Last name is Coholic.

MOE: Let me check . . . [calls] Phone call for Al. Al Coholic. Is there an Al Coholic here?[14]

Society can probably survive if future generations don't understand that joke; WhatsApp is worth it. In any case, the TV generation got along pretty well without newsboys taking to the streets to scream, "Extra! Extra! Read all about it!"

Now you can also stay in touch after trips, something that used to be reserved for only the most special circumstances: a new friend or lover who made such an impact that you'd be willing to handwrite letters and buy airmail stamps to keep in touch. And that was wonderful, especially when her name was Daniela and she sprayed it with her perfume so you knew it was there before you opened the mailbox and savored it for hours before curling up on your bed and reading it over and over and . . . what were we talking about again? You'd stay in touch afterward.

But now you can, at a level that befits (your perception of) the friendship: follow the friend passively on social media, exchange the occasional message, Skype with regularity. Of course, if they choose a higher friendship stratum that makes you uncomfortable, it's harder to avoid staying in touch. Texts don't get lost in the mail.

It has also changed romance. Last century, we were dependent on love letters to extend fleeting vacation romances. Those letters from Daniela, a girlfriend from a summer spent in El Salvador, were real, and went beyond the olfactory: she was an entertaining correspondent. Our romance went on for a year, even leading her to deceive her family to visit an invented female friend (played in photos by a friend of mine) to visit me in New York.

It was romantic—and impractical, torturous, and traumatic. I think we see the love letter with the same nostalgia we feel for pocket watches or pre-Tivo gatherings to watch *Cheers* or *Saved by the Bell*. If you measure the serotonin boost provided by one love letter per week in 1994 to fifty WhatsApp messages, five audio calls, and one video call a week in 2018, I suspect a convincing win for the modern era. And if you think WhatsApp messages aren't romantic, download them all into a Word document, print it out, and look at it a year later. If you did it right, you'll have something just as good as a love letter, minus the perfume.

MAPS AND GPS

In 2013, I traveled to Santiago, Chile, to write a "$100 Weekend" column—a vehicle I invented, then instantly regretted, to prove that you could enjoy yourself practically for free in any of the world's great cities. Usually I'd arrive in a city on Thursday to get my bearings and do some initial scouting. On Friday afternoon, I'd start chipping away at my $100 allocation. By Sunday, I was down to pennies and usually pretty hungry.

It was ten months after Google Maps was first released for iPhone, and I was a convert. I had quickly figured out how to predownload block-by-block details of a city so I wouldn't be dependent on wifi or roaming, and I had largely abandoned paper.

But in Santiago, Google Maps failed me. It's surely better now, but back then it couldn't find even half the places on my list. So I asked a human being where I could find a bookstore and followed the directions to the Librería Partenón, where I bought a city map. Like, a really, really good city map, the kind that folds out to bathtowel size and is made of tough paper that rips only when you set your mind to it. It cost 6,690 Chilean pesos, at the time worth $13.75—a huge expenditure for the Frugal Traveler, especially for something now seen as optional for anyone with a smartphone, or even the neighborhood maps found in most guidebooks.

The map obviously had been designed to look good on paper, not in pixels. It was gorgeous and detailed, and opening it up in the street felt like a cool retro move, kind of the way I feel when I read the actual newspaper on the subway. Reading the newspaper reminds me of my parents, but opening up the map reminded me of me, when I was a kid, spending hours paging through our world atlas.

As with many travelers raised in the twentieth century (and, presumably, before), it was looking at maps—in addition to the atlas, we had a spinnable globe in our family room—that first made me want to see the world. By the time I was seven or so, I had memorized the location of every country on that globe but Gabon, whose name I learned only later when my devious father challenged me to find it—hidden beneath the thin blue tape that represented the equator. I read about the countries in the encyclopedia, studied their flags in our almanac, and decided to paint copies of every single one as a special project for my second-grade teacher. (His definition of "special" may have been different than mine.)

I would never advocate going back to hard-copy encyclopedias or almanacs, but maps—that's another matter. For daydreaming about travel, there is no tool better than a big, solid atlas. My *National Geographic Atlas of the World*, Eighth Edition, resides on a shelf under my desk, and just now I pulled it out to make sure I was right, randomly opening to the map of Europe. My eyes settled on Sweden, its border defined with a thick, translucent yellow line, the width of a highlighter, that demarcates the country's shape starkly—even its western border to Norway (which in turn is outlined in green highlighter). Red lines—roads and highways—crisscross it like veins; mountains and lakes in gorgeous relief send signals straight to your brain about how hilly and waterlogged the country is. Dozens of cities and towns and river names fit into every crevice, yet everything is remarkably clear. There are Rivers Torneälven and Ljusnan and Ljungan, and there is the town of Kiruna, which by the boldness of the font and thickness of the dot I can tell is bigger than Jokkmokk or Kvikkjokk or Malmberget, its neighbors above the Arctic Circle. The airports are marked with red planes, as if to say, "Come visit us!" but you can also spot other ways in: at least two roads from Denmark and a ferry from Germany.

All this fits in a portion of the page that is no bigger than a smartphone. But when I type *Sweden* into Google Maps on the same smartphone, what comes out is more crime-scene chalk outline than map. No cities are shown, lakes remain nameless, and a thin gray line shows the border with Norway. Of course, as you zoom in, cities begin to appear, as do faint white lines, barely visible, that indicate roads, or perhaps provincial boundaries—it's hard to tell.

But by then you've lost context. You have no idea where you are in relationship to the rest of the country, forcing you to zoom out again (in which case you're likely to have trouble finding the place you had previously zoomed in upon). You have to get in close, really close, to see the towns or rivers I spotted in the atlas, and no matter what you do, there are no airports and no sign of the Arctic Circle.

Yes, but that's not the point of Google Maps, right? Google Maps is designed to get you to the nearest Bed Bath & Beyond, or to show you whether it's faster to take the subway or a taxi across Hong Kong. And, of course, it is completely searchable. But type in *airports* and you'll find exactly one—Stockholm's—far less dream-inspiring than discovering the ones near Gävle and Karlskoga. Type in *Arctic Circle* and you'll find . . . the Arctic Circle Snowmobile Park in nearby Finland. ("Perfect place for the kids!" reads one of the four reviews.)

And I had opened the atlas to the smaller of two Sweden maps, the one that includes the rest of Europe. The Scandinavia page has an even more glorious rendition, set over two huge pages and with even cooler above-the-Arctic-Circle place names. (Jukkasjärvi! Björkliden! Vuoggotjålme!) Carrying the atlas on vacation is impractical, of course, but you can easily order a Sweden map (or Stockholm map) for less than twenty bucks. Waste of money? You decide. For couples, that's the cost of skipping dessert once or twice along the way. If you end up not using it, well, the dessert might not have been that good, and anyway, you could stand to lose a few pounds.

In Santiago, I sat in a café and began marking up my map—with an actual PEN—circling places I hoped to get to sometime that weekend. And as I did, I noticed that the spatial relationship between my destinations, coupled with the clearly marked subway system (something Google Maps has yet to figure out), made it easy to design a route. You can create a similar customized map on Google—I've done it before—but it takes ten times as long, and of course, when it's on your phone, you can't see all of it at once.

Then, a few hours into exploring the city, another odd thing happened: I began to understand, intuitively, where I was in relationship to where I was staying and where I was going and where I had been. The city around me was not a chaotic mass of cars and buildings and delicious *empanadas de pino*, but instead an orderly place. I paused, looked around, and knew where I had been and where I was going. The markets I had visited were, yes, over there to the north; my next stops had been San Cristóbal Hill and Pablo Neruda's house, OK, over to the northeast; the Couchsurfing apartment where I was staying was to the west, and the Bio Bio neighborhood where I planned to go the next day was off to the south.

Unlike when I had followed step-by-step Google instructions in other places, I found myself leaving one place and knowing exactly which direction to go to get to the next.

There is some scientific evidence that following directions from apps on our phones or other GPS devices is actually debilitating to our brains, reducing our inborn ability to create mental or cognitive maps. Surely this rings true to anyone who lived in one city before GPS was invented, then moved to another city, and can still get around their old city better. When I was a reporter living in upper Manhattan and covering the Bronx from 2000 to 2005, I wore out an atlas of city streets as I drove up and down and across the borough countless times. But eventually, I barely needed it.

Moving to Queens and traveling often to Brooklyn by car from 2010 to 2016, I used mostly GPS. And beyond the orderly grid of my own neighborhood, I'm instantly lost without that soothing voice telling me to get in the right lane and bear left in two hundred yards.

I was surprised to learn that letting my smartphone lead me around may have literally shrunk my brain. A study from McGill University found that older adults who did not use GPS had greater activity and more gray matter in the hippocampus, which is associated with navigation and memory. Another study showed that a portion of the hippocampi of London cab drivers, who must memorize twenty-five thousand streets and know countless routes around the city to pass a licensing exam, was larger than that of the average person.

Other less surprising studies show that drivers using GPS to get somewhere don't pay much attention to their surroundings and thus have more trouble finding their way back than someone who went without a GPS in the first place. Even with years of pre-GPS driving behind me, I have been known to panic when I'm navigating and my cell-phone battery runs out or is out of cell range. But then I remember that I am not the last person alive on earth and I stop in a gas station to ask for directions.

Perhaps being on automatic pilot isn't so bad in your day-to-day life, especially when your phone routes you around traffic, saving a lot of time. But on vacation, you should be rewarded for spontaneously changing your route because you spotted something interesting or you think taking local streets would be fun. Instead, your device berates you: Recalculating . . . recalculating . . . recalculating. If you insist on driving this way, that's OK, but at least use a map when you wander an old city center on foot. Perhaps you've heard the French verb that refers to purposefully aimless wandering: *flâner*. It's not just a joy in Paris. In Cuenca, Ecuador, all I had to do was learn where my hotel was relative to the triple blue-tile domes of the Cathedral of the Immaculate Conception, and I was free to leave my phone in my room and explore. And let my brain grow. On the other hand, GPS could have a hidden benefit: one less verb you have to learn in French class. *Je flâne, tu flânes, nous flânons. . . .*

Not having to ask for directions, while an advantage in our daily lives, means we miss an easy way to meet locals while traveling. If you are the kind of person who chats with everyone anyway, this is no loss. But if you are like me and get butterflies every single time you approach a stranger, it's easy to succumb to your phone instead. Say "Where is Trattoria della Nonna?" to your phone and it will show you exactly how to get there. Say it to an Italian and he might say, "Why would you go all that way when the best pappardelle with wild boar sauce is right around the corner? Tell them Giuseppe sent you!"

When you consider how technology has changed travel for the better, it's vital to remember an obvious but easily forgotten truth: People were having plenty of life-changing travel experiences before the smartphone.

I sometimes think back to an interview I did with Richard Brackett, a forty-three-year-old traveler whom a *Times* photographer captured at sunrise on the Great Wall of China. It was 2006, with user reviews and OTAs going strong, but iOS and Android, as well as WhatsApp, map apps, and international roaming, were still unimaginable.

> I haven't had a calendar or a watch for the last year and a month. I don't need a whole lot of money to travel. In Mongolia, I spent $80 in two months. I start walking and hitchhiking and whatever happens, happens. Nowadays, travelers aren't really meeting people or opening up. Everyone's following each other with their laptops, waking up late, missing out on the good sunrises. The night before this picture was taken, I slept on the uneven stone slab floor of the highest fortress so I could wake up early and experience the dawn glory. The wall stretches out forever, I mean like, man, it's infinite. I kept wondering why they didn't build it across the ocean.[15]

Today, how many people would have slept on the stone floor if the Airbnb app's instant-booking option offered up a nearby bed? Or would have missed the sunrise because they stayed up too late Skyping with their girlfriend?

Avoiding the pull of technology even in 2006 was fairly easy: Like Richard, you went cold turkey. Practically no one's phone worked abroad, and it was also fairly easy to avoid email when reading it meant taking part of a valuable day to find a cybercafé. Once smartphones caught on, it became a bit more daring to wander empty-handed, but many people did it, leaving their phones at home, or, at the very least, in the hotel room during the day. I remember thinking it was incredibly weird, back in 2013, when a friend was doing business on a BlackBerry as we sauntered around the Dominican Republic.

But the last few years have changed all that—wifi is widespread, international plans are cheap, and our devices are so important to our daily functioning that many people would prefer to travel without their underwear. Going smartphone-free might work for a hiking or fishing trip, or in a beach resort, but for most people on most trips it would make them obsolete, or like some quirky time traveler who actually asked hotel clerks for wake-up calls, inquired about the nearest pay phone, looked at the sky to determine the weather. And how would you meet up with new friends (or even your travel companions) if they can't text you?

If that all sounds silly, and you still travel without a smartphone, you have my deepest respect. I approve. I love you. Never change.

But that's not me, and it's not most people. Pretty soon, we'll have access to unlimited data everywhere in the world, and left to our, ahem, own devices, we'll overuse them, just as we do at home. In fact, we should be using them in situations where they will improve our interactions with the places and people we visit, and avoiding them when they distract us, serve as a crutch, or make things too easy.

That's why I often wish that right under "Airplane Mode" in your phone's settings was something called "Travel Mode." If Airplane Mode shuts off the elements of our phones that (we've been led to believe) interfere with the plane's navigation but allows us to do everything else, then Travel Mode would shut off the parts of our phones that detract from our travel experience but not those that allow us to, say, see in the dark when the power goes out in our Albanian youth hostel.

The app would not simply block Facebook and Instagram. Instead, it would restrict usage of them, and other apps and functions, to encourage discovery by breaking habits that, while acceptable or unavoidable at home, are no benefit to good travel.

For example, live receipt of text messages would be restricted to no more than five preselected contacts: your sister, your mom, your dogsitter, etc. Everyone else would have to wait for the single one-hour period each day permitted by the override function. Social media could work similarly—you could take pictures all you want but post them to Instagram or Facebook only during the override hour. How many likes did you get? You'll have to wait until the next day and activate your brain's reward circuitry through local means, like ice cream. Alone in a café? With scrolling through your friends' feeds disabled, you'll have to read a book or talk to someone. (Or read a news app, if you've preallowed it.) In this Travel Mode, Google Translate works, but only after you've passed a test showing you know five basic phrases of the local language. Yelp works in your hotel room, but not as you wander the streets. You'll have to look around you or ask people for suggestions—using Google Translate where applicable, once you've greeted them in their native language.

I've taken it further than that. You'll find my detailed design for Travel Mode in appendix 1. Coders, call me. Better yet, send me a postcard.

So far, everything I've said applies to technology currently in existence. How can we apply it to new tools as they come along?

Here's what I'd suggest for future travelers. Use technology when it keeps you healthy, or safe. Use it when it enhances your experience in ways for which there is no substitute, such as figuring out why the person who "lived in this house, 1834 to 1852," was worth memorializing on that plaque in front of you. And use it, sparingly, to make the annoying parts of travel less taxing—podcasts for you and tablets for your kids on long flights, for example.

Don't use it if it removes you even slightly from your travel experience and brings you closer to home. And don't use it if it makes choices for you that you should make yourself or with help from those around you, or reduces potential discoveries by nudging you toward a standard, tried-and-true path.

All this assumes that technology is being used as a supplement to travel, rather than as a replacement. One day, virtual reality might advance so far that we put on our goggles and slip into our techno-skin, insert our iTongues and iNostrils (optional filter for raw sewage), and engage in "travel" experiences that might tempt us to stay home.

Could technology someday replace travel? To a certain extent, this is a naive question. It has been replacing it for centuries, starting with the printing press. I've already gone through the diffusion of formerly unknown cuisines that immigration has made part of our daily routines (or made part of mine, as long as the Thai lunch special at Kitchen 79 down the block remains under $8). After Koda-chrome was invented in 1936, we no longer had to rely on paintings to see what color French water lilies were. Now we can go onto Google Images and see photos of anything we want—including just about any Monet painting hanging in any museum in the world—and travel endlessly on YouTube and Netflix and cable and through 360-degree video and virtual-reality devices. You can pooh-pooh this as "not the same as travel," and of course it isn't. But for people who cannot afford to travel, or don't have time, or are physically unable, the possibilities are astonishing.

I would argue that such travel substitutes are undeniably positive. But what if virtual reality advanced so much that you could truly see, hear, smell, and even touch a place without going there?

I'd definitely want to try it. It would be great not to need sun-screen, or to have to take a plane. It could even offer attractions not available in the real world—leaping from a viewing platform into the Grand Canyon or heading over Niagara Falls on a raft would become significantly less risky and better than any video game. And, in theory, you might even be able to interact with other virtual travelers from around the world virtually visiting the same attraction.

But even if you could simulate skiing the Alps, smelling the tropical sea breezes, feeling the Szechuan peppers numb your faux tongue, you'd still be missing out. You might hear wolves howling in the woods near your campsite, but you won't really fear them—at least no more than you would in a horror movie. You won't feel butterflies in your stomach when you try to strike up a conversation with people unlike yourself, and the resulting rush when they invite you to tea, or even manage to understand your mangled Bulgarian. You won't actually be able to interact with real life on the ground—or at least I hope not, because the last thing I need is to share the sidewalks of New York not just with regular tourists but also with holograms.

But I'm being selfish. It would have its upside, potentially allowing the billions of people around the world who don't (or can't) travel a low-risk adventure. What if, after playing soccer with the village kids outside their school in Swaziland, I could have given them the exact coordinates of my block in New York and had them "visit" in winter to "feel" the cold and "touch" the snow? Maybe, through some futuristic Pokémon Go–like system, I could even walk around with them. It would be awesome. But it wouldn't quite be travel.

The author crossing a bridge in Papua, Indonesia.

Chapter 5

· · · · · · · · · · · · ·

RISK AND TRAVEL

Should you visit Rio de Janeiro?

Here's the upside. It's a 450-year-old city of modern towers interspersed with colonial churches and palaces and wedged into whatever narrow bands of flat land exist between riotous, rain-forest–draped mountains on one side and Guanabara Bay on the other. On sunny days (which are most days) white-sand crescent beaches teem with scantily dressed bathers whose bodies range, unabashedly, from finely toned to let-it-all-hang-out. But their bronzed skin pales in comparison to the dramatic granite monoliths reaching to the sky from the coastline and even from the water itself. A block or two from the beaches, uniformed staff squeeze fresh juices from often unrecognizable fruits—soursop, cashew apple, acerola cherry—at countless stands on practically every block for customers often still in bikinis and Speedo-style *sungas*. For vis-itors (heretically) not into the beach scene, the formerly decrepit port area transformed for the 2016 Olympics offers the brand-spanking-new Santiago Calatrava–designed Museum of Tomorrow and the almost-as-new MAR, which stands in Portuguese for Rio Art Museum and anything-but-coincidentally means "sea," lest you forget you're not at the beach. Come night, live music lasts into the wee hours, for both the hardest-core partiers and the most laid-back beer sippers. Natives adhere to a strict flip-flop dress code for all but the most upscale pursuits and exhibit a contagious charm that only a string of overcast days can dispel.

So, yes, you really should pay a visit.

No, you shouldn't. Crime is rampant and largely uncontrolled by the beleaguered state police, except when they themselves are the criminals. One hundred thirteen people were hit by stray bullets in the first half of 2017 alone; thirty-three died. The naked eye easily detects the chasm between rich and poor, as favelas on the hills overlook the richest beach enclaves in tragicomic juxtaposition; even the blind aren't exempt, for the stench of raw sewage wafting through certain parts of the city betrays the inequality by its shifting potency. The moneyed live in secure buildings where guards stand behind bulletproof mirrored glass, ushering residents and guests in through two staggered gates to protect the inner sanctum from opportunistic push-in intruders. (For a brief moment after the first gate closes and before the second buzzes open, inhabitants find themselves locked into what amounts to a cage.) During the 2016 Olympics, bullets shattered the windows of a bus, and the official in charge of security for the Opening Ceremony was set upon by knife-wielding assailants on his way home from the event. Need more? The state has since gone bankrupt and crime has risen. In February of 2018— just two days after a raucous, tourist-filled Carnaval celebration— Brazil's president put the military in charge of the city's (and state's) security forces.

Are you in or out?

Rio is but an extreme example of a destination that poses a confusing hodgepodge of incentives and deterrents to travelers. Are you safe taking the subway to a Yankees game in the South Bronx? How about attaching a bungee cord to your torso and jumping off a bridge into Africa's Zambezi River? Are cheap inter-island flights on Indonesia's discount airlines a bargain over national carrier Garuda Indonesia or an accident waiting to happen? And should travelers categorically avoid any city (or country or continent) recently struck by terror?

Risk assessment is woven into our DNA and our travel planning at all stages—from idle daydreaming (say, "Can a woman safely trek solo through India?") to concrete planning ("Do I dare rent an Airbnb in Bogotá's romantic but dodgy La Candelaria district?")

and on-the-ground decisions ("Should I risk a late-night walk home through the safe-looking but unfamiliar streets of Osaka?").

But we stink at it. In part, that's because travelers make decisions with imperfect information. I've given advice to many foreigners about Rio over the years, and their impressions about safety there fall over a stupendously vast but entirely comprehensible spectrum.

On one extreme was the New Yorker friend of a friend in his early thirties who asked me for contacts and nightlife suggestions. He was utterly unconcerned with risk. When I began my boilerplate warning, he waved it off. It would be OK, he said, because a good friend had recently returned and everything had gone fine. There is danger everywhere, but "you just have to use common sense," he said, an attitude that works perfectly until you're out an iPhone, a lung, or a life.

On the other extreme was a California woman who had a gig as a public speaker on a cruise ship that had just docked in Rio. I was there doing a story on tourism and violence, interviewing people on the Copacabana Beach promenade. In Portuguese it's called the *calçadão*, essentially, the "grand sidewalk," and it fits the description, with palm trees, sand, and coconut-water vendors on one side, the traffic of the seaside Avenida Atlântica on the other, and a black basalt and white limestone mosaic of stylized waves underfoot. (Under barefoot, for many.)

Fanny pack on hip, she assented to an interview on one condition: that we keep moving. A Brazilian worker on the ship had warned her that standing still in public would make her a target. "The vibe here is for crime," she told me. "I'm just not really as smart as I need to be."

Neither the foolhardy New Yorker nor the panicky Californian was definitively "wrong." The vexing problem with risk analysis is that there is really no right or wrong, often even in retrospect. Let's say neither got mugged. The New Yorker wasn't necessarily right— he may have just dodged a bullet (perhaps literally, in this case). But the Californian wasn't right either—she stayed safe but missed out on enjoying the city. Both got their advice from a plausibly reliable source: a trusted person with on-the-ground experience. Each turned that advice into a straightforward plan of action: "Don't worry, you'll be fine" for one, "Fear for your life at all times" for the other. And both plans will work the vast majority of the time: After all, if even 10 percent of tourists who went to Rio got mugged or hurt, we wouldn't call traveling there risky, we'd call it insane.

In the man's case, he relied on the experience of a single tourist, and an unreliable one at that. That's like getting a new car without seatbelts and concluding you don't need them anyway because you made it home from the dealer with no problem.

The woman, at least, got her advice from a local, but she applied it so badly that it could have backfired. I don't claim to understand the mindset of muggers in Rio, but a skittish blonde with a fanny pack and broad-rimmed sun hat speed-walking along the city's most touristy beach sure seems like a juicy target.

In an ideal world, you would make your decision based on accurate data about crimes committed against tourists in Rio. (Many of Rio's crimes occur far from tourist areas.) But even if such data existed, which, as far as I can tell, it does not, human beings are pretty bad at assessing risk.

For argument's sake, I've made up a crime statistic for Rio: A quarter of one percent of foreign visitors fall victim to a crime during their stay. The number is based vaguely on outdated and partial numbers I found, but let's just assume it's accurate. Now imagine I told our gung-ho friend: "Don't worry! Only one-quarter of one percent of visitors to Rio fall victim to any crime, aside from being forced to see pot-bellied old men in Speedos." He'd probably laugh (though I may be overestimating my own sense of humor) and be on his way, confident his friend's advice had been confirmed by a travel expert. 0.25% sounds like a very small chance, especially since the average tourist tends to consider himself savvier than the average tourist.

Then let's say that I spoke to the skittish woman, my countenance turning grim as I say, "Be careful out there. Five thousand foreign tourists a year fall victim to crime in Rio." I bet she'd pull that fanny pack just a bit tighter. Five thousand is quite a lot.

But studies have repeatedly proven that presentation of statistics matters more than the statistics themselves. My warnings to each contained the exact same information: About two million people visit Rio every year, and 0.0025 x 2,000,000 = 5,000. A fairer way to present the same numbers would be to adopt a neutral tone and say, "The average foreign tourist to Rio de Janeiro has a one-in-four-hundred chance of falling victim to a crime."

Alas, we're not very good at processing even accurate, fairly presented numbers. As Brian J. Zikmund-Fisher, a behavioral decision theorist at the University of Michigan, explained to me: "Risk is not something you actually experience. You experience outcomes. You don't experience something being 85 percent good."

Or, in this case, 99.75 percent good. For nonvictims, the experience is 100 percent good; for the unlucky few who are robbed or raped or shot, it's 100 percent bad.

Even if you could internalize a quarter of a percent risk, that number is an average. If your stay is shorter than most, if you're an experienced traveler, that reduces it. Being blond or fair-skinned, dressing like a foreigner, getting drunk every night and stumbling home on foot raises your risk. Passing as a local and taking a taxi home each night from an early dinner lowers it.

Zikmund-Fisher works on health-care decisions, where data tailored to a patient's specific circumstances are often available. Candidates for chemotherapy may now receive data on "reduced risk of death within ten years" based on their age, race, and variables describing their particular prognosis. That's a great advance, but such specialized data are not available for most decisions in life, including whether a specific traveler on a specific trip will fall victim to a crime. And, of course, there's no such thing as an average crime. Being murdered is worse than being carjacked at gunpoint, which is worse than being shoved and pickpocketed. None of those choices is pleasant, but you can be pickpocketed and still have an overall good trip. Such things happen. Being murdered, on the other hand, is a real downer.

It's natural, then, that we should be especially concerned with the chance we will die when abroad. And it's relatively easy to get information about that. But again, presentation matters. In Michael Moore's 2002 film, *Bowling for Columbine*, he gravely intones:

"How many people are killed by guns each year?"[1] and then doles out the shocking numbers:

In Germany: 381
In France: 255
In Canada: 165
In the United Kingdom: 68
In Australia: 65
In Japan: 39
In the United States: 11,127

I saw this movie back in the liberal confines of the Lincoln Plaza Cinema on Manhattan's Upper West Side, and, more than fifteen years later, still remember the people around me clucking and gasping in disgust. The statistics had reaffirmed their beliefs about gun violence in America.

I clucked in disgust as well, but at Moore. Wherever you stand on guns, this was a bogus comparison: He had not adjusted the statistics for the countries' vastly different populations. At the time, the US population was about nine times the population of Canada and about fifteen times the population of Australia. (I was far from the only one who noticed—A. O. Scott's review in the *New York Times* noted the "slippery logic, tendentious grandstanding and outright demagoguery" of the film.)

No matter, word spread. According to transcripts, CNN and CBS replayed that exact scene for its audiences without questioning the numbers. Here are the statistics, adjusted as though the other countries were as populous as America:

Germany: 1,284
France: 1,197
Canada: 1,451
United Kingdom: 319
Australia: 933
Japan: 86
United States: 11,127

The movie declared that the United States has nearly thirty times as many gun deaths as its nearest competitor, Germany. Adjusted for population, that's nearly nine times as many—still pretty startling, but a much fairer assessment.

It also turns out that Moore ignored the European countries with higher levels of gun deaths than the United States, such as Switzerland, which, at 5.4 deaths per 100,000 population in 2002, would come in at 15,530 once adjusted for the chart above. Finland would have clocked in at 12,663.

At the risk of sounding like an infomercial huckster . . . BUT THAT'S NOT ALL!

It doesn't really matter how unnatural deaths occur, only *that* they occur. What if people in countries with less access to guns simply stabbed each other to death more?

Bowling for Columbine was not about travel, of course. But the film did $36 million in box-office sales abroad. I'm guessing plenty of Germans and French and Canadians and British were as shocked as Americans—not to mention instantly less interested in taking their children to New York City or the Grand Canyon or Disney World.

Australians, too. I'm not sure whether Tim Fischer, former deputy prime minister and former chairman of Tourism Australia, saw the film back then. But he has suggested several times since that Australians avoid travel to the United States. When the US State Department warned American travelers about potential terror attacks in Australia in 2015, he told the Australian Broadcasting Corporation: "You are 15 times more likely to be shot dead in the U.S.A. than in Australia per capita. Let's start highlighting this. It's time to call out the U.S."[2]

Call it out, notably, by using *per capita* statistics. Using the Michael Moore system, he would have said, "Two hundred times more people are shot dead in America than in Australia."

So that set up the quirky possibility that Australians would avoid travel to the United States at the same time Americans were avoiding travel to Australia. All in the name of staying safe.

Back to Rio. You can find relatively recent numbers on murders in Brazil from the United Nations Office on Drugs and Crime. For 2016, per 100,000 people, Brazil had 29.5 murders, compared with the USA's 5.4.

But Brazil is a big country; a quick online search and you'll see that though Rio is certainly a perilous place, with 18.6 murders in 2015 for every 100,000 people, it was far from being the most murderous city in the country. (That was Fortaleza, with 60.8.) Rio was actually safer by that measure than Baltimore, St. Louis, Detroit, and New Orleans. Rio's Carnaval and New Orleans's Mardi Gras occur at the same time. Which one is safer for tourists?

If you really wanted to know, you'd have to research where murders occur, at what times of day and in what circumstances. You get the point: This can go on and on.

* * * *

We have a double problem here: The numbers we can get our hands on are misleading or incomplete, and even if they were accurate, we wouldn't internalize them very well.

Before the 2016 Olympics in Rio, there was a spate of news about how dangerous the city was. You probably remember the risk that terrified visitors most: the Zika virus. Images of Brazilian babies born with an often-devastating birth defect called microcephaly ricocheted around the globe, spurring countless potential visitors (and several athletes) to skip the Games.

Yet unless you were a pregnant woman, a woman trying to get pregnant, or someone having unprotected sex with one of those women, Zika was an extraordinarily minor risk. Most people infected with the virus never even noticed, and the vast majority of the rest developed minor, flu-like symptoms. Serious side effects were so rare that anyone who has ever texted while driving but feared death by Zika was an extraordinary (if unintentional) hypocrite.

BUT THAT'S NOT ALL!

News stories rarely mentioned that the virus was largely concentrated in northeastern Brazil, a thousand miles from Rio, and that by the time the Olympics rolled around, it would be winter in the Southern Hemisphere, which in Rio is mild and pleasant for humans but quite inhospitable to the *Aedes aegypti* mosquito. A few weeks before the Olympics, the numbers came out: 510 Zika infections in Rio during the entire month of June, down from 7,733 in January. Number of microcephaly cases linked to Zika in Rio: zero. When I spoke to Rio's secretary of tourism in July, he declared: "There will not be a single mosquito in Rio during the Olympics."

As with all politicians, he was exaggerating. But during my trip, I met not a single local who wore repellent on a daily basis. Assuming you were not in the risk categories for birth defects AND regularly applied repellant, you would be pretty darn safe from what was a largely harmless disease in the first place.

And you'd even be safe from more dangerous illnesses such as dengue fever and chikungunya, spread by the same mosquito, which had in prior months affected more Rio residents than Zika. I tried my hardest, writing in the *Times*: "If you're a man or non-pregnant woman more scared of Zika than dengue, it's too late. You've already been infected by the news media."[3] But statistics, even for the journalists who understood them, were no match for images of babies with shrunken heads and severe disabilities.

The World Health Organization later announced that there had been exactly zero reported Zika cases during the Olympics.

News coverage of Zika was already a steady drumbeat when another pre-Olympic story exploded into the headlines that June 2016. It was from Reuters: "Exclusive: Studies Find 'Super Bacteria' in Rio's Olympic Venues, Top Beaches."[4] Word spread. Here's how a particularly convoluted Australian news report summarized the risk:

According to the Centres for Disease Control and Prevention, at least two million people become infected with this kind of bacteria each year, causing 23,000 deaths. It can prove fatal for 50 per cent of those afflicted.[5]

Non-math majors take note: .50 × 2,000,000 ≠ 23,000. The article was numerically nonsensical, but "fatal for 50 per cent" sounds very scary. Those who read onward learned that more than half the samples taken at tourist-packed Ipanema and Leblon Beaches tested positive for the bacteria. A reasonable takeaway would have been that tourists accidentally swallowing seawater had at least a 50 percent chance of ingesting the bacteria, and that those who did ran a 50 percent risk of death. Death rate for not keeping your mouth hermetically sealed: one in four.

For those who read to the end of the story, though, there was another piece of (quite) relevant information.

> . . . the good news, according to experts, is that these super-bugs can only really cause problems for those who are chronically ill with immunity problems. Therefore, they may not pose a strong risk for athletes or healthy travellers.

Very few people read to the end of any story. I was in Rio when the Reuters article came out, and I asked the tourism secretary about the super bacteria. "Really, I never heard of it. It only showed up for the Olympics," he said.

A friend of mine in town had another take: "If it's so dangerous, why hasn't anybody died of it yet?"

In 2016, 1,909 people died in Rio of something else: murder.

✳ ✳ ✳ ✳

Another flaw in human risk assessment is that we are more frightened in unfamiliar places than we are at home, even if, objectively, the risk is no greater (or far less). Countless travelers from large cities in Brazil, for example, are irrationally terrified of New York City, where crime rates are comparatively infinitesimal. That may be in part Hollywood's fault, but another part is the instinctive and understandable fear of the devil we don't know. We tend to ignore risks we've become used to and fear them too much in places that are new to us.

I do, anyway. Here are two instances where I got it wrong:

1) On my trip up the Yangtze, I spent two days in the dreary but gloriously tourist-free Chinese river town of Fengjie. The Ro-

man alphabet was nearly absent on signs and menus, which was kind of fun, even when things went wrong. The mushrooms in the vegetable stir-fry I had ordered by pointing to the bowl on the table next to me were actually pieces of pig stomach. Hahahahaha. It was less hilarious when I headed to the port to see what time I could catch the next boat upriver and found no English signs and no English speakers.

Luckily, a student with rudimentary English took pity and helped me interact with the ticket agent. Via choppy phrases and an assist from Google Translate, I understood that the daily ferry to Chongqing left at 2 a.m., and that I could buy my ticket on board. But that night, when I returned a bit after 1 a.m., the port area that had been humming by day was deserted, the perfect setting for a murder on *Law & Order*. I waited on a dock as two o'clock passed with not another human in sight, let alone a ferry.

2) A few years before I took over the Frugal Traveler column, I landed a plum assignment to write about Tortuga Bay, then a new resort in the Dominican Republic owned by Oscar de la Renta. Joining me was none other than nontraveler Jon Chapman, lured by a weekend with his buddy and a once-in-a-lifetime chance to stay in a $600 room, not necessarily in that order. We were both particularly intrigued by the twenty-four-hour availability of a butler at the push of a button—specifically, the number 2 on the resort-issued mobile phone.

I knew the rest of the Caribbean country well after repeat visits over a dozen years, and was proud that my Spanish had picked up traces of the local accent after nearly a decade living in a Dominican neighborhood in New York. So whereas most visitors fly into the private Punta Cana International Airport to be greeted by sign-bearing drivers, I decided we would first tool around the capital, Santo Domingo, then drive two and a half hours out to the resort so Jon could see a bit of the rest of the country. I was proud and excited to show off my local knowledge during the drive.

So, where was I in more danger?

It's clear which felt riskier, that ferry landing in China, a strange country where I didn't speak the language and had no place to spend the night unless that ferry showed up.

But the ride in the Dominican Republic was more dangerous by far. In China, tourists might get scammed into overpriced tea ceremonies in Shanghai, but robberies and assaults are extraordinarily rare. I knew this in theory, as I shivered alone on that dock in the middle of the night, but my gut told me to panic. I sat there with my Kindle, trying to ignore the internal distress call, but didn't get much reading done. Around 3 a.m., a few people showed up with suitcases; at 4 a.m., the ferry came. Perhaps the student had inadvertently mixed up his English numbers. I couldn't really blame him; I could barely say "hello" in Mandarin.

But as I showed off my knowledge of the Dominican Republic to Jon, my gut was completely at ease. The figurative gut that handles instincts, that is, since the literal gut that handles nourishment was churning, thanks to the Dominican Republic's and my shared obsession with deep-fried plantains.

I did not know then what I know now, and what is perhaps the single most important piece of information on travel and risk that you will ever hear: More American tourists abroad die in motor vehicle accidents than by any other means. According to the State Department, which monitors citizens' deaths abroad, 201 Americans died in motor vehicle accidents abroad between July 2016 and June 2017, more than any other cause. (And that doesn't include twenty-one pedestrian deaths.) It's not an American peculiarity. According to a report by the FIA Foundation for the Automobile and Society, "Road traffic should be every tourist's greatest concern. . . . Road crashes represent the greatest fatality risks that international tourists are likely to face."[6]

Combine that with another useful and readily available fact: The roads in the Dominican Republic are among the most dangerous in the world. World Health Organization figures from 2013 show it had 29.3 deaths per 100,000 inhabitants, fourteenth worst out of

179 countries—and second worst among major tourist destinations. First—on both lists—is Thailand, at 36.2.

As I stood, fearful, on that dock in China, I knew of the low crime rates, but my gut didn't absorb them. In the Dominican Republic, the clues suggesting that I should have felt more in danger were clear—potholes that could swallow a subcompact like ours appeared out of nowhere, for example. But I was feeling so much at home that they didn't faze me, nor did the many cars, buses, and cargo trucks, swerving around the potholes in the lanes beside us, whose brakes could not possibly have met all inspection standards in the United States or Europe. Jon was rightfully terrified, but my gut was sending me the wrong signals, and my brain couldn't muster a fight.

Underestimating risk in familiar situations and overestimating it when our surroundings are novel and strange is useful in theory, and was in practice as well when our ancestors, say, emigrated from a land where the fauna ranged from kittens to puppies into a territory where cheetahs and wolves roamed free. It's not irrelevant for travelers: You do need to be more aware in strange places, but likely not as much as you think.

What to do about those gut feelings? If you have facts that indicate a place is safer than it feels, it can be helpful to seek out other travelers (perhaps in online forums) for reassurance. In the opposite scenario, when you suspect you aren't scared enough, try looking for stories of danger to give your gut a chance to catch up with your brain. It's not hard: A Google search for the country's name, plus *tourist* plus *killed*, should do the trick.

You also need to source your facts well. The best-known reference for travel safety recommendations is the US State Department's Travel Advisories (known until 2018 as Travel Warnings). Those are risk assessments written largely by diplomats who live in the country they're evaluating and whose job it is to be on top of the news there.

A network of professionals working in nearly every country in the world with a primary mission of representing American citizens' interests should be a pretty reliable source, especially as a starting point. Through the height of the Zika scare, the State Department did not issue Travel Warnings for affected countries, as they did with the genuinely calamitous Ebola virus in West Africa. For Zika advice, it referred potential travelers to their colleagues at the Centers for Disease Control (CDC), which gave extremely reasonable counsel: Travel need not be avoided for most, as the risk was extremely low. They recommended regular repellent use, just as your mom might.

State Department warnings can be overly cautious at times, to be sure. But that caution can also be misinterpreted, causing an overstated impact on tourism. This happens most often when travelers misunderstand a warning about one region to mean that the whole country is a bubbling cauldron of danger.

We have an extraordinarily hard time understanding that countries are big places. Travel to Mexico tanked after drug wars flared up there a few years ago. Places like Cancún were still safe, and with direct flights arriving there from all over the United States, you would not even need to be exposed to any regions affected by the violence. You might as well pack a winter coat for Disney World because it's freezing in Minnesota.

Our brains have another way of tricking us: by assuming information they absorbed long ago is still true today.

When I was growing up in the 1980s, civil war in Colombia was all over NBC Nightly News, which was part of the Kugel household's 7 p.m. family ritual. It was also on the front page of our morning newspapers. I usually just read the sports section, if I beat my brother to it, but I saw enough headlines to associate the country with jungles and guerrilla war and drugs and danger.

Colombia, like Brooklyn, has become a darling of many travelers over the last decade or so, and I've yet to meet anyone who didn't love it. But the message has only reached so far. When I recommend its gorgeous coffee-covered hills, unique musical traditions, heartbreakingly warm people, and direct flights from New York (Bogotá is closer than LA!), I sometimes sense doubt. Ask any Colombian in the United States how people react when they mention their roots— cocaine will usually be part of the first sentence. And the Netflix show *Narcos* hasn't helped.

No place got a worse rap in the 1980s than the Bronx, though, where the jungle was urban and the only guerrillas were the differently spelled ones in the Bronx Zoo. Though there are still high-crime areas, much of the Bronx is a great place to visit for a taste of what Manhattan used to be, and not in the bad way. Since gentrification has failed to make as much headway there, most places look more or less the same as they did when I taught there in the 1990s. In many neighborhoods, kids even still play on the streets unsupervised—something utterly missing from gentrified areas of the city, where unsupervised street play is no longer allowed, lest the kids come into contact with an inorganic head of lettuce (among other reasons).

While the Bronx still scares many Americans, its fellow borough, Brooklyn, long ago shed its similarly gritty rep and large swaths of it have been remade through radical gentrification into the very definition of cool.

But perhaps not as much as you think. When I started "Amigo Gringo" (the YouTube channel that helps Brazilians navigate New York and American culture), I received a startling number of questions from Brazilians asking whether Brooklyn was as dangerous as they had heard. I was puzzled, for I doubted the mostly youthful questioners had seen the car chase scene in *The French Connection* and concluded that traffic might still be hazardous forty-five years later. I finally figured it out when I asked viewers to send in questions about Brooklyn.

The culprit was the sitcom *Everybody Hates Chris*, loosely based on Chris Rock's life growing up in the tough Bedford-Stuyvesant neighborhood. It ran only four seasons and ended in 2009. But it is still wildly popular in Brazil, where it has become the primary reference about Brooklyn for a generation of now–twenty-somethings, despite its having taken place in another century.

And it's not just Brazilians.

In 2016, the *New York Times* documented a conversation between two visiting sailors during Fleet Week, when sailors practically take over Manhattan. Connor Vest of Maryville, Tennessee, nineteen, speaks with Colby Warren, twenty-three, of Landrum, South Carolina.

WARREN: I'm up for anything. Times Square, Central Park.
   They're at opposite ends of everything.
VEST: I don't like the idea of Central Park at night.
WARREN: That's when you get mugged: the real New York
   experience!
VEST: I don't want to get mugged.[7]

✳ ✳ ✳ ✳

Personal stories affect us even more than news. That's in large
part because humans have been programmed through the millennia to be influenced by storytelling and—like any other complex
species—have evolved to make fight-or-flight decisions based on gut
feelings. Making decisions based on careful statistical analysis, on
the other hand, is anything but instinctual.

Kenya will always be where fifteen-year-old me got hepatitis
from a contaminated water supply; I still fear more for my health
in Africa (anywhere in Africa!) than I do in regions with equal or
greater risks. I was an unequivocal advocate of taking public buses
around Latin America regardless of their condition—what an experience!—until I learned a colleague's niece had died in a bus crash
in Peru. Holding an entire continent to blame for something that
happened in one village in 1985 makes no sense. Buses didn't get
any more dangerous because I heard a story, but they sure felt more
dangerous to me.

My view of Rio de Janeiro also changed significantly a few years
ago when Daniel Pereira, a friend of a friend I had hung out with
several times over the years, was shot and killed there after leaving a bank. My Facebook feed was suddenly full of despair about
the tragedy and about violence in the city in general. On my next
visit, Rio seemed palpably more dangerous. That's a natural reaction, if imperfect for several reasons. Most notably, I absorbed his
death and its effects on my friends, but not the details of the crime,
which were somewhat irrelevant to most travelers. He was leaving
a bank in a nontourist neighborhood with about $5,000 in cash. A
gang specializing in such attacks had apparently placed a scout in

the bank who then alerted accomplices outside. It's not a story likely to happen to tourists, which doesn't make it less tragic, just less worrisome on a practical basis. On the other hand, I had become pretty carefree in Rio, so perhaps I needed a scare.

When I learned of my colleague's niece's death in Peru, I realized I might have been underestimating the risks of taking public transportation in South America for decades. So I went back and read about her, as well as other travelers' deaths over the years. It worked as a corrective—I still take buses in South America, because I love taking buses, and because they're cheap, and because there are some places you can't reach any other way. But I now look into bus safety in specific countries before I go, and I have—even as Frugal Traveler—spent more to use a bus company that is considered more reliable. If you realize you're not scared enough about something, I encourage you to seek out stories to recalibrate your sense of risk.

✳　✳　✳　✳

When experts talk about risk, the travel example that comes up most often is Americans' large-scale abandonment of air travel after the September 11 attacks. In the months that followed, many of us started driving more and taking fewer domestic flights. Predictably, the added road miles led to a significant increase in traffic deaths compared to previous years. The exact number varies by study, but everyone agrees on the number of deaths from airplane hijackings in the United States since 2001: none.

Those who drove instead of flew were not right or wrong. Many had probably even heard the often-quoted statistic that air travel is far safer, per mile, than automobile travel. But there was considerable uncertainty about air travel after September 11, and it was entirely reasonable to conclude that air travel had become more dangerous.

Of course, these days we have other terrorism concerns: truck attacks, airport bombs, mass shootings. Assessing how much risk to take on when you travel depends on many variables, but perhaps none more than where you reside. If you already live in a place that could be considered risky, there's little reason not to travel to a place of equivalent risk. For mass shootings, that's every American. But other kinds of attacks tend to be concentrated in areas tourists are likely to be: Istanbul's Atatürk Airport, La Rambla in Barcelona, a Bastille Day celebration in Nice. So if you live on a farm in Nebraska (or Switzerland or Peru), it is certainly rational to consider skipping big cities for fear of the next attack. It is irrational, however, to take a thousand-mile road trip instead.

On the other hand, it is also perfectly reasonable to continue traveling the way you did before. If something goes wrong, that doesn't mean you made a mistake. People often make reasonable decisions that kill them. Risk is not a true–false quiz.

You can, however, change how you travel to make your trips safer. Appendix 2 outlines a series of steps to take to evaluate and reduce risk when planning a trip and while on one. It includes a great number of practical measures that will reduce risk anywhere.

*   *   *   *

You already know that deaths in road accidents were the top cause of death of American citizens abroad for the year ending June 2017. What do you think the next four causes were? Take a minute and fill in the blanks (in your head if this is a library book):

1. *Vehicular accidents*: 201
2.
3.
4.
5.

I'll tell you mine. Before I crunched that State Department data, the causes of death I feared most were tropical diseases, plane crashes, terrorist attacks, and getting shot in a mugging gone wrong. If I could add a sixth, it would be freak infrastructure collapses in countries with lax code enforcement. You know, a rotted rail crumbles, sending an all-too-trusting American travel writer looking for the perfect Instagram post plunging to his death in the volcanic crater below. Guatemalan newspaper headline the next morning: *¡Gringo Estúpido!*

Turns out this gringo was being *estúpido* about his fears. The answers are:

2. *Homicides*: 158
3. *Drownings*: 142
4. *Suicides*: 131
5. *Other Accidents*: 108

So really the only crossover between my instincts and the truth was homicides. And even that is questionable—if you download the State Department data as I did, you'll see that many of the killings occurred in hot zones like the US–Mexican border, where the dead were more likely American citizens involved in drug trafficking, or perhaps Mexican Americans visiting relatives—something travelers will often do no matter what the risk.

I should note that illnesses are not included in these statistics, but the CDC website notes that less than 2 percent of American deaths abroad result from infectious diseases.

What about terrorism? It was way down the list, with eight. That includes three killed in the Nice truck attack on Bastille Day 2016, and one each in London, Bangladesh, Iraq, Pakistan, and Egypt. We'd be better off spending our risk-avoiding energy looking both ways before we crossed the street (pedestrian deaths totaled twenty-one), not to mention only swimming at beaches where there is a qualified lifeguard.

But it's not that easy. Terrorism will continue to terrify us more than it should—which is, of course, how it got its name. Count me among the terrified. And I doubt the comparatively low statistics on air accidents will make anyone feel better when their plane hits heavy turbulence over the Sahara. ("Honey, don't worry. According to State Department stats, you should be more scared of drowning!")

I learned another important lesson about vehicular accidents in, of all places, the airport in Maputo, Mozambique. I had always thought that the cause of high death rates on roads in developing countries was some combination of poor road conditions, poor driver training, and poor vehicle upkeep. Then when I landed in Maputo, the Mozambique Migration Service computer system was down, and no one who needed an arrival visa was getting into the country until it went back up.

So a big group of us were stuck for hours. I ended up talking with an Israeli-Canadian trauma surgeon who regularly came to Mozambique to train local surgeons. In my preparation for the trip, I had read that expats and diplomats regularly drove a couple of hours across the border into South Africa for even routine checkups, so I asked him for the lowdown. He surprised me by telling me that the Mozambican surgeons he worked with were quite skilled.

The biggest problem, he said, was the lack of emergency services—there was essentially no functioning 911 system in most of the country. Get in a car accident on a highway in Mozambique, he said, and you may die of injuries his Mozambican colleagues could handle easily—if only you could get to them.

The idea that you could call 911 after an accident and no ambulance would come as you bled out was terrifying to me in a way that potholes and a lack of guardrails had never been. It had never occurred to me before, but three days later, during my eight-hour bus ride from Maputo to Inhambane, it occurred to me many, many times.

If all this makes you think twice about traveling to less-developed countries, fine. Because when you do go, that hesitation will make you safer. The "Bad Trips" report shows that the average foreign driver is more likely than locals to be involved in accidents. But you won't be the average driver; you'll pay more attention, take more precautions, and be more prepared.

✳ ✳ ✳ ✳

Much as I wish travelers were better at assessing risk, their miscalculations do lead to opportunities for others. Traveling to a place that many people think is more dangerous than it is yields rewards in several ways. You will likely save money, as those countries are comparatively cheap. But, more important, by seeking out the safe places in countries or regions generally thought of as dangerous ("Africa," "the Middle East"), or actively questioning your biases about much-maligned places closer to home (i.e., the Bronx, Detroit), you will be rewarded upon arrival by finding far fewer travelers clogging its touristic arteries.

That means more things to discover and a population more motivated to interact with visitors from far away. Remember my rule: The number of visitors a place receives is inversely related to how nice locals are to those visitors. I'm a good example. When I'm in Manhattan and see gobs of tourists, I feel like running in the other direction. But when I bump into the occasional tour group in Jackson Heights (generally for a culinary adventure), I'm downright proud. How did they hear about the place? What do they think? Do they have any questions?

Anyone who has traveled to Colombia in the last ten years has likely sensed this. It remains an undervisited destination, despite aggressive marketing campaigns, including one that attacked its own outdated reputation head-on with the slogan: "Colombia, the only risk is wanting to stay." These days, their tourism board is on overdrive, and travelers and travel writers generally rave about the place—its mesmerizing landscapes, deep-rooted folk culture, even the easiest-to-understand Spanish accent in the world. But the most common comment is that the people were almost heartbreakingly kind. Colombians are indeed naturally warm, but part of that has to be the pent-up pride in their country and the relative novelty of welcoming outsiders.

Shorter-lived events—particularly shocking or tragic ones—can also keep travelers away longer than is warranted or from a geographical area much wider than that affected. The resulting drop in tourism receipts can doubly devastate regions already suffering.

It can feel unethical to visit a country recently struck by tragedy, especially if part of your incentive is the discount air and hotel rates. But I find it to be precisely the opposite. Of course, you should not go to gawk at, say, the destruction a cyclone has wrought. But traveling to an affected area or to other parts of the same country before mainstream tourism returns can be incredibly helpful, especially if tourism is a vital part of their economy.

Of course, not everybody will be convinced. It's a tough sell, as I found out in March 2011, when a severe earthquake caused the Tohoku tsunami and Fukushima nuclear disaster in northern Japan. I had tickets to fly to Tokyo less than two weeks later. It would be my first time in the country, and I was busy scouting out an itinerary that would have me crisscrossing the country to write at least four Frugal Traveler columns.

The obvious choices were: (1) cancel; (2) postpone. The uncertainty was huge. Tsunami footage surfaced on YouTube that was disaster-movie horrific: cars and houses swept away by a terrifying rush of pitch-black water. Images of the nuclear meltdown were harder to come by, but I grew up during the Cold War. I don't need footage to be terrified of radioactive fallout.

But hold on. How big was Japan, anyway? Where, exactly, was Fukushima Prefecture? (What, exactly, was a prefecture?) Could I visit other parts of the country safely?

The destruction, though large scale and horrific—nearly sixteen thousand deaths were eventually confirmed from the tsunami—was limited to a small portion of Japan. The evacuation zone around the nuclear plant maxed out at a twelve-mile radius. A few foreign governments advised nationals to evacuate wider zones. There was some unsubstantiated murmuring that Tokyo—170 miles away— could be affected.

I looked at a map. More than half of Japan lay south and west of Tokyo, in the opposite direction from Fukushima. That included Osaka and Hiroshima, places already on my itinerary. I noted that Fukuoka, Japan's fourth largest city, was geographically closer to Shanghai than to the meltdown.

After four days of heart-wrenching news coverage, the Japan National Tourism Organization (JNTO) put out a statement: The region affected by the tsunami could not be visited (and who would want to, anyway?) and Tokyo was still experiencing some rotating blackouts. But Hokkaido, Kansai, Chugoku, Shikoku, and Kyushu—regions that combined to form more than half of Japan's territory—were unharmed and tourism operations were normal.

Air and hotel bargains were sure to emerge over coming weeks to draw visitors back; fewer visitors would mean more attentive hosts, shorter lines, more upgrades. That was not only good for me but also for my readers to know. The Japanese—at least those in the tourism industry—really wanted people to come.

The antidote to fear, I decided, was information. So I forwarded the JNTO release to my editors and suggested that I reschedule the trip as soon as we had further confirmation the nuclear fallout was contained.

I heard back in sixteen minutes. "Are you out of your mind?" wrote one editor. "No one is going to want to go there. We need a Plan B."

I half agreed. No one is going to want to go there. But that's exactly why we should stick with Plan A: to show why everyone was wrong. I could convince at least a few people to visit, and others would at least learn that Japan was not as small or monolithic as they thought. (As for "Are you out of your mind?" that was a toss-up.)

The trip was off.

Tourism tanked that year in Japan, from 8.6 to 6.2 million visitors, the largest-percentage year-over-year decrease since at least 1964. Maybe more coverage would have helped around the margins, but some drop was inevitable: Humans have a primal instinct to stay away from places associated with death and destruction.

In case you were curious, tourism to the United States tanked even harder after the September 11 attacks. From September through December of 2001, 5.1 million foreign tourists came to the United States; over the same period of 2000, it had been 8.6 million.

I still haven't been to Japan.

*   *   *   *

For all this talk about risk, we have yet to consider what we should be measuring it against: reward. It's not enough to consider the dangers of a destination, or of certain activities in that destination, in isolation. You have to weigh them against what you will gain by going.

Travel is a vital part of my life, which makes some risks more tolerable. But not all. My desire to run with the bulls in Pamplona is approximately zero, so you'll never see me in white clothes and a red scarf scampering down the street during the Festival of San Fermín. You may feel differently: Perhaps running with the bulls is your (asinine) dream. As a result, though you might agree with me that the risk is significant, you'll still do it. Crossing Africa via public transportation sounds incredible to me; there's a pretty good chance that, even knowing the risk, I would happily go. I'm going to guess most people I know would not. One of them might want to climb Mount Everest, an extraordinarily dangerous challenge; that's of no interest to me. In fact, I'm not sure I'd go if there was a gondola to the top.

One final question to consider: In certain circumstances, might risk itself become part of the reward?

School shootings notwithstanding, most Americans (and Canadians and Europeans and . . .) who can afford to travel live in places where daily life is generally safe. Our cars have air bags, our children have car seats, our ambulances arrive promptly, our preschool teachers undergo criminal background checks, and our bridges, elevators, and tractor-trailers are inspected regularly. Even New York City hot-dog vendors are regulated by the city. When things go wrong, there's an outcry, a news report, an investigation. Products are recalled, new security systems are put in place, pledges are made by officials that this will not, cannot happen again. Worst-case scenario, we sue. Well, at least we Americans.

This sort of safety is not the natural state of human affairs, and in many places you might want to visit, it simply does not exist.

But our instinct is to try to re-create such conditions on the road. That's why plenty of travelers shun public transportation in developing countries, steer clear of large public gatherings, balk at street-food vendors, and avoid wandering off from the safari tent after dark. (OK, I'll give them the last one.) While some caution is of course prudent, might part of experiencing a place where life is full of risks be to accept and experience, to some degree, what it's like to live with them?

Perhaps my parents recognized this when they let me take that exchange trip to rural Africa when I was fifteen. When I went to the Dominican Republic, I certainly felt it was valuable to stay in the precarious neighborhoods from which my students had emigrated, where I learned that being electrocuted by a downed wire was, though tragic, not extraordinary. I took that bus ride in Mozambique after hearing about the lack of emergency services, but not without a knot in my stomach. I think about it often now when I drive, stomach-knot–free, on American highways.

I also realize this every time I go to Brazil. As a New York City pedestrian, I'm moderately careful, of course. But I'm pretty confident I won't be mugged in broad daylight, and I do assume, correctly so far, that cars will stop at red lights and generally cede to pedestrians. I realize there is a tiny risk they won't—enough to keep an eye out, but not to actively worry.

But the first time I set foot on Brazilian streets, I am jolted into "something could happen at any second" mode. I'm constantly scanning (subconsciously) for potential muggers, and (very consciously) remembering that drivers have no patience for pedestrians. I wish Brazil weren't like this, of course, but knowing what it feels like does have some value to me, a sort of subtle bonus gift from spending time there. It's not so much about "understanding Brazil" as it is coming back and understanding my own home better.

Another reason to go to Rio.

Street sign in Tripoli, Lebanon.

· · · · · · · · · · · · ·

Chapter 6

PEOPLE AND TRAVEL

You know what they say about South Carolina: Go for the boiled peanuts, stay for the alligator-trapping tutorial.

It was 2012, I was dating a woman named Cris, and we were on a road trip from Washington, DC, to Savannah, Georgia. Driving through South Carolina with ninety minutes to go before Charleston, we had just polished off our second lunch of the day—because even if you've just eaten, you don't pass up a barbecue buffet at a place called Hog Heaven that has a sign featuring three pigs in bibs and halos, salivating atop a cloud.

Cris showed some modicum of buffet control, but I was overstuffed with pulled pork and beans and banana pudding and something called Oreo Delight for dessert. So when I suggested we stop for boiled peanuts a few miles farther down, I assumed she thought I was crazy.

And she didn't even know I hate boiled peanuts, a mushy Southern tradition that proves once and for all why God created honey roasting.

It was really an excuse to see who and what would be at a place called the Carolina Country Store on a sparsely populated stretch of US-17 midafternoon on a Wednesday. Handwritten signs on the door (WE'VE GOT MILK and BABY CHICKS & DUCKS FOR SALE) were promising. Inside we found the milk, along with pork rinds, Old Milwaukee beer by the case, and David Bilderback, the memorabilia-collecting owner. He had decorated the whitewashed wood interior with an ancient meat grinder, a fin-de-siècle refrigerator, a battered washboard, and very much more; ancient wrenches hung from the ceiling. The livestock was outside, in Chicken City, a scale-model Wild West town sized for hens and roosters who spent their days clucking in the church and pooping in the bordello.

As I was buying the boiled peanuts, Cris somehow got into a conversation with a young African-American man in a gray T-shirt and baggy jeans bunched up at the boots who asked her whether she knew how to trap an alligator.

She did not. By the time I joined them, he was showing her how. (I missed most of it, but the gist was: "very carefully.")

His name was Marcus, and alligator control was (apparently) in his job description at a nearby plantation. In fact, the family that owned it was away, he said. Would we like to visit? We declined, since we had to be in Charleston by evening.

Yeah, right. We scrapped our plans and followed his pickup to a brick gate, with an allée of Southern live oaks draped in Spanish moss beyond. It looked like the nineteenth century.

Our first stop was at two ancient cabins, with thick wood shingles tilted outward like a Persian blind peeking open ever so slightly.

"Slave quarters," he told us. The roofs had been replaced, but the walls and the brick chimneys within were still largely intact. Marcus led us toward the door and pushed it open slowly, as if he were sneaking in.

"Anybody here?" he whispered.

"Who are you talking to?" I asked, thinking snakes.

"Spirits," he replied.

* * * *

When I think back to any trip, the first image that pops into my head is never a canyon or a city skyline or a beach sunset. It's a face. For China, there's no contest—it's Mei Mei and He He, adorable six-year-old identical twins who helped me learn to count in Mandarin while their grandmother did tai chi by the river in Yichang. For Sweden, it's the farmer who invited me to a friend's house for a whiskey-soaked evening of listening to the Beatles. He wasn't quite as cute. For Paraguay, it's Digna López, an eighty-seven-year-old woman who had been making traditional *ao po'i* embroidery since she was fourteen. (The exact image is of a sleepy version of her face, since she was napping when I knocked on her door.)

Maybe it's because I'm not a landscape or museum lover, though I do appreciate sublime views, especially when accompanied by a cocktail. And I have been known to find beauty in even the most abstract art, especially if an authoritative voice in an audio tour tells me to. But travel is about meeting people.

Some might quibble, arguing that it's just as much about scuba diving or spotting rare birds or tracking down your great-aunt's gravesite in Lithuania. And some might disagree with me entirely, as did Steve Herppich, a photo editor from Olympia, Washington, I interviewed in 2007 for a "Why We Travel" feature about his trip to Mount Hood National Forest:

> I try to get out in the woods on a backpacking trip at least once a year. What I do for a living is totally immersed in humanity. There's something I really love about covering assignments and meeting all different kinds of people every day. But to get out where, for all you know, there's nobody within miles is priceless.[1]

I get it. But I think for most people, meeting others—especially those with extraordinarily different life experiences—is a major factor in a successful trip. Not many great vacation stories start with the phrase: "So on the fourth day of my solo hike, guess which song got stuck in my head?"

"So this guy was teaching us how to subdue an alligator with our bare hands" works much better.

✳ ✳ ✳ ✳

Marcus led us from the slave quarters to a low-slung, modern building. "I got something to show you," he said, and disappeared inside. He came out dragging a wild-boar carcass, black as night with blood dripping from its nose. His plan was to use it as bait for gators, which he would then trap and sell.

"You make a little money off them," he said. "You don't get rich."

Then it was on to a weathered, three-story wood-shingled building, with windows and chute openings at oddly irregular intervals. It was the old rice mill, he said, leading us through an ancient door attached by a thick, hand-forged hinge and walking us by rusted plows and gear-and-belt-laden machinery. On a wooden column, someone had made hatch marks in pencil and scribbled dates from what appeared to be the 1900s. Was I looking at state-of-the-art early-twentieth-century rice accounting? Marcus didn't know.

He told us that employees of the plantation often use metal detectors to search for artifacts near the slave quarters and outbuildings, and showed us what amounted to a private history museum. It was a carefully catalogued collection of shoe buckles and slave uniform buttons, sconces and doll parts and plantation tokens (which slaves used to buy goods)—all found on the grounds. Many had been unearthed by using old maps showing the locations of long-gone slave quarters to go on treasure hunts, Marcus said.

Finally, we came to the owners' residence. Should we really be going in there? I asked. They wouldn't mind, he said, leading us into a living room where family pictures were on display.

Marcus was a charismatic, skilled, intellectually curious and dedicated man. Why would he show two total strangers around? Maybe it was pure Southern hospitality, maybe he was proud of his work, or had a crush on Cris, or was just lonely. He certainly did not know I was a writer, and when I fessed up as we said good-bye—alas, without running into any alligators—I expected he would panic and urge me not to write about the visit. But he was fine with it.

It's not hard to find a tour of a South Carolina plantation. But it will cost you $20 or so, and your guide won't be as knowledgeable, funny, or clearly in love with his job as ours was.

Of course, people who will drop everything to give you a tour of their workplace are rare. How do you go about finding them? Often it's just luck, but how does that old saying go? The more boiled peanuts you stop for, the luckier you get.

Advance planning helps as well. We were traveling on a local road when we could have taken the interstate. We were in a rural area where tourists are not that common. And we were in the American South, a region generally associated with hospitality. It's unlikely we would have had such luck along the Hollywood Walk of Fame or at an Orlando convenience store favored by Disney employees. (Although that workplace tour would be awesome.) Stopping whenever it struck our fancy was also a help. As was forcing myself to talk to people even when I'm not feeling social at all. Which is quite often.

There are some people for whom talking to strangers comes without fear and regardless of mood. But for most, it takes an uncomfortable effort to make small talk with random people. Back in the day, when I was a reporter, doing person-on-the-street interviews would make my stomach churn. I'd have to steel myself against the inevitable (and at times nasty) rejections from busy, stressed New Yorkers. It helped to lower expectations beforehand, and tell myself I was lucky if one in five people stopped, and one in five of those said something interesting. When someone brushed me aside or politely declined, I reminded myself, it was not because of me, but because they were late to work, had other things on their mind, or just hated reporters.

A similar attitude helps in travel. If you're an introvert, you're unlikely to become a social butterfly, but no matter the level of your talk-to-strangers game, you can certainly up it a bit when you're on a trip. Or even when you're not, as batting practice for your next trip, maybe by vowing to talk to three strangers a day (even if just to mention the weather in an elevator). I've already acknowledged that I might be an extrovert with friends and colleagues, but instinctively avoid talking with strangers. I can't think of anything to say, my stomach sinks, I fear rejection or that I'll say something stupid or that they just won't like me. And that's when I order at McDonald's. (Just kidding!)

The potential payoff is worth the discomfort, whether it's just exchanging pleasantries, getting good restaurant advice, or landing an insider's tour of a plantation.

So how do you approach strangers? The best advice I've ever heard was: "Smile and ask a question." It's simple and brilliant and I wish I remembered who said it so I could credit them here. Thought-ful questions are always preferable, but in reality any dumb ques-tion will do, even if you already know the answer or couldn't care less. "How do I get to the plaza?" "I like your hat, where did you get it?" "Excuse me, do you know what time it is?" The responder's tone and demeanor will indicate whether there is a chat to be had (or whether they speak English), but either way, you've lost nothing, and maybe even picked up some information.

Seriously, *any* question will do. In 2013, I stopped for coffee at a gas station/convenience store along US Route 212 in South Dakota. (By the tail end of that Baton Rouge to Fargo solo road trip, even a field with sunflowers filled to the horizon wasn't enough to keep me alert.) A young woman was pouring herself coffee from one of two self-service pots. She looked local—blondes abound in the Scandinavian-descended upper heartland—and I figured she might know a good place for lunch (or fall in love with me).

I smiled and asked, "What's the difference between those two pots?"

"I think this one is fresher," she said, with an accent that revealed she was from far, far away.

Hardly Mamet-quality patter, but, as I said, any question will do. And since her accent had given her away as nowhere near local, an obvious path of conversation had materialized. I found out she was a recent college grad from Estonia who had flown to the United States for the last four summers to live with host families. I remember one of them was a Nevada mining family, which sounded fantastic. She was turning her experiences into a book; I mentioned that I was planning a book as well. We became Facebook friends and almost met up in New York a few months later. (She showed up during Thanksgiving, while I was away.)

The exchange was of no real consequence. But how often do you meet an Estonian in a South Dakota gas station and learn a great new way to get to know the United States? And if I go to Estonia someday, I'll look her up.

✳　✳　✳　✳

So smile and ask a question, then do it again, and again, and again. Don't expect anything to come of it, and something eventually will.

Of course, if given a choice, an intelligent, well-worded question is preferred to a moronic, coffeepot-related one. There's a trick to this: Embed a mission into your trip that gives you an interesting thing to ask locals about. Perhaps you are really into rum, or secondhand-clothing stores, or street art, or something esoteric like intercity rivalries. So in a bar in Puerto Rico, you might ask someone which local rum is best. A funkily dressed pedestrian in Seoul might warrant a compliment and a "Where can I find something like that around here?" Someone photographing one work of Berlin street art might lead you to another one. And if you're in Australia, you might ask the guy stitting next to you at the bus stop, "Excuse me, I'm sorry to bother, but I'm asking everyone I meet here: Which is better, Sydney or Melbourne?"

The wording of a question can sometimes make a big difference. Perhaps the most common question travelers like to ask locals is, "Where do the locals eat?" This always makes me cringe, because though the spirit is right, the wording invites failure. The instant reaction of many people—especially those in professions who deal with tourists, like drivers and hotel staff—is to think, "Ah, these rich, picky tourists would never like the hole in the wall I take my family to—and don't Americans just eat burgers and pizza anyway? I'll send them to the place with a view of the harbor and photos on the trilingual menu."

So I try to hem them in a little, by asking something like, "Where's the last place you ate out with your family?" Or "Where do you go for a beer after work?" Mustering a little playful prodding can work. I have had a lot of luck talking about how sick I am of places full of travelers. "Before you answer," I've been known to say, "please realize that if I go and see a single other tourist there, I'm coming back to complain."

Nothing will work every time, because vast swaths of humanity have more important things to do than to help you. But you'll eventually find someone who doesn't, and you'll get good—sometimes even damn good—advice.

If you're really out to make friends, you also might consider more advanced tactics. Here's one that has worked for me:

You enter a restaurant and see a large, festive group. Instinct might tell you to sit as far away as possible. But instead, try to get a table right next to them, and, upon returning from a trip to the restroom, walk right by. Ask whoever is looking in your direction what the occasion is. People in good moods (or are well oiled) are far less likely to snub you, and, depending on local social conventions, you might be invited to join them.

Do this even if your traveling companions cringe. And note that it works extra well if you're alone in a country where eating alone is considered especially pathetic.

Here's another favorite tactic: As I peruse the menu, I ask the diners at surrounding tables whether they like the dishes they've ordered. More than once, I've had a nice chat and gotten a free taste, and exactly once a family at a Naples pizzeria shared the significant leftovers of their *fritti misti* platter.

Although it's usually more fun to dine in a place with a good crowd, it's sometimes even better to sit down in a place where every seat is empty—in other words, where the staff has nothing better to do than talk to you. ("Do you have any tables available?" I like to ask, testing the staff's sense of humor.) Same with shops at off-hours, ice cream stores in winter, museum staff on an off-season weekday—you name it.

If you're really shameless (recommended), you can dispense with all but the flimsiest cover story. Passing a group having a delicious-looking fried-chicken picnic in the park? Nothing wrong with saying, "Excuse me, you all seem to be fried-chicken connoisseurs. Where can I get the best fried chicken in town?"

Someone in the group will inevitably respond, "At Aunt Joan's house"—Aunt Joan being the person who prepared the picnic.

"Well, unfortunately, she's not my Aunt Joan, so can you recommend the second-best fried chicken in town?"

You may very well score a piece of chicken and, if you are really obviously from way out of town, an invite to join. If this sounds too shameless to you, don't do it. And for heaven's sake, skip the next anecdote.

For the final night of a four-day bike trip from Lexington, Kentucky, into Appalachia, I hadn't really planned out a place to sleep. I figured that if no charming inn offering sharp discounts appeared, I'd find a motel along the way or just bike the extra thirty miles or so to my destination, Paintsville, where I'd be picking up a rental car on Day 4.

But, rather like what happened to Cris and me on our way to Charleston, I ended up stopping way too often along the way. One irresistible pause was the tiny Country Side Community Church, on a gentle slope up from the country road I was taking. An EVERYONE WELCOME sign was handwritten on blistered white paint, so I decided to stop in to fill my water bottle. Or that was my excuse, anyway. I really just wanted to see the church. From the road, it had looked empty, but a bunch of cars were parked in the back, and the place was humming with a rehearsal for a Bible camp play. The kids had just gone back to work after a pasta buffet lunch, and it wasn't long before the family members who had prepared it "surprised" me with an invitation to fuel up before I continued along my route.

That was one of the more pleasant stops. Another unexpected delay was more frustrating. A rails-to-trails route I had planned to take was unpaved, and my bike wasn't up for it. That forced me to take a detour down not-very-scenic, not-very-bike-friendly Route 114.

Route 114 had barely any visible homes, let alone a single motel, so my options were looking like cutting through a mountain road and doing the last twenty miles to Paintsville in the dusk and dark— or finding a place to sleep under the stars that looked black bear and bobcat free.

Then I spotted a gas station/convenience store, crossed the road, and parked my bike. It was immediately clear this was not your generic Slim Jims, Dasani, and gas operation. Baggies of homemade Kentucky cream candy ($3) sat on the counter, and some folks had gathered around a somewhat-out-of-place table by the soda fountains, acting like a family in their living room.

As it turned out, it was a family—the Marsilletts. I removed my bike helmet and explained my predicament. Was there a motel nearby? Was there a quicker route that would allow me to make it to

Paintsville by nightfall? A kid named Jordan, who turned out to be fourteen, told me there wasn't, and there was no way I could make it over the hill in the dark. Around this time it occurred to Jordan's nineteen-year-old cousin Kevin that it might be fun (and kind) to have this weird outsider from New York stay over. His uncle, Jordan's dad Tom, approved.

So they took me down a road that led off the highway to a surprisingly large home in a densely wooded "holler"—the Appalachian term, I would learn, for a hollow or valley.

If you're thinking, "Marsilletts, you're insane, I would never invite a sweaty stranger to sleep in my house!" you're missing two important details: (1) I was not invited to stay in their house, but in a hunting shelter way back in the holler; and (2) they owned at least two dozen guns and were perfectly capable of defending themselves should I, say, attack them with my Swiss Army knife.

A few minutes later, ten-year-old Cody had joined us and I was hanging out at the pool with three cousins whose total age fell just short of mine. Judging by the pool (and their claim that the suburban-style house was once owned by Johnny Depp's mother), they seemed to be doing OK for themselves. I soon learned that, in addition to the convenience store, they owned a scrap-metal yard and bred hunting dogs.

I took a particular liking to Kevin, the one who had engineered my stay. He had graduated from high school the year before and was obviously plenty smart enough to be in college, though he wasn't. He was curious about New York, my work (I said I was a "writer," but, as usual, didn't tell anyone until I was leaving that I was writing about the trip), and the world in general. Becky, the mom/aunt, came out and recounted how the region had suffered from the decline of coal mining, forcing many families to leave. Others, like the Marsilletts, were sticking it out. "Everybody needs gas," she said.

Kevin, Cody, and Jordan gave me a tour of the house's "man cave." (A sign labeled it as such.) The sofa and chairs were outfitted in camouflage patterns; hunting trophies covered the walls. Cody told me they had once adopted a sick bobcat. "You're the first family I've ever met to have a bobcat," I told him.

He corrected me: "We've had two."

The boys took me to two safes in the master bedroom, where the family's huge gun collection was stored. It included collector's items like an intriguing double-barrel shotgun with a separate trigger for each barrel, as well as Becky's pink shotgun. They were as amazed at my explanation of New York City's strict gun laws as I was at their arsenal, and equally uneasy about how I would react. Like most in the region, they were acutely aware of how people elsewhere in the United States viewed Appalachia. They had heard the jokes.

It was time to show me to my accommodations, accessible only via an odd vehicle—it looked to me like a combination ATV and moon buggy. They called it a "side-by-side." I was the only one who had bothered putting on a seatbelt before Jordan gunned the engine and zoomed into the woods along a boulder-lined, impossibly rutted incline. How this thing clawed and jolted its way up without stalling or flipping over astonished (and relieved) me. Engine roaring, we made it to the shelter deep in the woods in what seemed like just a couple of minutes. What I had imagined as a rustic cabin was a retooled tool shed from Lowe's, perched on a platform high off the ground. It was dusk.

Kevin glanced at me. "This would be a good place to kill someone," he said. Then he paused for just a split second, monitoring my eyes for the slightest flinch, before cracking up. If there were a Savile Row for comedic tension, he had just tailored a bespoke "gotcha," measuring the dynamic between three Eastern Kentucky kids and a forty-four-year-old city slicker stuck deep in their woods with remarkable precision.

In the shed, we found a cot, a stove . . . and a half-dozen active wasp nests. Cody rummaged around for the stove lighter and then torched them, swatting at escapees with his baseball cap. Appalachian turndown service.

We returned to the house for dinner—I had offered to buy a pizza, which, of course, we got at the family convenience store. (Convenience stores, as you may know but I sure didn't, often include built-in, made-to-order pizzerias these days. If you are as clueless as I was, search "Hunt Brothers.") And then it was back to the holler for the evening's activity: target practice. As targets, we used glass bottles of the most Kentucky beverage there is—ginger-citrus Ale-8-One soda—placed horizontally in the nook of a tree.

Kevin handed me a loaded Smith & Wesson and granted me the first shot. I could hold my own here, I figured. I had taken riflery at summer camp, shot police-issue revolvers at pop-up metal gangsters during a (terrifying) training session for journalists in São Paulo, and killed a wild boar on my second shot during a daylong hunting outing in rural Florida. But it was not enough. I lost their respect (and caused them to duck in unison) by flouting basic gun safety rules and waving the loaded weapon around instead of pointing it at the ground until I was ready to shoot. But I did gain back some respect by knocking off the bottom half of the bottle with my first shot.

Except for two stings from wasps that had been torched or swatted enough to be immobilized on the cot but not quite enough to be killed, the night passed without incident. In the morning, I heard the side-by-side roaring long before I saw it. I thanked the family, got on my bike, headed over the hills, and reached Paintsville in under two hours. It turned out I could have made it the night before. Of course, I was glad I hadn't tried. My motel in Paintsville was quiet and anonymous. The Marsillett family experience had been neither.

❋   ❋   ❋   ❋

I had acted rather shamelessly with the Marsilletts. Though I truly did not have a place to stay that night, I had walked into their shop fully hoping someone would offer me a bed. Which raises the sticky issue of travelers' intentions with the people they meet on the road. When are we good-hearted humans out to make connections, and when are we fishing for freebies, "exotic" experiences, and self-congratulatory tales to tell the folks back home (or reading our column in the newspaper)? How do we monitor ourselves to make sure our interventions in other people's lives are ethical or, at the very least, cause no harm?

Here's a first stab at it. Travelers should never take advantage of people's good nature to the extent they become a burden, especially if those people are clearly worse off financially, which is often the case. I think I did OK on this account with the Marsilletts: This was a smart, business-owning, relatively financially secure American family. Kevin was wise to my maneuvers, and enough internal family debate preceded the invitation to indicate they were clearly not offering up a place because of some ingrained cultural hospitality. I could be wrong, but I also think we all had a pretty good time, especially the kids, who were out of school for the summer and didn't seem to have much else to do.

Making friends with the Marsilletts was invaluable. One objective of my trip to generally poor Eastern Kentucky was to test my own prejudices. Of course, one evening with one family was not enough to scratch the surface of Appalachian reality. But during my two prior nights in the region, I had hung out with Latino pipeline workers at a motel, and stayed in the Bowen Farm Bed & Breakfast (the very one you won't find on Booking), run by—no, presided over by—Joe Bowen, a politically active Democrat who once walked across the United States on stilts. My view of the region had, at the very least, gained some nuance.

Writing about the trip, and the Marsilletts especially, was a challenge. I did ask at the end of the trip whether I could use my experience with them in my story, and, as usually happens, they were totally OK with it. More OK than I was, in fact, because portraying a much-maligned region via a handful of experiences sure seemed like a minefield. And since several members of the family had friended me on Facebook (granting me access in coming years to some way-out-of-my-bubble posts), and Kevin would bug me regularly about when the article was coming out, there's no question the family would see it. When it did come out, I dutifully sent him a couple of print copies. He never wrote back.

Seven months after that, I noticed a few posts with Kevin tagged in them popped up on my Facebook feed. I finally read one: "Even at the lowest point in my life you would do anything just to make me crack a smile dude. Rest in peace Kevin Marsillett."

I clicked to his page. There were more:

I've been going through our conversations all day. It's like i'm waiting for you to send me something hilarious on Snapchat lol.

I miss you terribly.

Fly High Ratdad. There will never be another like you buddy.

We had some times. Realest motherfucker I knew.

There were also links to local news reports.

FLOYD CO., Ky (WYMT)—A Sunday night crash claimed the life of an Eastern Kentucky teen. It happened when two cars collided on Route 114 in Floyd County, Sunday night. Kevin Marsillett, 19, died after being transported to a hospital in Lexington. He graduated from Prestonsburg High School in 2014. A friend describes him as the class clown, life of the party and a good friend. "He was probably the goofiest guy I've ever met," said Marsillett's friend, Selena Kelly.[2]

Selena's quote was touchingly unsurprising. This sounded like an excellent description of the guy I spent an evening with. The article detailed funeral arrangements and ended in another, more gutwrenching nonsurprise: "Troopers say Marsillett was not wearing a seatbelt."

There's an odd imbalance when travelers meet someone who lives in the place they are visiting. We catch them during their real, sometimes stressful lives, whereas they meet us as we delight in carefree leisure. So I often question how real are the friendships I form with people while traveling. I've certainly forgotten far more than I remember.

But some people are too uniquely charismatic to be just "that guy I met on a trip once." Kevin's subtly subversive wit—the feeling that he knew exactly where we both fit into the world, that he was as entertained by me as I was by him, made him different. It felt more like a friend far closer to home had died. I regretted not writing to him to find out what he thought of the article.

Yet I got lucky. A sort of answer came three days later, after I heard from a Marsillett family friend who emailed me via my website to tell me the news. She thought I should know, which was touching. I wrote her back to say that I had seen the updates on Facebook and was writing a note to the family. She responded:

> Forgot that big city people use Facebook too, haha. Seems like such a small town forum and hardly any of my friends out of state use it. Silly me. Thanks for the quick response. Thank you also for the kind and respectful tone you used in depicting Becky's family. They're good people. Seems like we're the last group on the planet that it's ok to ridicule (and Lord knows there is plenty material to pick on). Your article didn't go there. I appreciated that very much.

How can you know whether you're taking advantage of a "local"? It's an impossible task, of course, and I'm surely far from innocent. But one test I like to recommend is to think about what would happen if they came to visit your hometown a year later. Would you automatically want to return the favor with similar treatment—having them over for a meal, taking them on a tour of town, showing them around your workplace, letting them take pictures of your children, whatever it may be? A genuine "Of course!" means you're fine. Anything less and you might want to think it through.

✳ ✳ ✳ ✳

Though being outgoing (or faking it as best you can) will go a long way in having good experiences with people you meet on the road, you can also stack the deck before your trip.

All else being equal, it's easier to connect in places whose people are known to be outgoing, unrushed, and hospitable. By *outgoing*, I refer to the kind of natural extroversion you might find in the Caribbean and in Italy, for example. By *unrushed*, I mean, well, the opposite of New Yorkers, who may be happy to give you subway directions but are unlikely to welcome you into their social life without a romantic or financial motive. And by *hospitable*, I mean a culturally ingrained custom of welcoming strangers warmly.

But again: all else being equal. That does not mean that if you love duck confit, dream of afternoons in the Musée d'Orsay, and know how to pronounce *arrondissement*, that you should skip Paris in favor of Istanbul because people are nicer. That said, if you have ten days, skipping out of Paris for a weekend to a far friendlier small French town might be worth it.

You could also set your itinerary to tilt toward places with fewer tourists, which, as you now know, I consider far better for meeting people. If you're dreaming of Peru, look for areas outside of Cuzco, Machu Picchu, and Lima that appeal to you, and try to make them at least a part of your trip. (Tip: Kuélap.)

And finally—again, all else being equal—favor places where you speak the language. A monolingual Mexican will likely make more friends in Spain than in Portugal, and the French might favor Tahiti over Fiji. Now, say you're an American planning a winter week in the Caribbean, where there are countless gorgeous, culturally rich islands. Assuming you don't speak very much Spanish or French, and are not obsessed with merengue or meringue, perhaps you should consider English-speaking Jamaica or Barbados or Dominica. Unless, of course, you have been learning a language and want to practice. Then, by all means, head to Curaçao and practice your Papiamento.

It's tempting for native English speakers to pooh-pooh this logic with "Everyone speaks English these days."

English is certainly the closest we come to a world language. But far from "everyone" speaks it. In much of the world, depending on English speakers means shrinking your potential circle of new friends to tourism-industry workers, the local elite, and teenagers. When someone comes back from Brazil and tells me, "Everyone spoke great English," I know precisely who "everyone" was. Places like Iceland or the Netherlands, where nearly everyone speaks English, also become more appealing. Just don't forget that "nearly" still excludes some of the most interesting people—typically, grandmothers, seven-year-olds, and those from small towns. And even those who speak decent English are less likely to confide quickly in you than they would in someone who speaks their native tongue.

Language should not be a deciding factor where you travel. But it is good to be conscious of what you might be missing. When I traveled to Cuba in 2000 and 2003, it was illegal for Americans to go independently, though many did. (Let's just say I went on a journalist visa and hope no one checks.)

Things were tough there, and like many living under oppressive regimes, the Cubans I met were uncomfortable confiding in outsiders. But language made a difference. I managed to make a few friends who, drawing their blinds and lowering their voices to near-whispers, told me just how bad things really were, how difficult it was to get medication or meat or milk. During those same years, I met several other Americans who had visited Cuba. They invariably fell into two categories: non-Spanish speakers who would say, "Cuba is so wonderful!" and Spanish speakers who tilted toward "Cuba is so depressing!"

Beyond handpicking a destination for the culture and the language, there's a far, far more effective way to ensure you'll have people to interact with: Choose a place where you already know someone, or know someone who knows someone and can hook you up. When readers asked how I chose my destinations for Frugal Traveler columns, I freely admitted that it was often because a friend, or a friend of a friend, or a grandmother of a friend of a friend, lived there.

Make finding contacts a part of your pretrip planning. A trip to Korea was greatly improved when a friend hooked me up with a Korean-American buddy living in Seoul; I ended up at his family's intimate Korean New Year's celebration. And though travel writers like me used to have an obvious advantage in our having colleagues scattered around the world, social media has evened the playing field. Don't think you know anyone in Italy? Post on Facebook. You don't have to say, "Hey, I'm going to Italy and really need a friend there because this book on travel said it's important." Try: "I'm planning a week in Sicily and wonder if anyone knows anyone who lives there that I can ask a few specific questions." Those "few specific questions" turn into a contact number in case anything goes wrong, and maybe even charm your way into a dinner invitation. Not everybody has international friends, but don't be surprised if an old high-school buddy you didn't even remember friending on

Facebook pipes up that he married a Sicilian whose family still lives on the island.

In the United States, most of us live near immigrant communities. New Yorkers have it easy—our city is home to people from all over the world, even exotic places like Texas. But it's hard to find any region in America without some immigrant presence. They might be your friends or colleagues, or (immigrant stereotype alert) your apartment building's superintendent or the neighbor's au pair. Only you can know how comfortable you are about asking for advice, but once people realize you want to visit their homeland, they sometimes get pretty excited and proud to share. They might also offer up relatives (and load you down with a package or two to take to them, but that's the least you can do). Once the parents of my Latino students in the Bronx got wind I had visited a student's grandmother in Santo Domingo, I was flooded with invitations.

Sound out people, even if you don't know them well. You may not get a personal connection, but you can get some great advice even from a casual conversation. If you're a regular at a coffee shop where the waiters are all Guatemalan (and how great that we live in a world where that could easily be true), just mention that you were thinking of visiting their country and see where they think you should go.

Their first instinct may be to send you to the places they think you want to go—touristy spots like Antigua, Guatemala's entry in the "beautifully refurbished World Heritage Site colonial city that is flooded with tourists" category. But their second instinct is often to send you to their home region. And if not, you can ask if it's worth visiting where they're from. What are the food specialties there? Chicken in pumpkin sauce? Oh, that sounds so good—if I go, will you tell me which restaurant does it best? Oh, the best is in your cousins' house? No, I couldn't possibly—er, are your cousins on Facebook?

Hostels, though not very useful for meeting locals, are also great places to meet people from around the world you might visit on your next trip. A couple of weeks on the hostel circuit could score you enough friends to visit for a decade of vacations, especially if you, like me, are willing to choose your destinations at least in part based on who you know living there. Just be sure you're willing to show equal hospitality when they visit you.

* * * *

Everyone knows that cultural differences can hamper making new relationships during travel. But knowing they exist doesn't mean they're easy to overcome. Our cultures permeate our behavior in ways we don't even realize.

In New York City, you can launch right into a discussion with a stranger, say, sitting next to you on the subway, sometimes without so much as an "Excuse me."

"I love that book you're reading," you might say, and whether that gets you just a nod or starts a conversation, you've not done anything wrong. (Of course, the person must actually be reading a book.) I once opened with "Great shoes," which scored me my only met-in-the-subway date. The problem is, it doesn't work everywhere, and I have occasionally forgotten that.

The NYC no-intro remark particularly bit me in the arse on a trip to Toulouse, France. My first day there, I sat on the grass on Prairie des Filtres, a pleasant stretch of green on the Garonne River. Four men of North African descent were sitting together playing a tune— two on the banjo, one on a guitar, and one on what looked like an overgrown mandolin. They were quite talented, and I decided to go over and chat. Smile and ask a question, I thought, as soon as they took a break. "That was very good, what's the name of that song?" I asked in my rusty French.

"Bonjour," said the guitar player.

"Really, the song is named 'Bonjour'?" I responded, before I figured it out. "Bonjour" was not the song, it was the greeting you must use to initiate any daytime conversation. He was derisively informing me I was a boor.

In my defense, Toulouse was my first stop in France, coming in from Spain, and it had been twenty years since I had spent any real time there. On the other hand, greeting people with "Bonjour" is literally the first thing I learned in French class in seventh grade. I apologized. They charitably asked me to sit down. It turned out they were a French-Algerian group called Nostalgérie, a clever combination of nostalgia and the French word for Algeria. They had a way with words.

We did not become fast friends, but the lesson vastly improved the rest of my trip, because I began to pay attention to the way people interacted in shops and museums, and imitated it. It was as if I had been cast in a play called "Wow, the French Are Really Formal," and was studying my lines.

Customer enters store
SHOPKEEPER: Bonjour, Monsieur!
CUSTOMER: Bonjour, Madame, how are you?
SHOPKEEPER: Fine, thank you, how are you?
CUSTOMER: I am well. Could I have a baguette?
SHOPKEEPER: Here you are, Monsieur. Ninety cents.
CUSTOMER: Here you are. Thank you, Madame!
SHOPKEEPER: Thank you. Good-bye, Monsieur.
CUSTOMER: Good-bye, Madame. Have a nice day.
SHOPKEEPER: Thank you! Have a nice day!
Fin

The same show, adapted for New York audiences, would have gone like this:

Customer enters store
BLEARY-EYED, UNDERPAID CLERK: Next?
CUSTOMER: Can I get a baguette, please?
BLEARY-EYED, UNDERPAID CLERK: Ninety cents.
CUSTOMER: Here you go.
Curtain

In France, the payoff was instant. When I followed the script, the French were suddenly quite pleased to interact with me. I had a number of lovely conversations in my remaining days in Toulouse, and on my next trip, the one to Besançon, I picked up where I left off. Once I even made a shopkeeper laugh. (That may seem like a small victory until you consider I had made jokes in at least ten shops before hers, to no avail.)

These kinds of etiquette tips are typically found in the front or back of a traditional guidebook in a section about cultural norms, pages we too often ignore. Or, these days, we skip the guidebook altogether, which is too bad, because though such information is sometimes available online, you may not think to look it up (and might not be connected to the internet on your red-eye to Paris).

Everyone knows you should learn a few basic words or phrases of the language in your destination. But a great people-meeting trick is to add a few startlingly advanced words or phrases as well. I have advocated for this ever since my friend Adam was due to speak to a Brazilian audience in São Paulo and asked me to suggest a culturally appropriate opening joke. I suggested he start by apologizing for not speaking much Portuguese. "In fact," he should say, "I only know three things." First came *Bom dia*, the basic hello, as they would expect. But then came *jabuticaba* (a very seasonal, only-in-Brazil fruit with an indigenous name difficult for foreigners to pronounce). And, after an initial laugh, *Crédito ou débito?* which is what clerks ask basically every time you pay with a credit or debit card anywhere in Brazil.

You hardly need a speaking engagement to make use of this tactic. Imagine meeting a tourist from China who apologizes for not speaking English and says, "The only three things I know how to say are 'How are you?' 'oysters Rockefeller,' and 'May I see your driver's license and registration?'" That would certainly charm me.

Another way to meet people—one that works in even the most touristy places—is to take a break from sightseeing and devote a few hours to wandering a neighborhood with no major attractions, no famous restaurants, and no blossoming hipster population.

Sometimes I do this on purpose, perhaps when someone recommends an out-of-the-way restaurant and I decide to make an afternoon of improvising a roundabout route to get there. And sometimes it's just a spontaneous detour when I'm out on a walk and a crooked street beckons.

It works just about anywhere, as long as you know it's safe. I've done it in Buenos Aires, Naples, even Knoxville, Tennessee, in 2015, where I saw that the highly recommended North Corner Sandwich Shop was a few miles out of the city center. I figured I'd walk to it. Scattered along the route were a bakery, a craft-beer store, a vintage shop, a record store, junky used-goods shops, and Original Freezo, a stuck-in-time soft ice cream and burger stand. (Frozen Mountain Dew, $1.30? No sale.) There was also a marker commemorating the former location of the radio station where Dolly Parton made her broadcast debut at age ten.

When I finally reached the sandwich shop way past lunchtime, I met the owner, who not only loves New York, but also loved having a beer after work with someone from New York. We are still in touch. (Granted, it was only four years ago.)

The wander-a-neighborhood system also worked out very well in Tripoli, Lebanon, the country's second-biggest and a largely Sunni Muslim city. Tripoli is not that well known as a destination because it has experienced intervals of violence, but in quiet times, like when I was there, it has an enticing mix of mosques, souks, and sweets, streets filled with women in conservative robes and everyone hustling for a buck. It was exceedingly conservative and equally friendly—a big help, since almost every sign was in Arabic script, making it hard to find my way anywhere. (Among the exceptions, at one pedestrian crossing light, was a sign urging me to PUSH AND WAIT FOR GREEN MAN, as though it were a Martian vending machine.)

I emerged from one of the souks into what looked like an ordinary working-class neighborhood and decided it was time to wander. In Lebanon for the first time, I thought the neighborhood looked straight out of a TV news report from the 1980s. That association made it seem dangerous, but I had heard from a good source that the city was generally friendly and safe, and since the friendly part had panned out, off I went. Lest anyone think I looked out of place— actually, lest everyone think I looked out of place—I kept my camera out, making it clear I was a tourist and nothing more.

As I trudged along a road that wound up a hill and was lined with five- and six-story apartment buildings, I noticed, in the open door of a ground-floor apartment, an elderly woman sitting pensively in a powder-blue robe and beige hijab. It was a photograph waiting to happen, but I had no idea what photography etiquette was here, or even whether the woman and I had any language in common.

From across the street, I smiled and lifted my camera tentatively, testing the waters. As it turned out, no common language was necessary: She started mugging for the camera, waving and smiling. I was happy to oblige, after which she called me over and invited me in for tea. (Score one for Middle Eastern hospitality.) Inside, I met her daughter, who spoke French, allowing us to communicate a bit. It turns out that my portrait subject, Wafaa, was ill with kidney disease, and didn't get out much.

Wafaa was clearly tickled to have a Western visitor in her home for what may have been the first time in her long life, and although I had been in two homestay-style accommodations elsewhere in Lebanon, I was curious to see how a family in Tripoli lived. It seemed a pretty fair exchange. Things got a little more complicated when they invited me to return for lunch the next day. I realized this would cost them money, but I decided to accept and take them a generous gift from the most famous (and pricey) sweets shop in town. They were happy with the sweets, and they brought out a platter of bread, tabouleh, French fries, and a spread or two—festive, but not elaborate. More family members joined. I knew there was little chance we would stay in touch, as no one there showed any sign of being on social media (or being under fifty). But I also didn't feel guilty: Wafaa easily passed the "if they visited you" test the minute she smiled at me. If she and her daughter did show up in New York and somehow get in touch, I would certainly have them over. Especially if they promised to bring sweets.

I tend to accept invitations to other people's houses unless something seems way off. Yet it's not an obvious decision for everybody. Occasionally a female reader would write to lament that the Frugal Traveler was a man, saying something along the lines of "I could never have done what you did." Of course, gay travelers, black travelers, and many-other-category travelers might have wildly different experiences from mine, and may in many circumstances face more risk or less openness. On the other hand, everyone travels differently—there are plenty of white men in their forties who wouldn't accept every invitation I accept, and plenty of women traveling solo who are far more daring than I.

Or differently daring. A few years ago, I talked to Amelia Thomas, a travel writer who had written for Lonely Planet about Lebanon, India, and Israel and the Palestinian territories. She had traveled the region both alone and with her children, and while she recognized a downside to traveling while female, she also saw advantages to being a woman that made up for.

"If women in the Middle East see you wandering around or walking into a café," she told me, "they always try and start up a conversation. So many times, I've been offered dinner—I think women and families look at you as this poor lost soul wandering around on your own for some reason. I've found people have been very open and generous.

"Of course there is danger, but I guess you have to go quite a lot on intuition and judge the circumstances and see whether you feel comfortable with them. My experiences have always been really positive. And the experiences I've had that have not been positive have had nothing to do with being female."

She echoed what others have told me, that things are sometimes safer for Western travelers in the Middle East than they would be back home: "In Paris or London, if a guy or even a family came up to you in the street and invited you to their house, you would assume there was something dodgy going on. I think it's hard to appreciate that the rules change when you go somewhere else. There are always threats and always dodgy people wherever you go, but it's just not the same rules of conduct."

At times, she said, a Western woman becomes an "honorary man," able to converse with men in a way local women never could, giving her the best of both worlds.

"I've always felt like it's a really great situation to be in, because you have the benefits of being female in that women will talk to you—women tend not to strike up conversations with men—but so will men, because you're kind of like an alien species to them." She said romantic advances by men from Egypt to India were easy to spot, tending to be clumsy and obvious and easily distinguished from a genuine invitation.

Around the same time, I also discussed gender and travel with Sita Conklin, who works with Save the Children and has also traveled the world solo. Whereas we all need to be careful about cultural norms, she told me that women need to be especially careful about importing body language from their home country. "Men immediately take it as an invitation if you're smiling, or if you're used to touching people and being very warm with them," she said. "I think it can be really scary for people who haven't experienced it before, this attention on them where they don't actually realize that what they're doing is encouraging it—they're just being themselves."

There is a lot more to say about how travel experiences are impacted by the traveler's gender, not to mention race, nationality, sexual orientation, and every cross-combination of these factors and countless others. I'm far from the expert, but there are many resources out there. (You'll find a list at facebook.com/globallycurious.)

But it is also important to remember that Amelia and Sita are experienced travelers, which is why I talked with them. Though what demographic or social groups you belong to will change your experience as a traveler, so will your experience level, your personality, and your language ability or other relevant talents. (Pro tip: Learn guitar.)

While there's not much you can change about you, at least not quickly, there is something you can do: Choose your companions. If you've tried traveling alone and it's not for you, go with friends or a partner or a group (or hang out in hostels until you find a willing partner to join you). And if you're always getting into squabbles with your travel companions, go solo.

✳   ✳   ✳   ✳

What about that other tool for meeting people on the road—romance? I'm not talking about flings with fellow travelers—what you do in an upper bunk of a youth hostel with an Australian rugby player or Belgian doctoral student is of no concern to me. But there are few better entrées into a place you're visiting than to have a relationship—define that as you wish—with someone from the place you are visiting. At least that's my conclusion after way-less-than-enough experience in this topic on the road: The interactions and discoveries that accompany it often provide insights and access to a place or culture you won't get any other way.

It's also dangerous territory. Such flings—when they are just flings, that is, which they usually are—can be disrespectful or devastating to either side, although more frequently to the local. Because I've been single for sizable chunks of the last two decades and usually travel alone, people imagine I lead a wild and crazy woman-in-every-port lifestyle. Not true; if it were, this would be an entirely different and almost certainly better-selling book. In fact, my late nights are usually spent alone in not-very-romantic rooms, poring over plans for the next day, writing the next week's column about wherever I was the week before, and anthropomorphizing a weak internet connection as I beg it to upload gigabytes of photos and video. I rarely built in time to relax, let alone engineer a well-plotted love story.

So this is not my top area of expertise. That said, a broken clock is right twice a day, and I have had the occasional romance on the road, for better or for worse.

When it's for better, it's great. It's one thing to be invited in for tea and an amicable chat. It's quite another to share hours of conversation and physical intimacy.

Let's start with a romantic and (I think) largely harmless example. One winter day, as I waited in line for 5 euro rush tickets to the Comédie Française in Paris, things went my way.

Anyone who has traveled while (unwillingly) single knows that you get a seat on a bus or sit at a café or get in a line, you're always hoping that maybe by some stroke of luck the person who ends up sitting or standing next to you will be attractive, age-appropriate, charming, and (this is key) a gender identity conducive to your yearnings. And by another stroke of luck, you'll play against type and strike up a witty conversation, somehow avoid exposing your myriad flaws, and end up dating or sleeping with the person, and who knows, even marrying them some day.

"Oh, how did you meet your wife?"
"Ah, in Paris, in line at the Comédie Française waiting for tickets to see Chekhov's *Three Sisters*."

That didn't happen. But I did meet someone who fit the bill: She was tall, with dark hair flowing down the back of a long blue overcoat. She was the second person in line that day. I was the first. Was I a charming conversation companion as we talked politics and art and theater and the composition of clever outgoing messages? I hope so. But she spoke great English, which helped, and Obama was president, which also helped. Regardless of your personal poli-tics, Obama's popularity abroad relieved American travelers of the pressure of having to defend or distance themselves from George W. Bush and the unpopular war in Iraq. (The Trump administra-tion has once again made travel more uncomfortable for Americans, whether they support him or not.)

Because we were in line together, we were seated together as well: horizontally stage left, vertically stratosphere. After watching the 70 percent of Chekhov's *Three Sisters* visible from our perspective, we went out for a drink, then kissed in the rain on the Quai des Grands Augustins.

Anyone interested in prurient details will have to hack my email, but don't bother: Our brief romance was far more interesting than our briefer sex life. She was awesome and I was temporarily in love as we spent the next day seeing her version of Paris. She led me on a tour of her favorite spots in the Marais, which, needless to say, was better than any self-guided or paid tour could possibly be. She even invited me to an unorthodox Catholic service, where we broke into groups and discussed the Bible. I'd read, as you may have, that Europe is becoming increasingly atheist, so it was interesting to spend time with a group of young faithful being faithful in untradi-tional ways, and a reminder that what you read about a place from afar is almost always a gross generalization.

We didn't even stay in touch. Since I sent her a couple of Facebook messages she never responded to, I'm pretty sure she was not pining for me. It was just a memorable and romantic evening. (To me, at least. It's possible that to her it was forgettable and dull.)

These days, you don't need to let fate decide who gets in line next to you. Tinder and its ilk (but mostly Tinder) have revolutionized romance on the road, and though I don't use it, I have heard plenty of success stories. One in particular stands out, both for the ingeniousness of the user and the travel discoveries that ensued.

It was told to me by a young Chinese-Canadian woman I befriended when we overlapped in Lisbon. She had recently spent a weekend in Madeira, a tourist-clogged Atlantic archipelago less than two hours' flying time to the southwest. After a day of using public transportation to explore the towns that ring the volcanic main island, she missed the last bus of the day and found herself stuck in a particularly small village.

What would you do? I probably would have tried to find a family willing to rent me a room, and left it at that. How unmillennial of me. She changed her Tinder profile to read: "Stuck in [name of town], can anyone give me a ride?" and swiped right on every reasonably good-looking man with a noninsane profile. Not only did she get a ride, but it turned into an all-night date, barhopping around the island without a tourist to be seen.

If only things were always that simple. In Western Europe, travelers tend to meet people who are usually in the same socioeconomic plane. In other parts of the world, it is not always so, and that complicates matters. Just about everywhere I traveled in my twenties and thirties was in Latin America, and often far from its wealthy cities. I had a lot to learn.

Approximately twenty years before Tinder was launched, I had my first overseas romance. It was during the summer I spent in the Dominican Republic with my student's family. I ended up taking a couple of weeks on my own to travel the country, ending up in that coastal town of Monte Cristi. (It fact, our first kiss occurred on the very day I visited El Morro, the beach that would later gain TripAdvisor's approval.)

It was my first solo trip anywhere, but somehow I fumbled my

way into an evening out with a group of young women. I asked
for directions as they sat on a porch I happened by. We went to a
basketball game at the town stadium, and then on to a merengue
club, where I ended up dancing with the one I found the cutest, a
nineteen-year-old named Solange. It was a thrilling night for reasons
far beyond the kiss. The prior month with my student's family had
immersed me not only in Dominican Spanish but also in merengue,
the overwhelmingly dominant rhythm of the island. It had become
custom for her mom and aunts to force me to dance whenever there
was music on, which was approximately always. My incompetence
was wildly entertaining, enough so to draw neighbors at times. But I
eventually achieved mediocrity.

The next night and the night after that, Solange and I escaped
on our own, kissing under a starry sky on an empty street behind
the town's courthouse. She was a virgin and was staying that way,
which was fine by terrified me. But we did go further than she had
before, and it had more impact on her than I had imagined. On the
last night, she broke down. Through her tears, she wailed: "I finally
know what love is, and you are leaving tomorrow."

In retrospect, that should have tripped an alarm. But I was
twenty-three and clueless, and instead found it very romantic.

A letter arrived a few weeks later to my West 102nd Street apartment in New York, postmarked Monte Cristi. "You're the sweetest
gift life has given me," she wrote, and asked me to save money to
buy a house in her town so I could visit whenever I wanted. Solange
was heartbroken. That was tough, but letter two was a shock: She
asked me to call her urgently, and when I did, told me her family
was going through tough times, and she needed $10. I sent it. Many
months passed before letter three arrived, informing me she was
twenty years old, married and pregnant. Meanwhile, I was a carefree twenty-four-year-old, living in New York City. The discrepancy
was not lost on me.

In fact, it would weigh heavily over my next decade of travel,
particularly when, just out of a two-year relationship in 2000, I
visited Cuba.

As a part-time journalist with a full-time regular job for the New

York City government, I had very limited vacation time. But Cuba was a great way to spend it. It was a fascinating, mysterious place for Americans to visit then—forbidden by United States law unless you went in a group (or wrangled a journalist visa), but circumvented with some risk by flying through Toronto or Cancún. The Cubans were happy to have us.

My fantasies of romance dissipated within hours of my arrival. Like any foreign man on the streets of Havana, I attracted half a dozen consecutive hustlers who offered me prostitutes (and cigars and illegal apartments and meals at private restaurants called *paladares*). The black market I had read about was far more overt than I had imagined: The only way to get ahead in a place where even doctors made $20 a month was to figure out what you had that you could sell to tourists for dollars.

By hustler number seven, a wiry guy named Abdel who swallowed even more syllables than the average Cuban, I was sick of it. And I told him so. He got such a kick out of it, and the fact that we were exactly the same age, that he decided we should hang out (free of charge).

Easier said than done—almost immediately, a police officer stopped to question him for the apparent offense of talking to a foreigner; that would happen twice more in the coming days. But we persisted. He took me to meet his mom and, after closing the blinds, started talking openly about Fidel. Like many Cubans, he practiced *Santería*, and took me to see their witch doctor, who cast bones and prophesied about my future. And he led me to a Carnival party, where barrels of utterly horrendous beer—the only kind available if you were spending near-worthless Cuban pesos—fueled the fun.

He was also a ladies' man, and, enticed by four women in extremely tight pants and tank tops walking in front of us, did something I would never have dared to do. He went up and just flat-out introduced himself to them, and then introduced them to me. One was blindingly beautiful, with shocking green eyes, a cherubic face, and, well, I already mentioned the tight pants.

Abdel engineered a double date with Miriam and one of her

friends the next day. He knew my travel MO by then—though I openly recognized I had far more money than he did and would be treating, I preferred the places that accepted grungy Cuban pesos, which usually meant no foreigners. (Legally, tourists could only spend US dollars and "convertible pesos," essentially dollars in the form of brightly colored banknotes with pictures of Che Guevara on them.) After greasy pork sandwiches, we ended up at my illegally rented apartment.

I spent the rest of the week with Abdel or Miriam or both. But not in that apartment—the owners, who had gotten wind of a police raid, kicked me out.

My romance with Miriam was mystifying and suspicious. She never asked me for anything, was far from a googly-eyed romantic, and spoke openly (though only in private) about how horrible Cuba was. The several times I saw her, we ate out in neighborhood places where you could spend Cuban pesos. I may have spent a total of a dollar on her. And she was far too beautiful to like me.

The day before I left, she had a request. Uh-oh, I thought, here it comes. "When you return to New York," she asked, "could you research Italian laws on divorce and immigration?"

It was not what I expected, but it soon made sense. She had a boyfriend—a fiancé, really—who lived in Italy. She was playing the guy. For him, it was love; for her, a business arrangement. He would visit her a few times a year, sending money in between, and now he wanted to marry her and take her to Italy.

It was one of the few ways to get off the island, which she wanted desperately to do. But she also had little interest in being stuck for life with a man she didn't love. She wanted to know how long it would be before she could divorce him and keep her Italian papers, and had no way to find this out on her own. The internet was nowhere to be seen in Cuba yet (and, frankly, it wasn't so great in the United States, either).

I was relieved that our affair had been just for fun. She appeared to genuinely enjoy hanging out with me and I with her—but much more than that, I admired her savvy in a desperate situation. (In fact, I also admired that quality in Abdel. "Savvy in a desperate situation" should have been inscribed on the Cuban flag.) I did find the information for her. If I recall correctly, after two years of marriage to an Italian citizen, you could apply for citizenship, which would then guarantee your right to stay. I called her number several times from New York, but never got through.

When I returned to Havana three years later with my friend Cesar to begin an island-long road trip in a boxy Russian station wagon, I stopped by the building where she had lived. She was no longer around, I was told. I imagined her in Italy, where I hope she still lives today—on her own or with a far less creepy guy.

It's hard to imagine a better lesson on how Cuba worked. And I was amazed when, a few years later, I found the whole system described in a novel called *Dirty Blonde and Half-Cuban*. In the book, through bizarre circumstances and bad luck, an American woman in search of her Cuban dad runs out of money in Havana. She survives by learning the art of cultivating foreign "boyfriends," much as Miriam had done.

What an education. Before that, I thought sex tourism was about tubby, balding European men paying for sex with (often underage) Thai prostitutes. But I had found in the Dominican Republic and again in Cuba that between pure sex for hire and pure romance there is a whole world of gray areas, varyingly shaded by power and fantasy and inequality and dreams and deception. I could have learned this at home, too, where similar shadows abound. But combine the economic inequality between tourists and locals, restricted earning power and independence for women in many developing countries, the accountability-free attitude of people on vacation—and sex and travel can get very complicated.

My experiences—and the Cuba book—spurred my interest in these gray areas along the spectrum between pure romantic love and pure prostitution. I started reading articles and realized that gender roles in sex tourism were not fixed. The 1998 film *How Stella Got Her Groove Back* famously switches it up, although *Paradise: Love*, a 2012 German-language film about a fifty-year-old Austrian woman who sleeps with several younger men at a beach resort in Kenya, is more raw and realistic.

Living in Brazil in 2010, I decided to do a story about it. So I went to Rio's Copacabana Beach, the epicenter of international "romance" of all shades, though mostly the shadier ones. Though pure money-for-sex exchanges are available, I wanted to learn about those gray areas from the women's perspective.

That left me with the intriguing challenge of going up to women on the beach and asking them about their sex lives, without implying they were prostitutes. I settled on "Have you ever gone out with a foreign tourist?" as a first question.

As soon as I arrived, I spotted two black Brazilian women in bikinis, likely in their late teens, sitting near roasted-red foreigners at a coconut-water-and-beer kiosk. Instinct—and a passing knowledge of how race breaks down in Rio de Janeiro—told me they might be there to meet foreign tourists.

As I drummed up the courage to approach them, one's cell-phone rang. She answered, shrieked in delight, and ran off gabbing. I walked up to her friend, introduced myself as a reporter, and asked question number one.

Her name was Natália, and she found my question to be a quite a coincidence, because her friend had just moments earlier gotten a call from another Rio woman visiting her boyfriend in Belgium. They had met in Rio and maintained a relationship over several more of his visits. Just recently, he had flown her to Europe to see whether she liked it, with a marriage offer in the balance. Apparently she loved it. Natália's friend would soon return with a report: She was getting breakfast in bed, overcoming her fear of riding a horse, and being treated like "a queen" by the man's family.

Natália had also dated tourists and was game to explain how the system worked, at least among her friends. Direct payment for a sexual encounter was not common. Dinners, drinks, and gifts were. "I like to combine utility with pleasure," she said. "The material aspect is part of it. But it is pleasant to be with a man who likes me, who treats me well." The ultimate prize, she said, is "to go away to another place, to have a good life." Belgium, apparently, qualifies as another place; horseback riding and breakfast in bed, as a good life.

Later in my trip, I met Mylla, an eighteen-year-old having a late-night hamburger at a Copacabana snack bar. She had come to Rio at sixteen from the central Brazilian city of Goiânia, escaping a bad (and early) marriage and chasing an acting dream. I went to question number one. Yes, she dated tourists. In fact, a week after she arrived in Rio, she said, she "fell in love" with an American musician in town on a gig.

"I didn't have any desire to meet a foreigner, none," she said. But during an afternoon with friends at the beach, she spotted a dreamily blond-haired, blue-eyed man. He was with his friends, and she couldn't go over and say anything, even if she dared—she didn't speak English. So she made sure he caught her staring. (Unlike wimpy Americans, Brazilians of either gender tend not to look away when the person they're staring at glances back.) "But he was very cold," she said. Translation: He didn't come right over to talk, as a Brazilian would.

A male friend in her group suggested she just go up and kiss him, but she refused. "In Rio, things happen like that," she said. "In my city, no." Eventually, her friends helped her break the ice, the two groups merged, and all went out to eat. On the way back to the beach, she dared to grab his hand. Still cold. She playfully pulled off his cap, and, finally, he pulled her in for a smooch.

"It was the most beautiful kiss of my life," she told me. They sat on the beach for hours, talking. Sort of. "He spoke and he spoke and I didn't understand anything," she said.

The next night, they went out dancing and she stayed over at his hotel. On subsequent dates, they went to an internet café to use Google Translate. (Today, of course, they'd have used their phones.)

"I never imagined I would find a person like you here in Rio de Janeiro," she remembers him writing.

They were together for a week, communicated by internet for a few months after that, and then he disappeared. Mylla was devastated, even asking me—six months after they had last spoken— what I thought had gone wrong. I gave a dishonest answer.

Though she missed him, she had met, dated, and slept with other tourists since (and even acted in a few plays). They sometimes gave her money and gifts, she said, but never directly for sex.

"I don't ask," she said. "It seems cold. I don't think that the fact that you are a tourist means you should give me money. You're not my husband! The only difference is you're from another country."

Most recently, she had been dating a Brazilian. So had she finally decided to kick the dead-end tourist habit and develop a lasting relationship? No, she said. She liked him because he had a nice car, expensive cologne, and plenty of money.

So things are more complicated than they appear, especially to travelers who are either unaware of reality or choose to ignore it.

If single travelers have their eyes wide open and are overtly honest with the people they meet, I'm all for it. But that's not as easy as it seems. I'll close this chapter with a look at what strikes me as an open-and-shut case of how not to conduct a travel romance. It's what happens when Sal Paradise, Jack Kerouac's fictionalized alter ego in *On the Road*, meets Terry, a "Mexican girl" (today we'd call her a Mexican American woman), during one of his road-trips-that-spawned-a-million-road-trips.

They meet on a bus en route from San Francisco to Los Angeles. Terry has just left her abusive husband. Sal is on a carefree adventure. What could go wrong?

They begin an affair, and soon she takes him back to her hometown; they pick cotton to make a living, eat grapes that fall off a truck, meet her son and brother and cousins. Though many in the area know of their affair, Sal still avoids her home and parents, shacking up in a barn nearby. She tells him she wants to go back to New York with him. But it's a no-go. Even as Sal prepares to leave Terry forever, lurking outside her house to say good-bye, he milks his intercultural adventure by eavesdropping.

Her five brothers were singing melodious songs in Spanish. The stars bent over the little roof; smoke poked from the stove-pipe chimney. I smelled mashed beans and chili. The old man growled. The brothers kept right on yodeling. The mother was silent. Johnny and the kids were giggling in the bedroom. . . . I hid in the grapevines, digging it all. I felt like a million dollars; I was adventuring in the crazy American night.[3]

Jack has had a grand old time. As he is about to leave after one final night making love under a tarantula in the barn, he says, insincerely, "See you in New York," and walks off. He turns back to see her one last time:

> She just walked on back to the shack, carrying my breakfast plate in one hand. I bowed my head and watched her. Well, lackadaddy, I was on the road again.[4]

Lackadaddy (I've learned) implies some regret, and I'm simplifying things, of course. For more insight, read Tim Z. Hernandez's book for which he tracked down Bea Franco, the real Terry. But from a romance-on-the-road perspective, it sure looks like he's been deceptive and a bit cruel, thrilling in the exotic and getting away scot-free.

On the Road was a travel model for many, but Sal Paradise was far from a model traveler. It's true you can't blame someone for flirting with a beautiful girl at a bus stop. And when you leave your day-to-day life behind to go on the road, it's easy to get lost in the carefree, responsibility-free fantasy that travel provides. A potential romance with someone from the place you are visiting may seem all upside, and it's easy to get starry-eyed and imagine it may turn into something more serious. But the more clearheaded you remain— and the more you remind yourself that the other person may have wildly different expectations—the better.

Kruger National Park, South Africa.

Chapter 7

MONEY AND TRAVEL

Heading down a gravelly road through South Africa's Kruger National Park, my driver slammed on the brakes and brought the vehicle to a screeching halt. The route ahead had taken on a lilac hue in the late-afternoon light. Sprawled across it, just feet from the car, were two sleeping lions: a full-maned male and a sturdy female. Farther up the road, two more adults and two cubs peered curiously at the car.

It was a stunning find, a safari-goer's dream. But after fifteen minutes (and hundreds of photographs in my Canon 7D later), they still showed no signs of budging. And if you're supposed to let sleeping dogs lie, jolting a pair of adult lions from a slumber is almost certainly a no-no.

But curfew at Kruger was approaching, and the map showed that backtracking to the closest detour would take more than an hour. In less than twenty minutes, the gates would close and the guards would abandon their posts at the entrance of my posh $400-a-night ecolodge.

Just kidding, I was not staying at an ecolodge, but in a tiny tent at Crocodile Bridge Rest Camp, one parking space over from a tattooed, whiskey-drinking Afrikaner war veteran. But anyway, our armed guide would surely know how to scare off the lions—perhaps by shooting his rifle into the air?

Just kidding, there was no guide, there was no rifle, and there was no *our*. It was just *me*—I was my driver—in a rented Ford Expedition 4x4 SUV.

Just kidding, it was just me in a subcompact Fiat Punto hatchback.

I considered my options. Staying out in the park after dark was clearly a bad (and illegal) idea. I had no cell-phone signal to call for help. Honking until the lions moved would break Kruger's rule against disturbing wildlife. But after eyeballing the space between them and the left side of the road, I thought there might be just enough clearance to creep around while keeping enough of the car on the road to avoid getting the low-hanging chassis stuck in the vegetation.

I edged close enough to see the dozing lions' hearts pounding in their chests. Were they chasing down a delectable impala in their dreams? As I nudged the Fiat closer, they opened their eyes and stared. All that stood between me and their (presumably) ferocious claws were about five feet and the thin glass of a driver's-side window.

Just kidding, I had left the window down. That had been on the advice of the Afrikaner, the better to hear the wildlife and feel the savanna air, he said. I hadn't thought to roll it back up just because I was sneaking up on a pair of deadly creatures that could be irritable if roused from a long snooze.

I rolled up the window, gingerly drove around them, and went back to camp to drink Black Label and hear Angolan Civil War stories from my tent neighbor.

✳ ✳ ✳ ✳

Safaris are, for many, the ultimate travel fantasy. In a 2017 spread, the British edition of *Condé Nast Traveller* stoked those dreams by raving about a Kenyan property called Arijiju and asking, "Is This the Most Beautiful Safari Lodge in Africa?"

Is it? If you'd like to take your family and find out, packages start at $7,500 a day for up to six people. That's about $50,000 for a week.

The same spread also suggests cheaper options, including a "vintage safari romance" at Angama Mara, also in Kenya, where low-season rooms these days start at $1,200 a night. Even if you abandon the glossies and do a simple online search for safaris, the path the travel industry and Google's algorithm send you down may convince you that seeing big game close up is beyond the price range of most travelers.

When I added "budget" to such a search, I fared a bit better—a *Travel + Leisure* article pops up listing a $4,200-per-week option in Zambia. There's even an operator that will equip you for a self-drive option (vehicle, camping equipment) in Botswana for two weeks for just $15,000. Sounds like a lot, but that's just $300 per person per night for a group of four—well, not including fuel, food, and park entrance fees.

Yet, as I found in Kruger, you can totally, easily, book your own safari for around $125 per couple per day. That's less than a middling all-inclusive resort in Aruba and includes literally everything except your flight to Johannesburg.

I didn't know this when I was looking into trips to Africa—in fact, I had previously concluded the Frugal Traveler would never go on safari. But then I asked a friend who had lived in Africa whether there was any way at all to reduce costs.

"Easy," he said. Embarrassingly easy, it turns out. Seeing game in a national park like Kruger is for South Africans what camping in Yellowstone is for Americans. Reserve a campsite online, rent a car, pack your tent, and stop at a supermarket for provisions along the way. (If your jaw is strong, consider a box of the slightly sweet, twice-baked biscuits called rusks.)

Of course, it is nothing like the luxury that Arijiju and Angama Mara provide. Being your own driver means a bit more work: checking out posted reports of game sightings the day before, conferring with fellow campers, and keeping a sharp eye out. You don't have to pitch your own tent, $22 extra a night gets you a sturdy furnished one with cozy beds and electricity. (For a bit more, you can upgrade to a lodge.)

It was a great trip. Yet the only other Americans I met at the teeming campsite were the Maurer family of Flagstaff, Arizona, on a yearlong trip around the world. Why don't more people know of this do-it-yourself option?

The answer is that the travel industry doesn't want you to. Whereas big companies with expensive services hire top marketers and publicists to make sure they get their product in front of your face, finding budget options depends on your own initiative. That means skipping past the big companies most people use, or at least remembering that their primary goal is to make you spend, even if they tell you otherwise. A hotel app does not ask for access to your contact information to remind you that your best friend from high school now lives in London and you could stay with her for free. When was the last time a waiter at the Hard Rock Café said, "You all had pretty substantial entrées, so I'd advise against the 1,276-calorie Oreo cheesecake"? And glossy travel magazines don't make money from their advertisers with headlines like "Go On Safari Without a Tour Operator, Save Tons of Money!"

In fact, they say things like this, from a 2015 article in the American edition of *Condé Nast Traveler*, "Everything You Thought You Knew About Safari Is Wrong":[1]

> MYTH #6: You can plan it yourself.
> FACT: Don't even try it. Putting your safari in the hands of a specialist is the only way to go.

Some people, of course, will be better off with a tour operator. But to categorically exclude planning your own trip is beyond wrong—it's suspicious. I don't think the authors were paid off by anyone, but I wonder what would have happened if the piece they turned in read:

> MYTH #6: You can't plan it yourself.
> FACT: You'll save a ton of money. Going with a specialist like the ones you see advertised in fancy magazines is a waste.

I suspect that might have run into resistance from the editors.

Let's say you do have money. The more you spend, the better your trip, right? That logic holds for most purchases. Orchestra seats are better than the second balcony. A decked-out sports car goes faster and looks cooler than a subcompact hatchback. Kettle-cooked, waffle-cut, artisanal potato chips are more delicious than a greasy store brand.

But I've come to believe that travel is different. I traveled on the cheap in my twenties and thirties, but that was out of prudence. I made relatively little money as a teacher, government worker, grad student, and freelance writer. When I was named the Frugal Traveler in 2010, just before my fortieth birthday, I believed my job was to help people spend less on travel without giving up too many experiences and without suffering too much discomfort.

It was my first full-time travel-writing gig, so I began paying more attention to travel media, to what companies were offering, and to what popped up on Google searches. As I skipped around the world, I talked a whole lot to fellow travelers, random strangers as well as friends making five or ten times as much money as I was, about their trips.

And I realized that the great experiences I was having on the road—a night out with the Brazilian women's boxing team in Barbados, conversations with the small-town Mexican cheesemaker who had rented me a room, a friend (and more) made in the line for rush tickets at the Comédie Française in Paris—were not despite my low budget, but because of it.

In other words, you get what you don't pay for. That's not so much a steadfast rule as a pretty good bet, a not-always-truism. If you're so wealthy that the difference between business class and coach is a pittance, go for it. Still, there can be surprises. During my extremely rare business-class flight from Panama City to Quito, everything was lovely. But as soon as we touched down, I heard muffled applause coming through the curtains from the hoi polloi in coach. I knew what it was—the lovable trait of passengers from some parts of the world to cheer the pilot and/or the fact that they're back home. It felt like watching an NBA playoff game from the luxury box when your team hits a buzzer-beating shot for the win—fans below are going crazy while you're stuck high-fiving a guy in a suit.

✳ ✳ ✳ ✳

Overall, business class is pretty cool if you can swing it—the fully reclining, angled-for-privacy, "reverse herringbone" seating can save you from days of sleep deprivation after an overnight flight. And why would you wait for the public bus from the airport when you could take a taxi or Uber? Stay at a hostel when you could be at a resort with a glistening azure plunge pool two steps outside your bedroom and the Champagne just a call away? Roam the potentially perilous streets of a new city for a hole-in-the-wall diner when the concierge can wangle a reservation at the farm-to-table bistro with a couple of Michelin stars?

Most people wouldn't, even in the best of circumstances. Rejecting the easy route is even harder if you're jet-lagged or faced with an unfamiliar language or worried about security. I want the taxi and plunge pool and crème brûlée infused with local organic jackfruit as much as anyone. I actually want it right now. But instead, I'm writing these lines at a $45-a-night Airbnb rental in a little villa normally inhabited by a twenty-something filmmaker in São Paulo. I'm working at her desk, a weathered wooden door on a jerry-rigged frame, as a black cat with a white streak down his chest patrols the desk and occasionally the rest of the house. He goes by the name of Bonifácio—to the extent he listens to humans at all—and part of the deal is that I'll take care of him.

The power went out here for thirty-six hours just minutes after I arrived, and the owner's bedsheets, while clean, are threadbare. In fact, the fitted sheet's elastic is so frayed I have yet to wake up any morning with less than half the mattress exposed. (Bonifácio is usually next to me, occupying prime sheet-covered territory.)

I'm here for the same reason people don't have French fries with every meal or have sex on the first date: trading in short-term pleasure to invest in longer-term goals. This isn't a Frugal Traveler trip. I could have sprung for something nicer. But I have a pet cat for the first time in my life, and we're getting along well now that we've come to an understanding and the scratches on my forearm have begun to heal. The ceiling fan is probably healthier than air-conditioning and no less pleasant, the location is as good as it gets, in the middle of rowdily hipsterish Vila Madalena, yet completely invisible from the street in a single-story home accessible through an alley. *Vilas* like this are typical of older São Paulo neighborhoods, though if you were walking by them like a regular tourist, you'd never know they were there. And I am able to stay for two weeks for the same price even a moderate hotel in an unneighborhoody location would charge me for a few days.

On the other hand, I've got to clean the toilet and there's a saber-clawed cat that likes to hang out between my face and my computer screen.

❋ ❋ ❋ ❋

There are three main advantages to traveling cheap, even if you can afford better.

First is the obvious one: You can do more of it. Turn a two-week summer trip into three, or stash the savings for a winter getaway. (Or get a new sofa or increase your charitable giving, what do I care?)

Second, you'll be less isolated from real life at your destination. If you've stayed at the Plaza on Central Park, did you notice the "neighborhood feel" when you emerged onto the street? Of course not, because you were surrounded by tourists and hot-dog vendors and a line at the Apple Store across Fifth Avenue. The more you spend, the more likely you are to be surrounded by other travelers instead of the people it's really worth being around. And though guides can be great, they add a layer between you and what surrounds you. Being cheap forces you to interact.

Finally, frugality leads to discovery. There is surely some overlap on the Venn diagram circles for "people who stay at luxury hotels" and "adventurers who scour the back streets, poke their heads into unmarked storefronts, and hop onto a crowded public tram." But not much. That's not necessarily because rich people aren't daring, it's because there's nothing pushing them to get out there and let great things happen. Instead, they're pulled back into the cocoon of concierge desks and taxis and carefully curated "real-life" experiences.

It's understandable—being in foreign places can be uncomfortable and sometimes scary, so it's tempting to make our trips as comfortable and safe as we can. I get it. Albert Camus, however, would have had none of today's concocted adventures:

> What gives value to travel is fear. It is the fact that, at a certain moment, when we are so far from our own country . . . we are seized by a vague fear, and an instinctive desire to go back to the protection of old habits. . . . This is why we should not say

that we travel for pleasure. There is no pleasure in traveling, and I look upon it more as an occasion for spiritual testing.[2]

So much of the unnecessary money we spend on travel today caters to that desire to make us feel comfortable and protected. Companies scramble to offer those services, and make them as tempting as possible. Your mattress has been dutifully imported; your tour guide's SUV air-conditioned; the route through the colorful working-class neighborhood vetted; the local people you meet, trained in your cultural quirks. And of course, no need to risk your stomach on fiery, exotic street food—there's a local chef (or five) who has tamed his grandmother's recipes and serves them with contemporary flair, and even silverware.

Yet the more we substitute pleasure for fear, the less we are actually traveling.

Assuming most people will not immediately abandon all comfort, grow dreadlocks, buy loose-fitting harem pants, and camp their way around the world, I have developed a list of characteristics that gauge one's potential as a budget traveler. See how you measure up.

1. **Nongermophobe:** There is a strong correlation between money spent and cleanliness encountered on the road. Street food is cheap. Motels have moldy bathrooms. Crowded buses mean sweaty locals. And, as we've learned, Yangtze riverboats mean pre-slept-in beds.

Germophobes will be tempted to shy away from some experience in parts of the world with sub-fifty-gallon annual per capita antibacterial-gel sales. For example, if you have a problem with sucking yerba mate from the same metal straw as three new Uruguayan acquaintances, you may have trouble making friends in Montevideo.

2. **Flexible sleeper:** These come in two varieties: travelers who can survive a few nights of imperfect sleep without ruining their trip or that of those around them, and those who can doze off under any condition, such as sitting next to a coca-leaf salesman on a thirty-six-hour bus ride from Guayaramerín, Bolivia, to La Paz. (True story. And you're unlikely to meet a coca-leaf dealer on a plane.)

3. **Strong-stomached:** You won't eat at a hole-in-the-wall taco stand or noodle place? That's going to cost you. I believe great stomachs are made, not born, so a note to the young: Eat anything in sight, and decades later you'll still be at it. (Or you'll suffer ignominiously from dysentery and decide never to travel again. But it worked for me.) Obviously, there are commonsense exceptions—raw shrimp that sits for hours un-iced in the equatorial sun, for example, should likely be avoided.

4. **Luddite:** Prices are dropping, but for now, phone calls and data use abroad can still cost you. Hotels with good internet service are also pricey. I'll confess—this one is not my strength.

5. **Highly organized:** Oh, sorry, THIS one is not my strength. I blow money all the time on chargers I forgot to pack and sweaters I didn't bring because I didn't think to check the average temperature in Melbourne in July. I've missed flights because I wrote down the wrong day or didn't write down any day at all.

6. **Accepting of disorganization in others:** No matter how organized you are, the world outside the luxury bubble can be chaotic. Things go wrong everywhere—more so in the developing world, and even more so when you are traveling on public transportation to a hotel that has an informal reservation system (and has lost yours). If you are devoted to routine, lack patience, or are nervous about improvising, caution-to-the-wind travel will drive you a bit batty.

7. **Highly social:** Extroverts have a far easier time making local friends and being led by them to cheap watering holes or dinner at home or a free place to sleep. Not to mention that talk is cheap— literally. A thirty-minute stroll in a Berlin park can provide the introvert with thirty minutes of free entertainment; when a guy I asked for directions to the zoo turned out to be an Air Berlin pilot, we ended up talking for an extra hour.

8. **Fearless (in situations where there's actually nothing to fear):** As I mentioned in chapter 5, uncomfortable or even unfamiliar situations make us nervous. It can take some time to get used to a new city, and that makes it very tempting to hire a tour guide or take a taxi.

❋   ❋   ❋   ❋

If even a handful of those traits apply to you, then congratulations. It's time to consider lowering your travel budget and reaping the rewards. Even a 10 percent cut can make a difference. The key is to reduce spending where it won't bother you so much and keep spending where you're unwilling to settle.

If you can't handle swapping boutique hotels or luxe beach bungalows for hostels or budget guesthouses, or, as I did in Kruger, trading ecolodge luxury for pitching your own tent amid crowds of locals, that's fine. Lodging is just one of the four main categories of travel spending. Chipping away at the budgets of the three others—transportation, food, and entertainment—can also reap benefits, as I found out on other legs of that same trip through southern Africa.

TRANSPORTATION

Taking trains, subways, and public buses instead of rental cars, taxis, and drivers hired by your tour operator are great ways to observe or even interact with people living their daily lives in your destination.

It sure worked for me in Mozambique. There are three ways to get from Maputo, the former Portuguese colony's chaotic, musical capital, to Tofo, a heavenly beach town 235 miles to the northeast that's popular with vacationing South Africans. The flight is $90 each way and takes an hour. Renting a car for the seven-hour drive is significantly more, though of course you also get to use it while you're there. Then there's a $20 public bus that gets you to Inhambane, where for less than fifty cents you can get to Tofo in a minibus so overcrowded that schoolchildren practically hang off the sides. In

Mozambique, this is called a *chapa*; in the United States, it would be called a lawsuit.

The public bus to Inhambane, on the other hand, is fairly comfortable (or at least was the time I went), if you discount the loud music and the lack of air-conditioning. A vaguely modern white minibus, it holds about twenty, along with a driver and a *cobrador*, whose two jobs are to collect fares and to recruit additional passengers from the sides of the highway by shouting "Inhambane" and seeing who flags them down. A similar system exists in much of the world.

The *cobrador* on my bus, Maurício, was particularly talented—he didn't just shout, "Inhambane." He tacked on apparently hilarious jokes in a Bantu language that had my fellow passengers and those on the roadside cracking up.

On this particular trip, Maurício, wearing a T-shirt from the Eagles 2010 tour of Australia that I'm guessing he did not attend, took on a third job: lay psychologist.

The lack of mental-health services in the developing world is well documented. You may have heard stories of families who chained or locked up relatives for lack of appropriate care or medication. (Or you may have read *Jane Eyre* in high school.) I had. (And I had.) But I hadn't thought much about all that until I saw Maurício in action.

Across the aisle from me was a young man; sitting between us was, I assumed, his father. The young man appeared restless from the start and gradually began attracting more attention by grunting, then cursing, and finally writhing. I finally stole enough glances to see that his father had lashed his ankles together with a fluorescent green cord and had tied his hands behind his back with the same. Each time his son acted up, he smacked him on the head with a stick. It was ineffectual. I was heartbroken for the dad, whose face had deep lines that I imagined were at most half from aging. But I was also outraged for the son. The obvious conclusion was that he was mentally ill. But I'll confess I found his reaction to being hog-tied and hit over the head in public to be quite sane. I might have done the same.

People did their best to ignore him, though when he started leering and screaming at some young women behind him, things got tense. This was when Maurício transformed from *cobrador* to social worker, coming back occasionally and soothing him with words I was frustrated not to understand, for they seemed to work better than the father's stick. At one point, the young man struggled so hard to wriggle free that his pants fell below his knees. Maurício climbed onto the seat, pulled up his pants, and embraced him from behind in a reverse bear hug. The young man calmed down and eventually even laughed a few times.

We arrived at Inhambane without incident, and I waited until everyone had left to thank Maurício and give him a tip. It wasn't a normal move for a budget traveler, but what I had witnessed was certainly not a normal move for a *cobrador*.

FOOD

It's easy to blow lots of cash ticking off the top-ranked restaurants at your destination. It also guarantees maximum likes on your Instagram account. But skipping the Michelin circuit in favor of supermarket-sourced picnics, street food, and cheap sit-down joints (broken up by the occasional nice restaurant, skip the appetizer) can yield interesting adventures and, often, better food.

But it can be tempting to take the easy way out in a new country with unfamiliar cuisine and uncertain sanitary standards. Hold your ground and use your instincts. After Kruger National Park, I had driven a few hours to the border of Swaziland. It was a pilgrimage of sorts. As a kid, I had been fascinated by the little landlocked kingdom that was smaller than an M&M on our globe, and during my second grade project its colorful flag was one of my favorites.

I had reserved a $14 hut at the community-run Shewula Mountain Camp in the startlingly green mountains of northeastern Swaziland. It was a gorgeous place without much to do, so I convinced the only other guest, a quiet young South African woman named Maria, to take a day trip with me. We chose the closest city of any significance, Siteki. Described in a government tourism handout as a "charming" regional capital, it turned out to be a rather dusty town with no obvious appeal.

It was a Sunday, and congregants were returning from church in their natty best, ranging from formal Western dress to brightly colored robes. The doors to the storefront High Praise Assembly church were wide open, so we poked our heads in. "We're just wandering around," I explained to a group of women perplexed at the presence of out-of-town (not to mention white) visitors.

"You should have been wandering around at 10 this morning," one said. "You would have seen us dance." An opportunity missed.

When we asked the women where to eat, they were unequivocal: the Siteki Hotel. We walked over and soon realized why they had recommended it. It was the town's stuffy attempt at a fancy "international" menu and wine list, and the place most frequented by foreign workers—if the vehicles emblazoned with "Columbia University Mailman School of Public Health" in the parking lot were any indication. It was, predictably, way too expensive. And we weren't foreign workers for whom a mediocre pizza or steak was a godsend so far from home.

So we wandered into a place named Lamatikweni Pub & Restaurant, which was empty and looked more like a Convenience Store & Steam Table. Shelves of sodas and snacks in front, a steam table and a few tables in the back. A woman with a white hairnet and a very easy laugh appeared to be the chef, so we asked what we should eat. She was unequivocal: "Beans with bones." I couldn't resist the name, so she served us a mash of brown beans studded with beef bones, each one with just enough meat hanging on to enable a significant amount of gnawing. Cost: less than $3.

Beans with bones, in Swaziland. The second grader in me was thrilled.

Actually, the forty-three-year-old was, too. The restaurant looked like it had never before seen a foreign guest. I doubt that's true, but, as of this writing, no one has mentioned it online. Three years later, Googling "Lamatikweni" and "Siteki" gave only four results—two from the Swaziland Electricity Company, one from my 2014 *New*

York Times article, and one from some guy who swiped my article and stuck it on his blog. If you Googled "beans with bones" in quotes and added "Swaziland," it was just the latter two. Even the electric company hasn't discovered Lamatikweni's beans with bones.

ENTERTAINMENT

Once you've gotten where you were going, slept and ate, the rest of your time is open, and you could spend as much or as little as you want to fill it. Taking advantage of free events and entertainment, settling for nosebleed rather than orchestra seats, and favoring loosely structured wandering to, say, helicopter sightseeing, is sure to reap rewards.

You may recall that, given twenty-four hours in Johannesburg before heading to Kruger, I rejected friends-of-friends' advice to see the newly Brooklynified neighborhoods of the city and visited Soweto. Instead, most tourists take a standard day or half-day tour and are conveniently picked up and deposited back at their Johannesburg hotels. "While it's possible to drive yourself, the township's layout can be confusing," an online travel site warns.

The website in question, no surprise, is TripAdvisor's Viator, which makes money on commission by selling you tours that average over $100. It makes no money if you choose the "confusing" option.

Why not stay in Soweto? There are some quite reasonably priced bed-and-breakfasts around. When I looked online, Flossie's B&B seemed an especially good deal, for $32. It was cheap partly because it was a full three miles from the tourism epicenter of Vilakazi Street, where throngs visit Nelson Mandela's modest house and, blocks away, the Hector Pieterson Museum, dedicated to the twelve-year-old boy shot and killed by police on the first day of the 1976 Soweto uprising.

But it included the hospitality of Florence Mondi (aka Flossie), who, no sooner than I had arrived from the airport, offered to take me around to some less-visited neighborhoods and then to a local pub for dinner. In the end, another engagement forced her to outsource the task to a neighbor, Shaun, who would meet me in the late afternoon. In the meantime, I made the (unconfusing) drive to Vilakazi Street to take in the main attractions. Mandela's house and the museum were intriguing and touching, but the highlight was yet to come.

Despite no promise of payment and no idea what I did for a living, Shaun led me on a sweeping drive that amounted to a tour of his friends' houses, important places from his childhood, and popular shopping centers. It was an entirely different Soweto from Vilakazi Street—a deeply personal one, skillfully placed in context for a foreign visitor by someone who had grown up there, left to see the world (as a South African Airways flight attendant), and moved back. We started by clambering up a rocky, brush-covered hill he called Kafushi to survey Soweto from above. On the climb, we startled a lone kid, maybe eight years old, who saw my camera and pleaded with me not to photograph him. Shaun calmed him down. "He's not supposed to be here," Shaun explained. "He's smoking." (And not tobacco.)

Shaun pointed out the Soweto neighborhoods that sprawled below, their distinguishing ethnic groups, social classes, and personalities. Though everyone studies English and speaks a native language at home—Zulu, Sotho, Swati, and the like—on the streets they speak in a mixture he called Sowetan.

Soweto was heavy on low-slung residential neighborhoods and vacant fields, with few commercial areas. Our next stop was one of those fields. Shaun had me park on a patch of grass at the edge of one such field. There he recounted how he would flee across it when police raided his high school in the late 1980s, when schools became a center of political meetings. I realized we were almost precisely the same age.

"They came with their dogs," he said. "We fled out the windows." He was never caught, though he told me about another time he was arrested for gambling with dice. The police took him to a graveyard where they forced him to fight a new police recruit undergoing initiation.

We had parked in this particular spot for a reason. He had always run in this direction because across the street was the house of a friend, the closest safe haven from school. He walked me around to the house's rear entrance, hard against the rear of a neighbor's house, and greeted an older woman in Swati. I was hanging back, and the woman, named Mashongwe, had not yet noticed my presence. When she did, she was visibly startled. Shaun reassured her I was a friend and turned to me.

"She thought you were here to arrest her," he explained. I asked him to find out why. They talked further, and he relayed the reason: Decades back, she had done housework for "the architects of apartheid," a label used to refer to the system's creators. That had been her closest contact with white people.

The house was a tidy, rectangular "four-room" with a floor plan like a checkerboard. There was a Christian sign on the wall in Zulu, which did not surprise me, and the *Steve Harvey Show* on TV at high volume, which did.

Mashongwe soon warmed up and was a gracious if still somewhat nervous host, offering juice and showing me the tasty-looking stew bubbling in the kitchen (alas, not yet ready). Later, we would stop in at two other houses, to similar reactions and similar juice offers, and at a mall where I tried "red cakes"—artificially flavored, coconut-covered snacks that were Shaun's childhood favorite.

In the end, I offered him 200 rand, about $18 at the time, for the tour. He said it was unnecessary; I said it was an incredible bargain. We went out again that night and he told me horrifying stories of the Inkatha Freedom Party attacks on African National Congress members—including his grandmother, who took a machete whack to the head and survived.

I returned to Flossie's and had trouble sleeping—the ceiling fan didn't work and the bed needed a new mattress, badly. So I spent some of the night sitting on the roof deck, listening to crickets chirping and dogs barking, looking out over Soweto's rooftops.

✳   ✳   ✳   ✳

By the time I went to Africa, nearly four years into my Frugal Traveler stint, the payoff of spending less and getting more had become almost an inside joke—with myself. I would start each trip feeling nervous about setting out on my own, fearing I'd miss out on some important sights each time I chose a more daring, less-structured, cheaper option even though risk-taking on previous trips had always paid off. On the other hand, the more money I spent, the narrower the blinders became: I often felt I was being led on a mostly straight line down a predesigned route, where even the deviations seemed preplanned.

Yet it's not an absolute rule, and budget travelers often take things too far. When saving money becomes the mission, rather than the means to accomplish that mission, it's time to loosen the wallet.

I will always remember the first excessive cheapskate I met as the Frugal Traveler, on the edge of Lake Titicaca, three weeks into my first trip. Bolivia is usually a dirt-cheap place to travel, and that was especially true for anyone arriving from booming Brazil in 2010.

On a choppy boat trip from the touristy town of Copacabana to see Isla del Sol, I was talking *dinero* with a grimy backpacker many more weeks than I into a trip through Latin America. When he told me his hostel in Copacabana was $7 a night, I suggested he move to La Cúpula, where I had found a room with a comfy bed, en suite bathroom, artistic touches, and a lake view for $12. "Something close to frugal heaven," I had written in my notes, and I was eager to share my find with a ragged traveler who looked like he could use a break. For five extra dollars, he'd get a one-night break from bunk beds and funky bathrooms. Actually, if he'd shared the room with a travel companion, they could have saved $2.

I expected a high five. I got barely a nod.

Perhaps he simply loved the hostel lifestyle. But to me, someone who doesn't see the value in a free upgrade for a few nights in a real hotel with patterned bedspreads and a view of Lake Titicaca isn't thinking straight. To me, he had joined the cheap-*uber-alles* club that values its own suffering in a twisted sort of self-Schadenfreude.

Discomfort, risk, or interminable delay, in limited doses and with good intentions, can lead to great travel experiences, or at least compelling stories. But suffering unduly just to put a little extra money in your pocket? That sounds a lot more like the job from which you're on vacation than the vacation itself.

✳   ✳   ✳   ✳

Cheapness can even cross the line into despicableness, especially when it comes to overhaggling—driving hard bargains over pennies with local residents for whom those pennies actually mean something. Backpackers are good at playing poor, but precious few truly poor people are gallivanting around the world for fun. They may have little money in the bank, but if an Ebola epidemic broke out during their travels, they'd likely find the funds to get onto the next flight out.

Cheapness is also counterproductive when you find yourself avoiding the very best aspects of a destination just to save money. You're in Rome, why are you eating ham-and-cheese sandwiches on supermarket bread when for a few extra euros you could be having *spaghetti carbonara* or *bucatini all'amatriciana*? You're on a once-in-a-lifetime trip to New York City and won't splurge on a Broadway show?

But exactly how cheap you should be is up to you. One of the most annoying aspects of writing the Frugal Traveler column was the constant pelting with comments saying I wasn't actually being frugal at all. They'd go something like this: "A $100 weekend in Paris? You call that frugal? When I was in college, I spent a month in Paris for $20!" This is not a competition, and it is silly to set universal standards for what a traveler should spend. Taking a late-night taxi instead of waiting for the once-an-hour bus is hardly despicable if you feel unsafe or need your sleep.

We all have our limits. For example, I will not give up eating out. It could be street food, that's fine, or local fast food, also fine, and I'm always happy putting together a picnic from a public market. But I will not depend solely on supermarkets in a city where I'll be spending less than a week. For longer stays, of course, I'll do some of my own cooking. But not always.

When I spent those two weeks at an Airbnb in the Príncipe Real neighborhood of Lisbon, I rarely went to nice restaurants. But I did eat breakfast out every day at the Padaria Beira Tajo across the street, despite a grocery down the block that easily could have fed me for less, but I had befriended the rather dour woman behind the counter, who served a perfect espresso and fresh buttered roll for about $2. I'd eat alongside workers (if I got up early enough) or gray-haired ladies blabbing about their grandkids (if I slept in a bit). By the third day, the woman behind the counter knew my order. I could have saved a little money, perhaps, but it was also the price of admission into a daily ritual in a little corner of a new city.

Papá Morales's soccer tournament in Quingeo, Ecuador.

Chapter 8

BAD INFLUENCES, GOOD TRAVELERS

People criticize old-school energy companies for their impact on the environment, commercial banks for prioritizing profits over clients' interests, and mammoth food conglomerates for pushing products that make us obese.

Yet somehow, many travel players get a pass. Not airlines, of course. We love to hate them. And Airbnb occasionally gets beat up. I've already aired quite a few grievances about user-review sites and online travel agencies. But plenty of other players we tend to think of as harmless operate in ways that impact our travel.

For most that means focusing on profit, growth, and getting bought by Google rather than making decisions to maximize the personal growth of their clientele. That's just capitalism. But the American government chips in one major impediment. And then there's the travelers ourselves, slowly but surely ruining the environment and harming the cultures we visit. At least we can do something about it: engage in what has come to be known as sustainable travel.

THE HOTEL FETISH

For the 2016 Frugal Traveler grand finale, I went rogue in Ecuador and spent the first half of a week there in luxury. It started with that business class flight from Panama City, and continued as I took a cab to what was then TripAdvisor's No. 1-ranked hotel in South

America, a lovely restored mansion in the center of Quito called Casa Gangotena.

Even the arrival process was an astonishing to-do for someone steeped in the ways of the grumpy check-in clerk, and it proved that I definitely would be uncomfortable if I woke up tomorrow as Queen of England. As my taxi approached the hotel, one staff member scrambled to remove the orange cones that protected it from parked cars. Another whisked away my bags, as a third (or maybe it was the cone guy again) practically tripped over himself to open the ornately carved hardwood doors. I was handed what looked like a magenta cocktail but the staff explained was an *agua de frescos*, a traditional, refreshing drink made of eight herbs and flowers and served to houseguests, they said, in the southern highlands of the country. I was uncomfortable drinking it as I checked in, but it was quite tasty.

The welcome was not over. When I arrived at my garden-level, no-street-view room, I found a handwritten welcome note from a manager I of course had never met. A tray of local fruits had also been left for me, along with a cute pamphlet explaining how to eat them, which I didn't see. As a result, I chomped down on the very bitter skin of a tree tomato rather than peeling it first. (I was pretty bad at luxury.) And on the bedspread was an odd little object that resembled a slightly misshapen ball of yarn. Upon closer examination, I realized it was an apparently handmade, stuffed tropical fish. Next to it was another scribbled note: "To: Your Inner Child."

I was encouraged to attend afternoon tea in the hotel, so I went. It was served in a sun-soaked covered patio, a refuge from the bustling streets of the still largely workaday colonial center. Afternoon tea is not an Ecuadorian tradition (though afternoon coffee may be), so they added some Ecuadorian touches—like a green plantain empanada. Mine was frozen on the inside, but what can you do? The hotel's efforts to blend luxury and local—the website is chockfull of their community involvement and Ecuadorian-ness—seemed forced to the point of confusion.

What accounts for my visceral reaction to the cloying, pampering, pseudo-perfection of Casa Gangotena? Perhaps I simply don't get it. Were these clunky touches what luxury travelers expect? It's not that I am anticomfort or antiluxury. Rather, it's that I can't believe that so many upscale hotels now feel the need to provide all-encompassing experiences rather than simply high-end lodging. They try to impress at every turn, and people eat it up—whether they can actually afford to be bathed in extravagance or simply aspire to it through the glossy pages of magazines. It's as if otherwise normal people now have an unnatural obsession with how much magic such places can create. I call this our "hotel fetish."

A fetish is "a form of sexual desire in which gratification is linked to an abnormal degree to a particular object, item of clothing, part of the body, etc." A hotel fetish, then, is a form of travel desire in which gratification is linked to an abnormal degree to where you spend the night. Not that people should be discouraged from, say, worshipping women's feet in stilettos or indulging in Bulgari amenities for lathering up in vintage copper bathtubs. But when they become the principal means of satisfaction in sex or in travel, that means we're really missing the good stuff.

Complicit in this are the travel media. When I see a "World's Best Hotels" story on a home page or magazine cover, I sigh. Oh, the meals that could be bought, the convertibles that could be rented, the trips that could double in length if people did not aspire to spend $800 a night for a place to sleep. How did travelers become so obsessed with the places where they should be spending the least time possible? What in the world could make a $600 hotel room so much better than a $300 one that you wouldn't be better off spending the difference on a two-star Michelin dinner (or giving it to charity)?

To me, the ideal hotel has a comfortable bed and a clean bathroom and is near public transport. If I'm traveling with a girlfriend, I'll tack "modern" onto "clean bathroom," concede that the staff should be pleasant, and reluctantly insist on soundproof rooms, though I kind of like hearing other couples argue in foreign languages.

A touch of style is a nice bonus—no complaints if room design subtly reflects local surroundings, or if a local artisan's work accents the lobby. Owners charming, hilarious, or wizened-with-tales-to-tell, even better. But. That. Is. It. No magenta beverage thrust into my face upon arrival. No custom-knitted fish for my inner child. No afternoon tea in the lobby. (No lobby at all would be fine with me.) Four pillows max on the bed; any more and the time spent removing them starts cutting into your sleep. Any disincentive to leave the premises as soon as breakfast is done is unwelcome. Actually, breakfast out sounds good, too.

But hotels are moving in the opposite direction with spas, afternoon teas, organized activities. The 21c Museum Hotels actually include a museum, integrating contemporary art exhibits with common spaces in each hotel. Craig Greenberg, the company president and CEO, told the Skift Global Forum in 2015 that "there are a growing number of travelers who . . . want to see something they've never seen before. They want an authentic local experience and want to meet new people."

OK, I agree, but why should that happen inside your hotel? If your destination city does not provide enough local experiences or people to meet on its own, perhaps you should consider going somewhere else.

I do see the point for business travelers. For people in town for reasons other than the town, it provides a taste of what they would be doing if they had any free time. Here's a Renaissance Hotel commercial:

> Why can't a sales meeting also have an inspiring taste of Paris? Why should honeymooners and blissfully unplugged people on vacation be the only ones with giant smiles wandering our lobbies? When you check into a Renaissance Hotel anywhere in the world, you should be greeted by amenities and local inspiration.

What a great service for those who would otherwise be scarfing down a breakfast buffet and rushing off to meetings without even noticing that the people outside were speaking French. But why should honeymooners and blissfully unplugged people be in a Renaissance lobby at all?

Alas, it is an intrinsic problem in the hospitality industry that business and leisure travelers, two groups with utterly conflicting objectives, so often share the same spaces and services. It's like trying to run a steakhouse and a macrobiotic restaurant out of the same kitchen.

Business travelers prioritize efficiency and predictability and thus love having everything they need under one roof: conference rooms, fast internet, a plush lobby for a tête-a-tête, a gym to sneak in a morning workout, a bar that serves a good nightcap. A leisure traveler values charm, romance, local quirks, and a relaxed feel—the lack of a gym might even be welcome.

Thus, few corporate travel departments seek out cozy bed-and-breakfasts. Many business travelers would recoil if required to say in advance what time they wanted breakfast served, and then face chatty guests sharing the communal table while an idiosyncratic owner poaches eggs, rather than scan their smartphones or go over the day's PowerPoint.

The worldwide standardization of the modern chain hotel is rooted in history and business sense. In the first half of the twentieth century, most European hotels forced guests to share bathrooms, a setup we still call "European-style." (Note: Those that remain can be excellent bargains, considering what an anathema they are to many Americans.) Worse yet, they served water without ice—which may actually violate the United States Constitution.

After World War II, European countries (and Marshall Plan planners) saw great rebuilding potential in tourism, and prosperous Americans were their prime targets. So they scrambled to make their hotels more appealing, sending experts across the pond to study how things were done stateside. The resulting improvements included weaker coffee, reading lights over beds, and complimentary soap. Ice and water also met with far greater frequency.

* * * *

American standards would spread beyond Europe in the following decades. Hotel chains flourished, then were bought out by other hotel chains. These days, they survive as mammoth hospitality conglomerates, like Marriott International.

Marriott has more than 6,500 hotels in 127 countries, many of them acquired—from eight Protea-brand hotels in Zambia, purchased in 2014 from a South African group, to the ornate Armenia Marriott Hotel Yerevan, opened in 1958 as a state enterprise of what was then the Armenian Soviet Socialist Republic and acquired in 1998.

Tacking "a Marriott International Hotel" brand onto your name offers the promise of dependable standards, historically a plus. But in recent years, as travelers began to value "localness" and could access user reviews on just about every property under the sun, such hotels have found themselves in a bind—they are by definition as unlocal as you can get.

And thus began the hospitality trend in which massive corporations break out farcical initiatives to reverse-engineer a local touch. I would receive press releases like this one:

> In support of "National Homemade Soup Day" on Feb. 4, Omni Hotels & Resorts is launching a month-long initiative, "Sensational Soups," to offer restaurant guests a different regionally-inspired, homemade soup at Omni properties across the country.

Smarmy enough to evince a chuckle, but well short of certain other appallingly transparent efforts:

> *Dear Seth,*
> *Travelers today continue to crave local hidden gems over cli-chéd tourist sights. They look to immerse themselves in local cultures, making surprising discoveries beyond the online reviews.*
>
> *Hilton Barbados Resort is meeting this demand for unusual experiences, offering a dually immersive and truly local experience now through Dec. 15, 2014 with its Off the Tourist Trail package. . . .*

Of course! All it takes to get off the tourist trail is a stay at the Hilton Barbados Resort! Why didn't I think of that? For just $469 a night, the package included trips to sites like Joe's River Tropical Rainforest (with a local adventure guide), Gun Hill Signal Station ("the hidden gem of Bathsheba"), and seventeenth-century Sunbury Plantation House for lunch ("at the great room's grand mahogany table").

$469 is almost precisely what I paid for my entire trip to Barbados four years earlier, including plane fare and my $40-a-night hotel. But, setting that aside, let's delve deeper into their curious definition of "Off the Tourist Trail."

Joe's River Tropical Rainforest is in most guidebooks and is a relatively popular destination. Gun Hill Signal Station is No. 29 of 204 "Things to do" in Barbados on TripAdvisor. And the Sunbury Plantation website notes: "Many tour operators include a stop at or tour to Sunbury Plantation House."

It's actually an appealing-sounding list of activities. But if this is the experience you want in Barbados, why would you need a Hilton resort to help you? Barbados is a manageable-size island where everyone speaks English and it's quite possible to get around without being shepherded everywhere. I loved Bathsheba, for example, where I got dropped off by a new friend after a 6 a.m. hike with about sixty Bajans organized by the Barbados National Trust. Later, I hopped a bus back to the guesthouse.

TRAVEL MEDIA

Sometimes in medical emergencies, doctors must act outside their specialty—a dermatologist delivers a baby on the side of a highway, for example. And sometimes, in a financial emergency, a freelance writer must do the same—a budget-travel writer reviews a luxury hotel for *Condé Nast Traveler*, say.

It was January 2010, I was living in Brazil on a shoestring and taking whatever assignments came my way. (A preposterously uninformed review of a luxury spa for *Interior Design* magazine comes to mind.) So by the morning of February 8, when I paid the bill for my room at the Tivoli Mofarrej São Paulo, I had spent the previous sixteen hours carefully examining something I had never thought much about before—what $642.57 should get you beyond a place to sleep.

My notes praise the pool area ("endless fluffy towels"), the lobby ("very chic"), the room-service lamb chops ("meaty") and basmati rice ("clove-scented"). I took note of the complimentary his and hers Havaianas flip-flops—complimentary, that is, except for the $642.57. I duly noted that the negatives included the three times I called for room service before someone picked up, the package for someone else I found on my bed upon arrival, and the pool heated to bath temperature.

The 350 words I turned in were packed with things I couldn't care less about. But to *Condé Nast Traveler*'s credit, I visited anonymously and they covered the tab. The hotel had no idea I was not an everyday customer. That is rarely the case when you read professional travel writing these days, at least beyond the most elite publications (and not always then).

The way it looks to me as I delete-delete-delete my way through the press releases that show up daily in my in-box, travel-industry publicists are desperate. Does anyone fall for their faux-personalized blather? ("Hi Seth! Hope you're having a great week! I'm reaching out to you because I think your readers would enjoy . . .") But I've been lucky enough to work for a publication with a budget to pay (however meagerly) for my travels.

Marketing departments have a much easier way to get the message to travelers: bribery. Most magazines, newspapers, travel bloggers, and online video personalities accept paid trips or media rates from hotels and tour operators, and—surprise, surprise—almost always have a great time with them.

The vast majority of today's travel content is produced this way (or without traveling at all, which is more common than you think), with only a few publications still ponying up for their writers to visit anonymously. (*Condé Nast Traveler* now accepts some comps; the *New York Times* is holding out.) Writers and other content creators who accept invitations and freebies predictably defend their independence along these lines: "Even though I accept media rates and take press trips, I don't guarantee coverage and would never recommend a place that didn't meet my standards. I give my honest take."

They have to say that, of course, and I don't doubt many do the best they can. But I think most know it is not—in fact, cannot—be true.

It's simple: When a hotel, resort, restaurant, or airline pays for your trip, they know exactly who you are. Only the most incompetent company would treat you as a regular customer. What are the chances you'll get the room that looks out on the alley? What are the chances you'll be in a standard-tier room at all? If you're part of a press trip, even worse: Your group is coddled the whole way. I know this not from experience but from the preposterously fawning social media posts I've seen colleagues post from luxury suites with ocean views, sometimes of their own accord and sometimes, in the case of social media influencers, as a condition of their stay. It is obviously impossible to give a fully independent assessment of such a place. They've been bought, you've been sold.

Some cases are worse than others. In my Amigo Gringo role, I was invited on a YouTubers trip by Vibe Israel, a nonprofit whose goal is to "strengthen Israel's brand in the world." For Amigo Gringo, I am a bit more flexible than with the *Times*, since we work with sponsors in much the same way a podcast might. I have accepted free nights in a hotel, for example, in exchange for thanking the hotel at the end of the video. But Vibe Israel would be taking us on a fully orchestrated tour of exactly the Israel they wanted us to see. Obviously, I refused.

It's also easy for writers to forget, when they go somewhere on a visitor's bureau or hotel company or tour operator's tab, to evaluate whether a place or service is worth its price tag. Of course, a $2,000-a-night resort in Tahiti is a great deal when it's free. But is it worth a once-in-a-lifetime splurge for your honeymoon? That's a different story, and the story that readers need.

Standard, but far from universal, practice for travel publications is to be transparent. If someone else paid for the trip or hosted you, let the readers or viewers know. But some attempts at transparency can be disingenuous. I remember confronting Ross Borden, a colleague of mine who founded the entertaining and innovative travel site Matadornetwork.com, upon the publication of a 2014 feature about his trip to South Africa with a photographer.

The article—mostly a slide show with descriptions—ran under the headline "African Safari Perfection: A Look Inside Singita's Resorts in Kruger National Park." It raves about Singita, calling it the "most successful high-end safari brand in sub-Saharan Africa" and noting its "architecturally impressive" common spaces and "super stylish" suites. Its guides have a "wealth of knowledge" and its "culinary experience will blow your mind."[1]

At the end—the very, very end—of a protracted three-dozen-photos-with-descriptions slide show came the line: "Matador visited the Lebombo and Sweni lodges as guests of our friends at Singita."

I wrote and pressed him on this tiny disclaimer, noting it came "at the end of a very, very long piece where I'd guess 3 percent of readers would see it." To his credit, he asked a colleague to move the disclaimer to the top, though that never happened. But he was largely unrepentant, writing:

> but for real, that place is the slickest hotel i have ever been to and the safaris were the most amazing wildlife experiences of my life (and i have been lucky enough to go on lots of safaris). your objections are noted but i was not embellishing and although we were hosted, this was not produced with a budget. singita is legit.

Quite frankly, I'd guess most of my colleagues would agree. And perhaps Singita is fantastic. Probably it is. I don't doubt my friend thinks he produced an unbiased piece about the place. We just disagree about the way travel writing works. The way I see it, any hosted visit by a travel writer is biased by definition, simply because the hosts know you're writing about them and have forgone revenue in exchange for—at least the way they see it—publicity. It's just the way it works. Singita may or may not have given him and the photographer special treatment—a room with a slightly better view, a top guide, or simply an extra managerial eye out to make sure all went smoothly—but even if it didn't, there's no way for my friend to know. Also, like most reviewers, he probably felt subconscious pressure to write a positive piece. And about that statement that Singita has the best safari lodges in Africa—perhaps, but are they the best for the money? There's no mention of cost or value in the article. If someone treated me to the $595 lunch menu at Masa in New York City, I guarantee I would rave about it. But would I think it was worth $595?

Ross also pointed out to me that Matador does clearly mark sponsored content—features for which his company receives payment, not just comps. That's consistent with a relatively new and most welcome FTC rule spurred by shameless influencers pretending to love brands as they receive handsome payments.

The blurring of the lines between journalists and marketers has another consequence: It disadvantages small operations with minimal or no marketing budget. If writers only write about places that reach out to them to travel for free, it is the companies that can afford publicity operations that will get the press.

Alas, we're stuck with this system, so travelers must become savvy readers. Any time I'm reading a travel piece in an unfamiliar publication, I scroll right down to the bottom before I begin, and I look for something like this:

Most gracious thanks to Viking River Cruises for hosting our recent stay at the Budapest Hilton.[2]

That's at the end of an article on the website Hotel Scoop that begins the night before the author docks in Budapest. A couple at her dinner table raves about their next stop. He calls Budapest "the gem of the Danube . . ." His wife jumps in: ". . . And the Hilton Budapest the icing on the cake." The author pokes fun at the clichés. But still: "There had to be something pretty extraordinary about the city of Budapest. And, of course, the Hilton."

You'll never guess how the review turns out: a total rave! The way the (modern) Baroque facade blended in with the (old) Baroque neighborhood was "entirely flawless." Each room had a king-size bed and a chaise longue, and the breakfast buffet was "wonderful," with coffee "just the way I like it." She stayed in the King Suite, its modern décor a "downright striking contrast" with the view across the Danube River to the late nineteenth-century Parliament Building.

Forget her gushing praise—let's check her facts. It takes just a few clicks at Booking to see that "each room" does not have a king-size bed. Many of the less expensive rooms have queen or double beds. And though she loved looking out over the Danube, she fails to mention that you pay a healthy premium—34 percent on the date I checked—to have a river view at all.

It turns out the King Suite is much more expensive even than that. At this writing, the least you'll ever pay for it is $450, compared with $135 for the least expensive room (or $202 for the least expensive room with a view).

So to extract the right conclusions from the article, you would need to use information from a review of a $450 room (written by someone who did not pay a dime for it) to determine whether you would want to stay in a room worth about one-third to one-half the cost (that you'll actually pay for).

As for the wonderful buffet with the perfect coffee—it actually costs $35 à la carte via Booking, somewhat less if you purchase it with the room. For a breakfast buffet to be worth $35 to me, it better include a back massage.

Alas, this is just the way business is done. "As is standard practice, our group of talented and experienced travel writers will often accept hosted stay invitations in order to facilitate more detailed reporting," states Hotel Scoop's disclosure page, going on to explain that there is no other way for a low-budget publication to do its work.[3] That's true, though some general travel publications find a middle ground when tourism ministries and local convention and visitors bureaus subsidize travel and hotel fare and let writers out on their own, though not without passing on a few, ahem, suggestions.

When I reached out to Hotel Scoop, the editor defended his site, noting this was an atypically "gushing" review written by a less experienced contractor. Such gushing may or may not be typical of the site, but it certainly is typical of travel content today, from blogs to Instagram to YouTube. What to do? Abandon newspapers and magazines and blogs and shows and depend exclusively on user reviews? That's one option. But to me, the best advice comes from an unexpected source: *Do Travel Writers Go to Hell?* the controversial memoir chronicling Thomas Kohnstamm's misbehavior as a Lonely Planet writer. "Maybe if people see what arbitrary bullshit goes into the making of a guidebook, they will realize it is just a loose tool to give basic information and is not the singular or necessarily the correct way to approach a destination," he writes. You should not follow a guidebook "word for word, recommendation-for-recommendation."[4]

I'd guess even the far more dependable Lonely Planet writers I know would agree, and I would say the same about my writing. I can never believe it when people follow my advice to the word, or attempt to re-create my trip precisely, even when it's in the *Times*'s highly researched, thoroughly fact-checked "36 Hours" series. I stand by my work and come by my opinions honestly. But it's my trip, not yours. Follow it too closely and you might as well be on a bus with a tour guide.

POINTS OF CONTENTION

You're planning what you hope will be a discovery-filled trip to Istanbul. Describe your ideal lodging. Is it an inn run by a local historian with an adjoining wine bar operated by her oenophile husband? An apartment in a building whose hallways are filled with the rich scents of neighbors' cooking? A spick-and-span private room at a sociable hostel beloved by travelers of all ages? Or an international chain hotel?

A few years ago, a friend came to me for advice on what to do in Istanbul.

"Where are you staying?" I asked.

"The Ritz-Carlton."

"That probably wouldn't be my choice."

"I had Starwood points from work. Why would I pay for a place when I could stay for free?"

It's irrefutable logic. Offered a free room in a dependably elegant hotel, few would bother researching other options. I wouldn't.

But it's also horrible travel. I hadn't been to that Ritz-Carlton (a Marriott hotel, FYI), but I could just about guarantee him that, despite its hammam in the spa, a (now apparently discontinued) weekly Mother's Breakfast, and a "chic interior inspired by Ottoman style," it bears a striking resemblance to Ritz-Carltons everywhere. Again, nice for business travelers stuck in meetings all day, but I'd guess vacationers would be better off getting their Turkish bath, Turkish breakfast, and Ottoman design elsewhere in town.

Points programs are another covert enemy of travel. And they are a behemoth, growing from the first airline frequent-flyer miles program in the 1970s and spreading into hotels and credit card companies as well. Most people love them too much to ponder why so many companies would give away tickets and hotel nights for free.

But they could probably figure it out. Without loyalty programs, there's not much left to distinguish among their competitors. The coach experience on American and Delta is basically the same, and if you vehemently disagree, I'll bet you hold elite status on one of the two. Given no other incentive, most people faced with a choice between two major carriers flying at the same time to the same destination will choose the cheaper one. There might be some slight overall differences in service between the two, but there is far more variety between two specific United flights than the average United flight and the average Delta flight.

Compare that with, say, Coke versus Pepsi, which obviously taste very different. That makes Coke drinkers willing to pay a bit extra to avoid drinking Pepsi. That's why there's no Coke loyalty program.

Hotel chains don't have a secret formula like Coke does. What are the substantive differences between the average Hilton Garden Inn and the average Courtyard by Marriott hotel? If you know, I congratulate you on your intimate knowledge of industrial-rug quality.

Loyalty programs help keep customers of largely indistinguishable products less willing to change brands on a whim (or to save $1). By offering free nights or flights, upgrades, or other extras to anyone who sticks with them, they've created distinctions where none previously existed.

And pretty soon, you've been locked in. There's only one rational lodging choice in Istanbul: the Ritz-Carlton.

That's bad for travel but good for companies and arguably good for some individuals. But which ones? Not leisure travelers who spend their own money to hit the road once or twice a year. They toil away, saving up points over time until either their points are devalued or, yippee, they've earned that one free night at the Comfort Inn. Their neighbors who travel for work reach elite levels quickly, thanks to countless business trips they don't pay for themselves, and are showered with perks and upgrades and bonuses they can use for their private travel.

You could argue that business travelers deserve the rewards—being on the road away from family and all. But in our society, we already have a mechanism in place for that. It's called salary.

There are ways leisure travelers can game the system—in fact, there are plenty of "points gurus" who claim to be able to teach you to take your family to Disney for free, or who always seem to be posting photos on social media of themselves sporting sea-kelp–infused pajamas in the latest Emirates first-class cabin. Many are, of course, sponsored by airlines and credit cards. They do often have good advice, as long as you have the leisure time and organizational skills to juggle credit cards with introductory bonuses, make a last-second "miles run" to Hawaii to bump up your status, and charge every last Snickers bar to your credit card. Do all that and you too can earn that free weekend at the Ritz-Carlton in Istanbul. Let me know how the hammam is.

These programs cost the hotels and airlines. They have to be administered. The services they are giving away have value—less so for the rooms and airline seats that would have gone empty, more so for those that wouldn't. But either way, every occasional traveler who pays for a flight or a room is at least slightly subsidizing the executives and credit-card jugglers who are not paying at all.

To cite a concrete example, on your next flight you may be subsidizing the travel of recently retired sportscasting legend Brent Musburger. In 2017, the Associated Press reported that one of the reasons he gave for calling it quits was "to use some of the millions of airline miles he has earned for recreational travel."

I would love to have millions of airline miles. In fact, people usually assume I do, along with quintuple platinum status. But when I'm not on a bus, I always take the cheapest flight I can (without crazy layovers), and that often means discount airlines like XL or Spirit or Vueling, a different one every time. Believe me, I'd rather take American. I will occasionally scrape together fifty or sixty thousand miles from regular flights to Brazil, or from a credit card sign-up bonus. But I have never achieved platinum or gold or even silver status on a single airline. A good flight for me is when I get upgraded from middle seat to an aisle seat next to a particularly smelly lavatory.

Many people who accumulate points don't even use them, resulting in a double win for companies: People get all dedicated to a brand for little reason, spending extra bucks to fly one airline over the other, and then don't even cash in. A study by Switchfly showed that the vast majority of points from the major airlines and rewards programs go unused in any one year. In 2015, there were 517 billion available points out there—*half a trillion*—and only 121 billion were redeemed.

BLAME THE GOVERNMENT

A final thorn in the side of travelers—at least those who are gainfully employed Americans—comes not from the travel industry at all, but from the government.

A 2013 report from the Center for Economic and Policy Research compared how many paid vacation days the world's developed nations guarantee workers by law. The French have it best, with thirty days. The British get twenty-eight, the Swedish twenty-five, the Germans twenty. Poor Canadian and Japanese workers only get ten.

Americans get none. Federal law has no code or clause or section requiring employers to grant even a single paid vacation day to their workers. All they get is federal holidays.

Kidding! They don't even get that. According to the US Department of Labor website, "these benefits are a matter of agreement between an employer and an employee (or the employee's representative)."[5] So if you got a paid day off last Thanksgiving, thank your employer, not the federal government. A full 23 percent of American workers receive no paid leave or holidays.

Not that the 77 percent who got paid holidays used them. Another study, by Skift, found that 40.5 percent of Americans didn't take a single nonholiday off in 2015, and only 27.3 percent took more than ten days.

How little time off do we take? Australia-based Intrepid Travel created special shorter itineraries for Americans. Others largely forgo the United States market, according to Darrell Wade, Intrepid's cofounder. Even those Americans who did get more time off don't prioritize travel, he told me: "An Australian or an English person, they're not necessarily any more or less affluent than the average American, but they choose [travel] to be a priority. Americans take work too seriously. They work too hard. They live to work."

Studies abound that claim American workers would be happier and more efficient if they took more time off. But who needs a study when I have my Brazilian friends' Instagram feeds? Their vacations seem endless—I remember seeing a selfie of a friend in Italy and thinking, *Didn't I see her post from France nearly a month ago?* Yep—and she was still on the same vacation.

That's because most formally employed Brazilian workers are guaranteed thirty days off a year—matching France. It's not as great as it seems—companies can require workers to take some or all of these collectively—for example, by shutting down the office for two weeks over Christmas and New Year's. But it's still pretty good. And many leave for a month at a time, whereas the mere idea of someone leaving for a month would strike fear into many an American who imagines his company could not survive without him. The company often agrees, sometimes pressuring employees to remain tethered to their smartphones on their ten-day jaunts.

Yet somehow, the Brazilians, the French, and more—pull it off. I suppose once businesses get used to their employees leaving for a month, they come up with systems to fill in for them.

Remember the fellow in Manhattan who told me that, with only two weeks of vacation a year, "I need nothing to go wrong"? When time off becomes so precious that we believe each day must be perfect, something has already gone wrong.

IRRESPONSIBLE US

Most of this book has revolved around what makes travel better or worse for you, the traveler. But what about your travel's impact on the world, on the cultural and physical environments you visit? Despite wanderlust-infused platitudes self-proclaimed travel addicts share on social media ("I wish I had never gone traveling. Said no one ever."), there is no inherent human need or right to leisure travel. If we're causing damage, maybe we shouldn't do it at all.

So it's worth some thought—or, at the very least, some afterthought—about what we can do to ensure that our travels are not beneficial just to us, but are helpful, or at least not harmful, to the world beyond us.

The answer is not always what we want to hear.

"No tourism is responsible," John Urry told me in our 2014 interview. "It's all transformative, it has unintended effects. The good tourist would stay at home and would find pleasure and interest in their local area. They would buy goods and services locally, maybe develop it with a heritage center, a museum, and find pleasure in local walks."

More hopeful thinkers believe that sustainable tourism—travel that minimizes negative impacts on environmental and cultural resources, while generating fairly distributed economic and social benefits to the communities we visit—is the answer.

Remember that human beings made more than 1.2 billion international trips in 2016—versus 25 million in 1950. The term *sustainable tourism* came about by necessity in the 1980s, around the time the number hit 300 million.

Some sustainable concepts are obvious: We should not plunder ancient Egyptian tombs, or take a motorboat leaking oil through endangered wetlands. But far more is in a gray area, especially when we are trying to fit in culturally.

For example, the day before a midnight-sun party above the Arctic Circle in Norway's devastatingly picturesque Lofoten Islands, I volunteered to cut a ten-pound hunk of raw whale meat into steaks. Whaling and the selling of whale meat is illegal and widely considered abhorrent in the United States. In Norway, it is eaten widely and nonguiltily.

What were my options? I was an invited guest at a joyous occasion in a faraway land with a well-educated, politically sophisticated, and (otherwise) socially conscious crowd. I suppose I could have become enraged, voiced protest against Norway's whaling industry, and stormed out of the party, though I'm not sure where I would have gone. I could have made a silent stand and avoided preparing or eating the meat. I wouldn't hold either of those two choices against anyone, especially since I could see myself taking a stronger stand on an issue I knew more about. But instead, presented with free lodging and ready-made friends in a fjord-filled summer paradise, and then asked to carve the flesh of an intelligent mammal, I asked, "How thick?"

I wasn't a complete pushover. Later that evening, I respectfully challenged several of my hosts to convince me that eating whale meat would not condemn me to hell. The result: I failed miserably in defending my own country's practices in killing, processing, and eating the more terrestrial mammals we consume daily. We were all going to hell together.

I'm not embarrassed that I carved and later ate whale meat. Every day, tourists submit to cultural practices they condemn. Western women who find conservative dress requirements in Muslim countries abhorrent still cover themselves before going out in public, for example, rather than defying norms and/or trying to rouse the oppressed to revolution. Being a responsible traveler can be tricky.

Not to mention, we're hardly in peak ethical form when we travel. Home is where we recycle, donate to charity, sacrifice for our children, volunteer in the community. Vacation is where we let loose.

But that's no excuse. We must make at least reasonable efforts to avoid leaving destruction in our travel wake. Urry's argument is sound: From the moment your airplane emits its first carbon molecules as it taxis onto the runway, it becomes tough to argue you're impacting the world less than if you had just stayed at home. We love to travel so much that we wish it weren't true, but it is.

I sometimes compare travel with something else I love: doughnuts. No one would argue that you will lose weight and lower your cholesterol by eating them. But you can certainly indulge occasionally, perhaps skipping the ones embedded with bacon, and then offset your doughnut footprint by having a salad for the next meal.

I'll admit, reluctantly, that more good comes from travel than from doughnuts. Hundreds of millions of people in practically every corner of the world are employed directly or indirectly by the travel industry. Travel has great potential to educate, to create connections, and to reduce intolerance. And luckily, many people and companies and governments are working on reducing its negative impact on cultures and the environment while increasing its positive impact on economics and human exchange. I'm aware of no such movement to create a healthy doughnut.

Carbon emissions are probably the most talked-about negative environmental impact of travel. Most people (except maybe truck drivers) use more fossil fuels on vacation than they do in their daily routines. Luckily, this is also the easiest problem to deal with.

In the short term, we can contribute to carbon-offset programs, which presumably remove from the atmosphere as much carbon as your travel pumped into it. This is admirable as long as you take the time necessary (like, five minutes) to verify that the company is legitimate and its processes are certified by a respected independent agency. In the long term, we should press for higher environmental standards for airplanes (and cars and boats and trains).

We can also reduce our impact simply by traveling fewer miles (or using cleaner or more efficient vehicles). Problem is, not many of us want to skip dream destinations because they're too far, or reject bus travel in countries with poor emissions standards.

A good compromise is to reduce our carbon footprint by visiting fewer places per trip. I've already made my pitch for spending more time in fewer places, and here you have another good reason. By the way, shorter flights are more harmful (per mile) than longer flights, so don't think you're a saint for skipping the Europe–Asia–Africa trifecta and instead flitting all around Europe on Ryanair.

If you are putting large portions of your trips in the hands of a single tour operator, hotel, or resort, you can do more. Search online to be sure the company you're considering hasn't been in the news for any disturbing reason, then look for them (or ask about them) on travel forums like Fodor's and Lonely Planet's Thorn Tree. You were already going to TripAdvisor to see how they do, so scan the reviews not just for ratings but for any complaints. Better yet, search for keywords like *green* or *pollute* or *responsible*. I highly recommend this for any company with the letters *eco* in its name. *Eco tour*, *eco resort*, and the like are terms to be treated with great skepticism. If you find nothing that says, "Calling this place an eco resort is a joke!" that's a good sign. Sometimes you won't be so lucky.

But sustainable tourism is about more than eco buzzwords. A number of groups have put together standards for sustainable tourism that are quite helpful for travelers trying to spend their dollars responsibly. To give you an idea, here is a tidy summary of the Global Sustainable Tourism Council's criteria for environmental sustainability of tourism businesses. They must:

- Have a long-term sustainability plan and communicate it to clients.
- Follow all environmental and other relevant laws.
- Involve themselves in local sustainability efforts.
- Conserve resources by managing water and energy use and waste systems effectively.
- Reduce emissions, including from transportation used by suppliers and staff.
- Manage client interactions with wildlife and guard against introduction of invasive species; assure ethical treatment of any captive animals, if applicable.
- Maximize social and economic benefits to the local community in their hiring practices (including at management level), purchasing practices and support of local entrepreneurs.
- Treat workers properly and offer strong labor protections.

- Not use community resources to the detriment of the community.

- Contribute to the protection, preservation and enhancement of properties, sites and traditions of significance and not impede local access to them.

- Maximize sensitivity, minimize adverse impacts and maximize positive impacts on visits to sensitive sites such as indigenous communities.

- Incorporate elements of traditional culture into its own operations (such as in decor or cuisine).

So before you commit, scan the company's site to see whether it has a sustainability plan and shows any substantive proactive signs of following the standards listed. (Serving regionally inspired homemade soup once a year does not qualify as "substantive.") Perhaps the company has received an environmental award or certification, that's always good. Keep a keen eye out during your trip, as well. Ask questions of staff and of local community members, complain when necessary, and weigh in with user reviews (or, in extreme cases, a report to relevant authorities) afterward.

There are plenty of other things you can do on your own. I'll assume you know not to litter in national parks and transport flora and fauna across national borders. But not everyone thinks to check whether the tap water in the country they're visiting is safe, and if it is, avoid bottled water, filling up reusable bottles before going out. (I was surprised to find that Barbados water was safe.) Shower less. Pack lightly. You obviously can't look into whether each dumpling stand you choose uses responsibly raised meats. But you can go out of your way to patronize local businesses and buy local rather than international brands.

You should also be generous with individuals—leaving tips in cash where appropriate to make sure they get to the right people, and never sweating small change when bargaining or negotiating a discount, especially if it's likely the person you're interacting with needs it more than you. (It is.) If you can, make volunteering a part of your travels, or perhaps go out of your way to share knowledge: If you meet young people studying English, go out of your way to help them practice. Watch the way locals act and try to fit in, instead of assuming your own norms apply (like by saying, "Bonjour" before you ask French-Algerian musicians a question). Triple your efforts when you find yourself on someone's property or in their home.

A further step is to favor destinations with sustainable laws and practices. Costa Rica, for example, is a long-celebrated model of ecotourism, so by going there you are supporting their efforts. You can find plenty of online rankings of the greenest destinations.

What about those "off-the-radar" (but somehow on your radar) stretches of coast beginning to develop their own tourism industry? Just by going there you're already encouraging the transformation, but that's no excuse for sticking with huge resorts. If you do find yourself in a beach town or mountain village being developed for tourism, spend your money at the local, rather than gringo, shops— even if that means watery coffee rather than iced latte—and seek out local artisans in their studios rather than spending at the hotel gift shop.

The ideal attitude is to assume that all actions cause damage until proven otherwise. You are not absolved just because you're on a volunteering trip or religious mission. The history of tourism is full of unintentional misdeeds, as the world's coral reefs will tell you. It would be easy enough to say, "Today's travelers are different," and, to be fair, the modern traveler is at least a bit more conscientious than the typical explorer. But if you've ever come upon an unspoiled beach or quaint coastal town and thought, if just for a second, "I should buy land here," or "I should open up the first bed-and-breakfast here," you are, in a sense, channeling Columbus.

Tourism's damage goes beyond the developing world. The most famous example is Venice, where the rare Venetian still living in the historic center does so in lieu of considerable Airbnb profits. This is also true of the old city of Dubrovnik, and I've already mentioned Barcelona and Lisbon as cities in the midst of irreversible transformations brought on by mass tourism.

Not that you shouldn't go to those cities, of course—they also benefit from tourism. But they would benefit more if you skip Prada,

Zara, and Starbucks. Uprooting local shops and bringing in luxury brands and fast-food restaurants only succeeds if travelers spend money there.

* * * *

In a 2013 TripAdvisor survey, 62 percent of travelers pretended that they often or always consider the environment when they travel. Even if that were true, how much are they willing to sacrifice to make their trip sustainable? Another study showed that 100 percent of junk-food lovers would buy an all-natural, fat-and-salt-free version of Doritos, as long as it tasted and cost the same. True, the sample size was one—me—but I think I speak for many of us in saying that I'd do everything possible for the good of humanity (and our waistlines) as long as it took absolutely no effort.

I admit that any resemblance between me and someone who deeply researches the sustainability of his trips is purely coincidental. I rarely volunteer and I doubt I've ever chosen a destination by how conservation-minded its government is. I'm embarrassed to say I never bought a carbon offset—I will from now on, if you will. I also pledge never to eat whale again.

I do follow a rule that I think is useful—before I do anything even borderline controversial, I think about how I would feel about someone doing it in my neighborhood or city. I'm always tempted to peer into windows of quaint houses. Would I be OK if a group of, say, Lithuanian tourists walked into my neighborhood of Jackson Heights and tried to peer into a neighbor's first-floor apartment windows to see what New Yorkers' apartments actually looked like? Obviously not.

For some reason, this is easier when traveling to a place where the people who live there can also afford to travel. We must especially monitor ourselves when we are in poorer countries, raising the bar on our behavior when the tides can't be turned.

This dynamic is clearly at play in one of Western tourists' most beloved activities: taking pictures of adorable local children. Put a cute three-year-old Kenyan or Bolivian or Thai kid outside a hut playing with a rustic toy as a group of tourists approach and see what happens.

On the other hand, put an adorable three-year-old French girl in Luxembourg Gardens in Paris comically holding a baguette almost as tall as she is, and the same group would be much more hesitant. Can you even imagine the carnage if a group of Chinese tourists started snapping pictures of a class of second-graders from a posh Manhattan private school as they filed in two orderly lines down Fifth Avenue on their way to the Met?

There are plenty of ways to rationalize the double standard. There is less expectation of privacy in certain cultures! The kid smiled when I picked up my camera and laughed when I showed him the picture, so it must be OK! It can be irresistible to start snapping when kids ham it up for your camera, and I'd be a hypocrite if I said I always resisted.

Next time your friend posts a shot of a group of uniformed schoolkids walking home somewhere in the world, check how white they are.

"But I'm taking photos for an article!" was long one of my personal favorite rationalizations, until I saw it crumble at a medieval festival in small-town Sweden. I was indeed there to do an article, and the adorable blond kids in knight costumes having sword fights were as picturesque as they come. Yet I cringed to think what would happen if their parents caught me. I could no longer deny that I had different standards with more "exotic" subjects. (I resolved the hypocrisy in the jerkiest way possible: taking shots of the sword-fighting kids surreptitiously.)

The group Global Volunteers, conscious of the sensitivity of photos as travel trophies, asks its participants to keep their cameras in their rooms for the first few days of each trip, until they've gotten to know the people with whom they're working. That's a great idea.

But you don't always have extra days. On my trip to Tofo, that beach town in Mozambique, I ran into the cute-kids-in-photos dilemma and a peer-into-the-house dilemma and I'm not quite sure whether or not I did the right thing.

Tofo is tucked into the south end of a five-mile stretch of sand that curves gently in the distance and disappears. There was a community around the tip called Barra that I spotted on a Google satellite-view map, but nothing before then. So I grabbed a bottle of water and set out for a five-mile hike. After a couple of farther-flung Tofo houses and lodges, there was nothing but sand and water, and a dune that prevented me from seeing what was past the beach.

But maybe a mile out, a sign of human life. In fact, one of the better signs, kids playing. Up ahead, five Bitonga-speaking kids, two boys and three girls maybe seven to thirteen, splashed in the knee-deep water. The boys were in underwear and the girls in pink shorts and no tops.

"Hello, how are you?" she shouted, in English.

"Fine, thank you, how are you?" I replied.

"Fine, thank you, how are you?" she answered. When I told them I spoke Portuguese, things got a little more interesting. (Portuguese is Mozambique's official language, the one they learn in school.)

They saw my bulky camera and—I swear—asked me to take photographs of them. A boy asked to see the pictures of "your country" on my phone. (I was clearly not their first tourist encounter.) I swiped through what I had—a hippo from earlier in the trip, which they easily identified; snow in New York, which surprisingly did not faze them; and then a picture of a Chicago-style pepperoni pizza. Now they were stumped.

"Food?" the older girl said.

Either there were still places in the world where pizza had not reached, or places in the world (outside New York) where deep-dish pizza is baffling.

Before taking my leave, I asked where they lived, and they pointed back over the dunes.

I kept walking for a bit, and soon enough a man approached from the opposite direction. I had underestimated the midday Mozambican sun, so with the tip of the peninsula looking quite far away, I asked whether I could cut across the dunes to a road I remembered seeing on the satellite map.

"It's very complicated," he said. "It would be longer than turning around and going to Tofo."

Challenge accepted.

He was not joking. It was tough going, scrambling over the dunes and then a few minivalleys beyond them, but eventually I found a sandy path that leveled out amid palm trees, cassava fields, and scattered clusters of rectangular houses with reed siding and thatched roofs. But no people.

Finally, outside a hut with a festive green door, I saw three women under a shady tree doing one another's hair. I waved from afar to test their friendliness, and they waved back gamely. So I went over to ask directions. Or, really just "direction"—there were no roads.

Then I noticed something peculiar: a huge pile of shells, thousands of them, under the tree, an obvious topic of conversation. They turned out to be the material the family would use to make the foundation for a new house.

Obviously, I would have loved to see their houses. But after a ten-minute conversation, we ran out of things to talk about. After conferring in Bitonga, they said their two children, Dulce and Manito, would lead me to the road for twenty meticais, less than a dollar. So they did. When we got there, I gave them fifty. And took their picture.

Could my hike count as sustainable tourism? Was it OK for me to wander down a beach, snap pictures of children in their underwear without their parents' knowledge, and then "stumble across" a Mozambican village I was kind of hoping was there? In the words of the aforementioned standards, had I maximized sensitivity and minimized adverse impact when visiting an indigenous community?

Stopping to talk to kids on a beach surely is OK. Taking pictures, though? Not sure. (One was published in the *Times*, so, um, I'm a journalist?) When I entered the village, I tried not to overstay my welcome, asked what I thought were nonintrusive questions—was there a school nearby? where did the people who lived there work?— but I have no idea whether I succeeded. I did resist the (very strong) temptation to peek inside their homes. And they did make a couple of bucks out of it, assuming the kids forked over the money. If I asked ten people what I did right and wrong, surely I'd get ten different answers. But at least we'd be talking about it.

An Istanbul park.

EPILOGUE

For the second half of that final Frugal Traveler trip to Ecuador, I went back to my frugal ways. First was a $20-a-night stay with an indigenous Saraguro family in southern Ecuador, where the youngest daughter, mischievous six-year-old Genesis, picked herbs and flowers that her mother made into *agua de frescos* far better than the one thrust in the face of arriving guests at the Casa Gangotena. Then I headed to Cuenca with two unplanned days before my flight home. It was pretty clear how I should spend my final days in Frugal office: head to a random town and see what happened. I scanned Google Maps for places within what looked like an hour's bus ride from Cuenca.

Anything on a major highway was not of interest, so Capulispamba was out, and so was Cumbe. Baños was big enough that I had heard of it, strike that one. Santa Ana? Boring name. Then there was Quingeo, nestled in the mountains, seemingly not a road in sight. Even when I zoomed in, the main routes going out of Cuenca did not even get close. A nearly imperceptible white line meandered to the little town—a line so faint that if it were a vein, not even the world's greatest phlebotomist could draw blood from it.

A quick search turned up no tourist information, no user reviews, no guidebook mentions. So far, so good. A municipal government website proved it did exist. And then I came to a Spanish-language article from 2008. The writer called Quingeo "an isolated and surprising town" that seemed nearly abandoned during the week but comes alive Sundays as residents who work in the fields and in Cuenca arrive for Mass and music and food. By luck, it was Saturday.

But when I started asking around, no one had even heard of Quingeo, let alone knew how to get there. So I went to the bus station and started asking the people working the counters at the astonishing number of local bus companies headed to every town in the region. Except Quingeo. Finally, I was directed to Sigsig Express, a company so insignificant that its office was cut off from the rest of the terminal. I had to walk out one door and in another to get to it. There was a once-daily bus that stopped in Quingeo, but I had missed it. A young woman explained that I should just get a cab to "the stop across from the Garaicoa School," and look for the bus headed to *El Valle*—The Valley.

The *El Valle* bus showed up promptly. It was the archetypal Latin American bus—with Greyhound-type cushioned seats in tatters, and no room to sit, anyway. I stood and listened to merengue blasting over the speakers. The driver let people out, anywhere they wanted to go, at their request. I asked several people if they would alert me when we got to Quingeo.

"Sorry, but I'm getting off before then," said one after another. The bus gradually emptied, and the man sitting behind me (for I had finally gotten a seat) told me it was the next stop. "Manuel," he shouted to a man a few rows up, "can you take this gentleman into Quingeo?"

Manuel and I stepped off the bus and headed up a dirt road. He was going home for the weekend, lugging a sack of root vegetables over his shoulder. "Is there a hotel or guesthouse in town?" I asked. He laughed.

"We'll ask the priest," he said.

It was a very, very quick walk to the center of town. Actually, the town was little more than a center, and it was a thing of my travel fantasies: a landscaped square surrounded by brightly colored buildings two or three stories high, with old-fashioned balconies held up by wood columns. Beyond were a few scattered houses, then mostly farmland. Quingeo was like a Wild West film set, except that the façades had been replaced by three-dimensional, inhabited buildings. The semimodern monstrosity of a church was the only disappointment, and it was also my destination.

Manuel walked me up to the rectory door and knocked, to no avail. He spotted an older woman walking by. "Doña Laura," he asked, "could you find a bed for this gentleman?"

She could, in one of the best-preserved buildings on the plaza. It was painted a mustardy yellow with a second-story balcony held up by chocolate-brown wooden stilts, and belonged to her family.

"What can I pay you?" I asked.

"Ah, pay what you think is right, but tomorrow," she said, asking a young woman to show me to my room, a cavernous space jam-packed with mismatched beds of all sizes. I had no idea whether I would be sleeping alone or with half the town. Either way would have its advantages.

I went out to walk the square, fish for friends, and find where I might eat that night. As I did, a loudspeaker crackled: "We will have a meeting tomorrow night at 6 p.m. to discuss Carnival activities," it said. Ah, a municipal public-address system. How I love those as a traveler, how I would despise them as a resident.

A one-story building at the west end of the square caught my eye. Well, its sign did: "BAR." I expected it to be a typical local dive, but instead, the walls were twinkling with Christmas lights and decorated with Bob Marley posters and 45 RPM records. The bar was empty except for a man dressed in a suit in the DJ booth. He introduced himself as Lennon—spelled like the Beatle he was named after—and told me he did not usually work in a suit, but he had been at a wedding earlier that day.

I left in search of a restaurant, but the only one on the square, Papá Morales, was closed. Odd, I thought, for a Saturday night. I had returned to my room, resigning myself to a dinner of nuts from my pack, when I had to go to the bathroom. Oddly enough, Laura had told me there was no bathroom in the house, so I would have to go out the back door and use the one in the house across the street, which also belonged to her family.

Coincidentally, the family was sitting down to dinner—and I was invited to join them. A man named Patricio and his adult son,

Paulino—relationship to Laura unclear—promptly invited me to join them after dinner at their grocery store across the plaza. Things were shaping up. I had eaten, I was headed to hang out on the square with some locals, and I had a bar to check out later.

We sat outside the store drinking Zhumir, an Ecuadorean sugarcane spirit, and discussing their jobs as public-school teachers in Cuenca. Like Manuel, they would spend Monday through Friday in the city and return home on the weekends. Patricio put on a cassette of something a bit unexpected: a pirated copy of *Concert for George*, the 2001 concert held in George Harrison's honor on the first anniversary of his death.

Patricio, it turned out, was a huge Beatles fan, and Lennon, the bartender across the square, was his son. Paulino and I eventually left Patricio and went to join a young crowd at the bar. Pretty soon we were eating chicken dunked in beer and grilled over a little campfire that burned on the dirt floor of the surprisingly unventilated bar. I left at 12:30 to sleep because I didn't want to miss the Sunday morning market. I'm pretty sure Paulino stayed quite a bit later, given how sick he looked in the morning.

I wasn't expecting much from the market, and I wasn't disappointed at how disappointed I was. A couple of farmers selling onions, tomatoes, and peppers; a few stands of cheap Chinese toys; Doña Laura displaying clothes that hung from lines strung under her balcony. The most interesting find was *encebollado*, a traditional fish stew served up for $2 a bowl at a stand labeled PAPÁ MORALES, maybe a hundred yards from the still-closed restaurant of the same name.

As I ate, the action picked up, with a six-on-six soccer tournament in the square. A man in his thirties gave the play-by-play over speakers that may or may not have been the same ones used to make the Carnival announcement the previous evening. If you closed your eyes, you might think he was announcing to a crowd of 150,000. He delighted in hamming it up for the players, who made up the vast majority of the nonexistent audience.

"Representatives of Barcelona and Real Madrid are here, looking for talent, so show them your stuff!" he announced.

"Who is that?" I asked at the Papá Morales stand.

It was Papá Morales. I went over to chat between games, and I learned that in addition to operating a (seemingly never open) restaurant, he also ran the four-month soccer league for teams from villages across the region. They pay an entry fee and the champion splits $1,500, and the league-leading scorer gets a dollar per goal.

He asked why I was visiting. I told him I had simply found the town on Google Maps and was curious. I also told him I loved his soup, a significant exaggeration. Minutes later, he was back on the loudspeaker.

"Seth from New York is visiting the greatest soccer tournament in the world," he announced, his words echoing across the town square. "He found it on the internet and has come from New York just to try Papá Morales's *encebollado*."

It was an absurd moment that confirmed forever the theory that how tourists are treated somewhere is inversely related to how many tourists visit it. Unlike the Mozambique hike, it's hard to imagine the trip to Quingeo being more sustainable—I took public buses there and back, I did nothing the people already living in the town didn't do, I pumped maybe $50 into the local economy, and I made an evening at least slightly more entertaining for a handful of people.

✳　✳　✳　✳

In 2015, Skift published a telling "manifesto" about the future of travel for its audience, the travel industry.

Among its messages: "Brands should build a business around helping travelers connect to their immediate surroundings and the people around them, rather than just digital connectivity." It noted that "the most forward-thinking travel brands are delivering experiences to travelers by focusing on three things above all else: inspiration, personalization, and a path toward self-discovery."

I'm glad to see the industry head in that direction. But if travel is moving that way anyway, how much do we really need their help?

The travel industry will always be needed to transport people to their destinations, provide them with places to sleep, and get them some basic information and advice on their destination. But inspiration, personalization, and self-discovery? Perhaps we travelers can be trusted to handle those three on our own. Inspiration can come from books and films and maps and our friends and clever online searches. Who better to create personalization than the actual person? Finally, envision a few potential paths to self-discovery through travel. How many of them involve Hilton, Carnival Cruises, or Lufthansa?

Of course, not everyone wants to spend their vacation riding a crowded bus en route to a "solitary and surprising" town like Quingeo with no idea where they will eat and sleep that night. Some might find this too adventurous, some nowhere near adventurous enough. I just wouldn't want anyone to skip out on it because they heard Doña Laura doesn't accept Starwood points.

ACKNOWLEDGMENTS

First off, I'd like to thank the world for being such an interesting place. That includes canyons and atolls and fjords and warthogs and humpback whales and giant anteaters, but I'm even fonder of its 7.6 billion human beings, their cultures, their societies and their many ways of deep-frying foods. Of course, some deserve more thanks than others, and I know what you're thinking: doughnuts. But I actually mean some of the people.

There are two elements to travel writing: the travel and the writing. (That may sound obvious, but a surprising number of people think travel writers just travel and the rest takes care of itself.)

Being a good traveler is a bit like being an expert Paraguayan *ao po'i* embroiderer: You can probably figure it out on your own, but it's much easier if you learn from your parents. So thanks to my mom and dad, who loved traveling enough to take a couple bickering kids along on our first foreign trip to London when I was eleven and thought sticking a Cadbury Flake in vanilla ice cream counted as exotic. Thanks for letting me go on a homestay in Kenya when I was fifteen (and there was no Skype or cell phones to stay in touch), and for taking care of me when I came back with hepatitis and no desire to ever travel in a "normal" way again.

I had no intention of being a professional writer at all until I was twenty-eight, and two people were largely responsible: My friend Jeanny Pak, who sat with me in some Upper West Side bar back when the Upper West Side was cool, and suggested I stop complaining about my government job and take a writing class. And Susan Shapiro, the person who taught the class, whose name, Writing for New York City Newspapers and Magazines, turned out to be literal. She insisted I fax(!) one of my class assignments to the *New York Times* op-ed page, which I thought was insane but totally worked. Other class assignments would end up in the *New York Post* and *Time Out New York*. My "humiliation essay"—Sue's famous first assignment—was bought by *Playboy*, which never published it, thank God.

Another Sue Shapiro assignment ended up in the City section of the *Times*, which would become my (freelance) home for five years. Thanks to everyone there who didn't care (or didn't know) that I had zero journalism experience and let me write about every corner of the city, but especially Dominican corners and Bronx corners. That includes Connie Rosenblum, Frank Flaherty, Dana Jennings, Mike Molyneux and Suzanne Spector.

I'm not even sure I knew travel writing was a thing until 2004 when the new travel editor at the *Times*, Stuart Emmrich, stopped me in the old *Times* building and asked me "Where have you been recently?" Turns out I had been floating down the Amazon River learning Portuguese from my hammock-mates, which was a pretty good answer. Six years and many assignments later, Stuart asked me to take over the Frugal Traveler column and then promptly handed the section over to Danielle Mattoon, who handed me over to Monica Drake who a couple years later handed me over to Dan Saltzstein, all three of whom helped shape my columns with patience and skill and absolute intolerance for bad jokes. Together we—and copy editors Florie Stickney and Carl Sommers, and others—put out over 250 Frugal Traveler columns over five wonderful years.

Sometime in 2012, Phil Marino, then an editor at Norton, called me in to see if I was working on any "book-length projects." I was not, and then, thanks to him and my agent Dan Mandel, I was. Slowly. Very slowly.

Phil would eventually abandon me (er, I mean move on from Norton), but not before he did one very good edit on the book and left it in the very dedicated and capable hands of Gina Iaquinta and Bill Rusin, whose hands-on and hands-off skills (respectively) made this thing happen.

Many others helped the along the way. My parents, both writers-on-the-side themselves (have you read my mom's blog, 80-Something .com?) read many versions—even the versions when the romantic stories were much more explicit—without complaint. Sue Shapiro, Alex Cuadros and Eric Zuelow, an actual expert in the history of tourism, read chapters and gave invaluable advice. I should also thank Eric's book, the theoretically academic but in fact very entertaining *History of Modern Tourism*, which was immensely helpful in putting together chapter 3.

Finally, thanks to the people who have provided advice and support and ideas and tolerated the (figurative but maybe slightly literal) insanity writing a book can provoke. Cris, Doug, Jon, and my brother Jeremy and his family were constant presences throughout, as was hot yoga, but there was also randomly occurring but excellent input from the likes of Zack, Marcelo, Adam, Caroline, Candy, Eric, Vanessa, Seth R., Neil, Frank B., Tomás Lin, Timbo, Todd, Mike L., and _____ . (If you've read this far and I haven't mentioned you, you probably belong in the blank, so just write yourself in.)

TRAVEL MODE

The smartphone is an ever-more-dangerous threat to rewarding travel, tethering us to life back home and preventing us from being fully present in the places we visit.

Yet it is also an ever-more-indispensable tool for travel— improving communications, facilitating spontaneity, and indispensable in emergencies.

Enter Travel Mode, the app.

Modeled after Airplane Mode, which restricts smartphone usage to functions that (allegedly) don't interfere with an airplane's instruments, Travel Mode restricts the use of apps that detract from travel while allowing free access to those that improve it.

"Restricts," I said, not "forbids." This is not a draconian app. Before your trip, you can program Connection Time, when use of some apps—such as Facebook—is allowed. Options are infinite, but the default setting limits you to sixty minutes of use per day, after 10 p.m., during which you can post and like and chat to your heart's content. Alternatively, you can program Connection Time for the early morning, or during a midday siesta, or even by geolocation, to be activated only when you're in your hotel, say. Once your trip begins, alterations go into effect only after a twenty-four-hour delay. Travel Mode is not stupid.

But it does have one major weakness: It is imaginary. Luckily, the concept works almost as well in analog form. Just draw up specific Travel Mode restrictions with your travel companions and pinky-swear to police one another vigorously. Solo adventurers will have to monitor themselves, but I can tell you from personal experience that it is possible—in that I have seen others do it. I'm way too weak.

Here is what is restricted, what is not, and why.

TEXTING AND MESSAGE APPS

Whether it's SMS or Facebook Messenger or WhatsApp or Telegram or whatever they use in China (which seems to have its own version of everything), messaging is our primary means of communication online. And Travel Mode follows the Hippocratic oath. First, it does no harm to your efforts to communicate with your travel partners, guides, and new friends made along the way.

What it does do is block all but the most urgent messages from back home. Messages that come in are quarantined until Connection Time, with the exception of those you can't afford to miss, say, from close family members, babysitters, or your boss. JUST KIDDING, NOT YOUR BOSS! And, of course, that can include both travel companions and any new contacts you make on the road, like, say, the ice-blonde barista whom you meet one morning at a Stockholm café who offers to give you a tour of the city after work. That way, she can text you and you can immediately drop whatever you are doing, rush to meet her, have a glorious day browsing bookstores and cute shops and back streets, and then, when you try to kiss her at the end, she has a boyfriend. I mean, or so I've heard.

Hard-core add-on: An automatic reply to texts that reads, "Sorry, I'm on vacation and this text will be deleted immediately. Send me an e-mail."

EMAIL

Email is an aging form of communication, but radio is still around, so we're definitely not getting rid of subject lines and bcc's anytime soon. Its nonimmediacy makes it the least intrusive form of communication short of the postcard, but it still needs to be controlled.

In the 1990s, I would get home from work, pick up my "real"

mail first, and then rev up my modem to download whatever email had arrived over the day. Travel Mode mirrors this old-fashioned system, disabling your email entirely until Connection Time. That should give you plenty of time to respond to friends or work emergencies or Nigerian princes who require your attention.

Optional hard-core add-on: A two-minute maximum for composing each message, approximately equivalent to the amount of time people used to take to write "Wish you were here" postcards.

SOCIAL MEDIA APPS

Facebook, Twitter, Instagram, Pinterest, and the like can mostly be given the email treatment: turned off during the day and available only during Connection Time. (Personally, I'd adjust settings to restrict morning Connection Time to emails and texts and leave social media as evening-only.)

Wait, so you can't post stuff about your day? Of course you can! The app is cruelty-free. The need to show off to friends is a deeply ingrained (if stupid) human habit. You'll still be able to. It's just that you can't post your photo of the Great Wall of China the instant it's taken, which is completely unnecessary anyway, considering there's a pretty good chance your friends are sound asleep in another time zone. Another bonus: Your travel companions won't get annoyed as you hold them up saying, "Wait, let me just finish tagging this photo!"

GPS-based exceptions are allowed. There is an option to set social media to work in airports, so you have something to do while you wait in the security line. But don't even think of trying it when you're feeling socially insecure for dining alone at a Tegucigalpa café.

There's also an option, discouraged but perhaps inevitable, to allow Instagram Stories or Snapchat or any such telling-the-story-of-my-day apps to function, since the whole point of them is to post over time. But any such exception would be a one-way street. You can post your own Instagram Stories but can't see others' comments, or their comments on yours. That's right, you'll have to miss the serotonin boosts we know come from "likes" and laughing emoji comments until the evening. Maybe you can figure out a way to make up for it with, say, the ten trillion incredible things there are to see in the world.

RELATIONSHIP APPS

Tinder, OKCupid, and the like are definitely permissible, but only to search for local dates, not to preplan dates for when you get back home. Restrict your swiping to Connection Time if you wish, but I recommend that any notifications and messages reach you immediately, lest you miss your chance.

MUSIC AND PODCAST APPS

Does your life depend on listening to your favorite bands—or *This American Life*—for hours on end? Then opt out. But for everyone else, Travel Mode sets a prespecified weekly time limit. When those hours (or minutes) are exhausted, you can still use the service, but it restricts content to music and podcasts that originate in or are about the place you are visiting. In a similar vein, use of apps to listen to local radio is utterly unlimited, unless the geolocator senses you're in a park at a time when the birds are particularly chirpy. Travel is sometimes about the ears as much as the eyes or the taste buds.

GOOGLE TRANSLATE

Unlimited use of Google Translate is allowed once you have passed Travel Mode's Five Basic Travel Phrases Test for the local language. It's just ridiculous to use Google Translate to say, "Hello," "Good-bye," "Thank you," "You're welcome," and "Where is the bathroom?" in the local tongue. Once you've proven you can do that, go for it. Translator apps are a great communication tool that will only get better. We're not that far away from having a near-instant translation of spoken conversations, something rather like the Babel fish in *The Hitchhiker's Guide to the Galaxy*, but less wriggly.

GOOGLE (AND OTHER) MAPS

Use of map apps is restricted, but not tyrannically.

For drivers, all uses, including step-by-step instructions, are allowed, though I highly recommend that you orient yourself by looking over the whole route on a paper map before you get started.

For walkers, there are limits. Pedestrians trying to get to know a city center or quaint town should be using paper maps, preferably beautiful big ones, and asking directions of locals. In those places, Google Maps will only activate after your phone's microphone has first heard you ask two people for directions.

There are some exceptions for emergency use—say, to search for the nearest pharmacy or hospital or ice cream shop. Searching public-transportation routes is not only allowed but also rewarded with an extra minute of Connection Time that night. If you're lost in a forest and it's getting dark, fire it up.

ONLINE TRAVEL AGENCIES AND OTHER TRAVEL APPS

Since you may need OTAs to search for hotels and check flight times, you can use them without restriction. In fact, they're an incredible spontaneity tool. Say you're enjoying Rome when you get a message from a friend who just got tickets to the UEFA Super Cup final (that's soccer) in Skopje, Macedonia. When's the next flight? How much will it cost? Is there a cheap hotel available? Fire up the app!

The exception is for the "user review" sections of such apps. You can certainly use them during Connection Time—or even free them up for unlimited use while you're at your place of lodging. You can also use apps like Yelp to find restaurants in less-populated areas. But in urban areas dense with eateries, they should be deactivated, encouraging you to wander around, peek into windows, ask locals for advice, and take a chance.

OTHER APPS

There are plenty of apps that you can use to your heart's content: Your phone's camera, for example—how else are you going to take that Great Wall picture to post that night? Currency exchange apps are obviously great, helping travelers to avoid rip-offs at shady money exchanges. Vivino can help you choose a wine, should there be no sommelier on hand. Shazam, which identifies music being played around you, is a great tool to identify local music you like and look it up again when you get home—and it can also be a good conversation starter. Say you're in a Gdansk nightclub and check Shazam surreptitiously to identify the artist of a particular song. You can then break the ice with someone by asking, "Isn't this Monika Brodka?"

"You like her?" the person will respond, tickled that a foreigner follows local music. "Famous in Poland! Won Polish Pop Idol 2004!" You promptly add the new friend to your texting "allowed" list and are invited to his or her house the next day. (Please remember that this is a fantasy app.)

A MINI-GUIDE TO RISK ASSESSMENT AND REDUCTION

No one is perfect at assessing the risk associated with travel, but most people don't really try. Here are some steps for thinking more carefully about risk as you're pondering a trip and wondering, "Hmm, is it safe to go there?"

PRELIMINARY THINKING

1. First, realize that you're not perfectly safe back home, either. Recognize the risks in your daily life—car accidents, gym injuries—and use them as a baseline when you evaluate a destination. If you usually text and drive on your way to work, but on your trip will be hiring drivers or taking a bus tour, your risk may actually be reduced on vacation. If you're a police officer, it almost certainly will be, even in moderately dangerous locations.

2. Then consider that risk tolerance is very personal—in fact, it may be partially determined by your DNA. If you think you're either way more timid or way more reckless than your friends or family, travel can be a good opportunity to grow and change. A good exercise is to consider how much you value your life. "Infinitely" is not the correct answer. If it were, you would be doing everything possible to reduce risk of death, like cutting down your potato-chip consumption to prevent heart disease and using the savings to buy a 2019 Subaru Outback or another of the world's

safest cars, which you'd be driving to your daily yoga class right now and thus not reading this book. (If you're listening to the audio version, I stand corrected.)

Instead, you take risks to make your life more enjoyable. You have dessert, you drive over the speed limit, you skip the gym to hang out with an out-of-town friend. Or maybe you don't. Some people value their lives more than others do, for reasons that vary: They have children that depend on them, they want to live to be a hundred, or they love doughnuts too much.

3. Distinguish among different kinds of risk. Risk to your physical safety is different from risk to your possessions is different from risk that you will feel embarrassed in a social setting. These should be calculated as separately as possible.

4. Unless you're traveling alone, be aware that your travel partner or group will have different risk tolerances, and be ready to compromise. None of you are "wrong."

CHOOSING A DESTINATION

1. Imagine that travel posed no risk at all. Jot down the names of a few places you'd most like to (and can afford to) go.

2. Now examine your preconceived images of your proposed destination. Where did this information come from? Is it current or ancient or somewhere in between? Is it geographically specific ("When I think of Beirut, I think of bombings"), a broad-brush national or regional impression ("The Middle East is unstable"), or pinned to a single event ("Remember that bomb in the Istanbul airport?")?

3. Consider how past trips have impacted your thinking. Personal experiences can be more powerful than a ream of statistics. If you've been robbed or assaulted or you became seriously ill on the road, you may be (understandably) overly cautious. If you've never had anything go wrong, you may think you're invincible. Dial back either feeling.

4. Do some research. Seek information from multiple credible

places. You might start at the US State Department website and cross-check it against the Australian Department of Foreign Affairs and Trade's smartraveller.gov.au. Other good starting points are online travel forums for traveler experiences and the "safety" section of a guidebook to learn from an expert who knows the locale well. Feel free to look up crime and murder rates, but if they are high, try to figure out whether crime is concentrated in certain parts of the country. Definitely look up transportation safety and traffic-related death rates, which are easy to find—that's the most common cause of traveler deaths. And don't forget weather events—do you even know when hurricane season is in the Caribbean? (June through November.)

5. Check with friends or acquaintances who have been there. All will be biased in some way, so try to gauge their attitudes toward safety and how they compare with yours. Just try not to let stories overwhelm dry numbers and advice from more official sources.

6. If your conclusion is "close call," consider ways to reduce the potential hazards: Skip a particularly dangerous city or focus on seeing it by day rather than partying all night. Use a tour operator instead of going solo; hire a driver instead of braving the roads; stick with more dependable local bus lines and airlines, even if they are pricier.

7. Check your gut. If you have gathered good evidence that a place is safe enough, but you still are terrified, choose another destination. How fun is a place if you're (even irrationally) terrified of it?

PRIOR TO DEPARTURE

1. Well in advance of your trip—months, if possible—find out what vaccinations and prophylactic drugs are recommended (or required) for your destination. First check the cdc.gov/travel site, and then visit either your doctor or one of the travel clinics that exist in most major cities.

2. Find out precisely what your health insurance covers while you're abroad, and how it works. Not being able to access quality

care—or hesitating before getting treatment you might not be able to afford—are risks in and of themselves.

If you're on Medicare or some other government-provided health plan, chances are you have no coverage. If you have a private health plan (including subsidized plans through state and federal exchanges), you may very well be covered. But that coverage may work differently when you're abroad. You need to find out exactly how.

You can do this by reading the fine print in your policy—not the basic summary, but the thick booklet or PDF file you've never even looked at. But calling works better. In my experience—as a freelancer, I've changed health insurance every year the Affordable Care Act has existed—the representatives frequently have to put you on hold to find out the answers, but it's worth it. They'll usually tell you that your plan only covers emergencies. But what is an emergency? Can you go to any hospital? It's worth pressing for details.

You also should ask how you will be repaid, and what documentation you'll need to collect. Most insurance companies require you to pay for care and fill out a claim later (which makes sense—why would a Mongolian hospital take Mutual of Omaha?), but there are exceptions. Members of Blue Cross plans can visit a worldwide network of hospitals that will accept their insurance.

You'll also want to find out how hospitals work in the countries you're visiting. In some places, you should have cash or a credit card with you at all times and be sure you've notified your bank that you'll be abroad—not something you want to deal with as you're vomiting blood in a Laotian youth hostel. In other countries, you can just waltz in. But be sure you leave with contact information for the billing office. I once received a bill from a German emergency room more than two years after I had hobbled in with a calf injury from an ill-advised pickup soccer game.

If you're traveling to the developing world, you'll want to figure out which hospitals meet Western standards (or Eastern standards or whatever standards you go by). Consider downloading an app such as Allianz's Travel Smart, which is free and rates hospitals around the world. That's easier to do over a cup of tea one month before your trip than when you're on an IV drip in the back of a *тургэний тэрэг* (that's "ambulance" in Mongolian).

3. Should you get travel insurance? If you're not covered abroad by your regular insurance, you absolutely should. But which one? Beware: Some travel insurance policies cover way more than health care, and those extras are not free.

    Policies can also be riddled with loopholes, especially if you're going to be engaging in certain adventure sports. So never just check a box as you're buying a plane ticket. Read the fine print. Mountain climbing is often not covered, but what does that mean? It surely excludes a trip up Mount Everest, and definitely covers tripping over an anthill, but how much in between?

    You can also look for user reviews, but if you do, ignore the ones from people who didn't get sick or injured. It's easy to be a good insurance company to clients who stay healthy. All that matters is how the company performs when something goes wrong.

4. Consider evacuation insurance. Even if you don't buy travel insurance (I never do), you should consider evacuation insurance (I often do), especially if you're headed somewhere that lacks modern transportation or emergency medical care. Evacuation insurance is best understood in Mad Libs format. Rustle up your worst travel nightmares and fill in the blanks.

    You're in an out-of-the-way corner of [DEVELOPING NATION] when you are hit by a [LOCAL MEANS OF TRANS-PORTATION] and suffer [LIFE-THREATENING INJURY], but local doctors speak English with a strong [OBSCURE LAN-GUAGE] accent and lack [TYPE OF ADVANCED MEDICAL EQUIPMENT] necessary to save you.

    Or maybe you're on [REMOTE ISLAND] and are stung by [SCARY-SOUNDING INSECT] that gives you [RARE TROPI-CAL VIRUS], and the nearest clinic doesn't stock [EXPENSIVE MEDICATION].

    What happens next? Without evacuation insurance, the best-case scenario is that you or your travel partner have your wits enough about you to pull out all the stops and arrange transportation to the nearest airport and onto an air ambulance to somewhere equipped to take care of you. Now imagine how much that would cost. (Actually, you don't need to imagine; it can easily break $100,000.) Alternatively, evacuation insurance can cost less than $100 a trip, and for those who travel a lot, a yearly plan is a bargain. (Often, the plans include additional services, such as a number you can call in lesser emergencies, and evacuation from a place when, say, a military coup occurs while you're there.)

5. Buy a high-quality, compact first-aid kit. Get your doctor to prescribe Cipro or another high-powered antibiotic, and stick it in the kit.

6. If you're an American planning to rent a car abroad, be sure you know how to drive a stick-shift vehicle. Well. If you don't, be sure to reserve one with automatic transmission well in advance, and call a few days beforehand to be sure you'll still get it. You do not want to experience the double discomfort (and increased risk) of awkwardly using a manual transmission in a country that drives on the "wrong" side of the road, or has poor roads and crazy drivers. While you're at it, read up on the country's driving etiquette, speed limits, and other driving hazards (such as driving after dark on unlighted back roads). A standard guidebook is your best bet here.

7. If you're a street-food aficionado, look into local food-safety standards. In general, people overestimate the health risks of eating on the street, although as hipsterish food-truck culture sweeps the world, it's easy to forget that old-fashioned food carts don't always adhere to the same health standards. Online travel forums are good at this, though you must block out the inevitable hysterical fringes on both the eat-anything-anywhere and eat-nothing-outside-the-hotel ends of the spectrum.

8. Before you go, check the latest news from your destination. Search its name together with the words *tourist* and *crime*. (Touristkilled .com aggregates such stories and is a good resource.) Then download one of the newfangled apps that tracks where you are and alerts you to any news reports of riots or disease outbreak or the like.

DURING THE TRIP

1. Ask around to get the basic lay of the land: What's the crime level? Are there neighborhoods to avoid? Is showing jewelry or using your smartphone on the street advisable? If you think you have a good sense of when a New York neighborhood "feels" dangerous and you assume that will work in Jakarta, you're wrong. Just be aware that hotel employees aren't the best sources—they often err on the side (or on the far edge) of caution.

2. Up to now, I've mostly been talking about risks to your health. Now for a brief digression about valuables. Unless you're in a pristine, crime-free city or town or jungle or island, here's a simple rule: Leave anything you can't stand to lose secured in your hotel or hostel or apartment when you go out. Back up your phone, leave the good jewelry at home, and carry one credit card, a good bit of cash, a piece of ID that is not your passport (like a driver's license), and a color copy of said passport. The cash, by the way, is not for you, it's for your assailant, so that he'll go on his merry way without, say, forcing you to an ATM at gunpoint. Shortly before the 2016 Olympics, a woman in Rio was stabbed to death in front of her seven-year-old daughter when she had no money to give to a mugger. A $100 bill in your wallet will satisfy most muggers (and be impossible to spend in many foreign countries, so you won't be tempted).

3. Be careful (but not obsessively careful) with new friends. Think back to the time I accepted a stranger's invitation to a family home in Turkey's pistachio region. Women who have heard that story often say they would have flat out refused to go. (Some men, too.) But being aware of local custom can affect your decision. In some places, it's utterly normal, and sometimes almost required, for locals to invite a traveling stranger to their home. If you do decide to accept an invite and are not sure, tell someone where you are going, and with whom.

4. Reduce the amount of driving you do yourself, especially when tired. Depending on local drivers is better, if feasible. Except

when they're drinking. You might be tempted to tolerate drinking and driving as a culturally acceptable practice, but if you do, your cadaver may learn about culturally acceptable practices in funeral homes.

5. Dare to ask taxi drivers to drive more slowly, and, if they refuse, dare to leave the taxi—but be sure you're in a safe area if you do.

6. When booking tours or packages, ask about the safety of the vehicles and the training of the drivers. It's worth $10 extra to go with the company with the modern minivan rather than the romantic but likely more dangerous rickety one.

7. Be prepared for phone-battery failure and cell-signal–free zones. In other words, don't count on your phone to save you. Always travel with a paper map, even if you refuse to take my advice to use it in nonemergencies. If payphones exist in your destination, figure out what you will need in order to use them. If the language of your destination is available offline on Google Translate, download it. And carry a phrasebook with a section on emergencies should your phone battery die. That chapter on emergencies that you never use only needs to come in handy once in a lifetime to be worth having it every time.

8. Memorize the local emergency numbers. Most Mandarin speakers don't understand what "Someone call 911!" means in English. (And even if they did, the number to call for an ambulance in China is 120.)

9. Carry a whistle wherever you go. (Though sometimes called a "rape whistle," it's not just for women—you could also call it the "I'm lost in the woods and it's getting dark" whistle.)

10. Wear sunscreen. Dying of skin cancer after twenty years of travel isn't much better than dying of a gunshot wound after twenty years of travel.

11. Register with your country's embassy, and keep its emergency number for citizens on a piece of paper, not just in your phone. (It might already be in your guidebook. See how many times guidebooks get mentioned here? You really should be carrying one.)

Finally, remember that things go wrong, and people get unlucky. If your trip goes badly, even tragically, that does not necessarily mean you made a mistake. If you did your research, knew what you were getting into, assessed the potential consequences and still felt comfortable with the decision, you should not blame yourself for the consequences. Things go wrong. But luckily, far more often, they go right.

NOTES

Chapter 2: ORGANIC EXPERIENCES

1. Jennifer Beese, "Social Hospitality: How 8 Hotels Engage Their Guests On & Offline," *sproutsocial,* August 27, 2015, http://www.sproutsocial.com.
2. Mark Twain, *Mark Twain on Travel,* ed. Terry Mort (Guilford, CT: The Lyons Press, 2005), 127–128.
3. Ibid., 127.
4. E. M. Forster, *A Room With a View,* (Urbana, IL: Project Gutenberg, 2008), eBook, chapter 2.
5. Arthur Frommer, *Europe on 5 Dollars a Day,* 50th anniversary ed. (New York: A Frommer's Book, 2007), 80.
6. Ibid., 39, 37.
7. The quote is a combination of the following *New York Times* articles, accessed via hyperlink on nytimes.com: "A Cleveland Arts District Hustles and Rebounds," November 15, 2017; "A Gritty Warsaw Neighborhood Adds to Its Allure," August 11, 2013; "Montreal Street Gets New Life," January 22, 2010; "In West Asheville, N.C. Bistros Mix With Tattoo Parlors," February 13, 2014; "Near Yale, a District Booms," August 26, 2012; "In Istanbul, a Spray of Style," February 10, 2013; "In Singapore, Head for the Hill, Hip Duxton Hill," March 25, 2012.
8. David Amsden, "Discovering the New San Juan, Puerto Rico," *Condé Nast Traveler,* April 2014.
9. "Best in the US 2015," *Lonely Planet* [no exact date], http://www.lonelyplanet.com/.
10. "La Globalización Comercial de Barcelona," *El Periódico,* June 14, 2016, http://elperiodico.com.
11. https://www.elperiodico.com/es/opinion/20160613/la-globalizacion-comercial-de-barcelona-5202598.
12. Mary H. Kingsley, "Travels in West Africa," originally published 1897 ("A Public Domain Book," prepared by Les Bowler, St. Ives, Dorset).

Chapter 3: WHY WE TRAVEL

1. Ellen Barry, "Two Children, One Rich, One Poor, Gasping for Air in Delhi's Smog," *New York Times*, November 23, 2016, http://www.nytimes.com.

2. Pablo Neruda, *Twenty Love Songs and a Song of Despair*, trans. W.S. Merwin (New York: Penguin Books, 1993), 37.

3. James Boswell, *The Life of Samuel Johnson*, vol. 3 (London: J. F. Dove, 1824), 31.

4. Alain de Botton, *The Art of Travel*, 1st Vintage International ed. (New York: Vintage Books, 2004).

5. "Punta Cana: Caribe All-Inclusive," *Viaje na Viagem*, 2018, http://viaje-naviagem.com.

6. Eric Zuelow, *A History of Modern Tourism* (Basingstoke, UK: Palgrave Macmillan, 2015), chapter 2.

7. John Urry and Jonas Larsen, *The Tourist Gaze 3.0*, 3rd ed. (London: Sage Publications Ltd., 2011).

8. Christopher Columbus, "Journal of the First Voyage of Columbus," in *The Northmen, Columbus and Cabot, 985–1503: The Voyages of the Northmen; The Voyages of Columbus and of John Cabot* (New York: Charles Scribner's Sons, 1906), 119, 143, 144, 113; facsimile edition at http://www.americanjourneys.org.

9. https://www.franceinter.fr/emissions/un-ete-avec-montaigne/un-ete-avec-montaigne-17-juillet-2012. Full text here: https://artflsrv03.uchicago.edu/philologic4/montessaisvilley/navigate/1/5/10/.

10. Francis Bacon, "Of Travel," in *Essays of Francis Bacon*, Public Domain Books, http://www.authorama.com/essays-of-francis-bacon-19.html.

11. Dean MacCannell, *The Tourist: A New Theory of the Leisure Class* (Berkeley and Los Angeles: University of California Press, 1999), 39.

12. Ibid., 101–2.

13. Photo caption from Seth Kugel, "In Papua, Indonesia, a Visit to the Welcoming Dani People," *New York Times*, August 6, 2015, http://www.nytimes.com/.

14. Gary Arndt, "7 Reasons Why the 'Authentic' Travel Experience Is a Myth," *The Atlantic*, March 8, 2011, http://www.theatlantic.com/.

15. De Botton, *The Art of Travel*, 19.

16. Paul Bowles, *The Sheltering Sky* (New York: HarperCollins, 2005), 6.

17. MacCannell, *The Tourist*, 9.

18. Ibid., 10, 94.

19. Roman Krznaric, *How Should We Live?* (Katonah, NY: BlueBridge, 2014).

20. John Urry and Jonas Larsen, *The Tourist Gaze 3.0*, 3rd ed. (London: Sage Publications Ltd., 2011), 165.

21. Walker Percy, "The Loss of the Creature," in *The Message in the Bottle* (New York: Picador, 2000), 47.

22. A. McKay and C. S. Matheson, "The Transient Glance: The Claude Mirror and the Picturesque," http://www.uwindsor.ca.
23. Zuelow, *A History of Modern Tourism*, p. 19.
24. "Daniel Kahneman: The Riddle of Experience vs. Memory," TED Talk video, 7:53, recorded February 2010, http://ted.com/talks/daniel_kahneman_the_riddle_of_experience_vs_memory.
25. Mark Twain, *Innocents Abroad* (Hartford, CT: American Publishing Company, 1869).
26. Jiyin Cao, Adam D. Galinsky, and William W. Maddux, "Does Travel Broaden the Mind? Breadth of Foreign Experiences Increases Generalized Trust," *Social, Psychological and Personality Science* (December 5, 2013), downloaded from Sage Publishing, December 29, 2013.
27. Twain, *Innocents Abroad*, in Cao, Galinsky, and Maddux, "Does Travel Broaden the Mind?"

Chapter 4: TECHNOLOGY AND TRAVEL

1. Milton Bracker, "Old Inca Citadel," *New York Times*, July 16, 1950.
2. https://www.youtube.com/watch?v=F8E4u5uVJiI.
3. Zagat review, http://www.zagat.com, accessed 2016.
4. "'The Grand Canyon? It's Nothing Special'—Meet the World's Grumpiest Travellers," *The Telegraph*, May 5, 2017, http://www.telegraph.co.uk/.
5. "Breatakingly [sic] beautiful!—The real Bali!!" CJW913, TripAdvisor review, June 15, 2015.
6. Bart de Langhe, Philip M. Fernbach, and Donald R. Lichtenstein, "Navigating by the Stars: Investigating the Actual and Perceived Validity of Online User Ratings," *Journal of Consumer Research* (April 1, 2016), https://doi.org/10.1093/jcr/ucv047.
7. http://www.booking.com.
8. http://www.tripadvisor.com.
9. "Improve your local ranking on Google," https://support.google.com/business/answer/7091.
10. Zack Stone, "Living and Dying on Airbnb," *Medium*, November 8, 2015, http://www.medium.com.
11. Benjamin Edelman, Michael Luca, and Dan Svirsky, "Racial Discrimination in the Sharing Economy: Evidence from a Field Experiment," *American Economic Journal: Applied Economics*, vol. 9, no. 2 (April 2017), https://www.aeaweb.org/articles?id=10.1257/app.20160213.
12. Gwen Moran, "How CouchSurfing Got its Start, and Landed VC Millions," *Entrepreneur*, December 9, 2011, http://www.entrepreneur.com/.
13. Steven David, "From Cities to Small-towns, People Change Their Lives Through E-mail's Instant Nirvana," *India Today*, Jan. 10, 2000, http://indiatoday.in.

14. "Bart Prank Calls Moe—Al-Coholic," posted by The Simpsons Legacy, June 24, 2016, https://www.youtube.com/watch?v=83rIZIgSYwQ.
15. "Why We Travel: China" (as told to Seth Kugel), *New York Times*, December 10, 2006.

Chapter 5: RISK AND TRAVEL

1. Michael Moore, *Bowling for Columbine*, quoted on *Piers Morgan Tonight*, CNN, July 29, 2012, http://www.transcripts.cnn.com/.
2. Stephanie Anderson, "Tim Fischer Urges DFAT to 'Muscle Up' and Change US Travel Advice to Reflect Gun Violence," ABC News (Australia), updated December 3, 2015, http://www.abc.net.au/.
3. Seth Kugel, "An Informed Traveler Is a Safer Traveler," *New York Times*, February 23, 2016, http://www.nytimes.com/.
4. Brad Brooks, "Exclusive: Studies Find 'Super Bacteria' in Rio's Olympic Venues, Top Beaches," Reuters, June 10, 2016, http://www.reuters.com.
5. Gavin Fernando, "Brazilian Scientists Have Detected a Group of Drug-Resistant Bacteria in Rio's Waters," news.com.au, July 10, 2016, http://news.com.au/.
6. John White, *Bad Trips: International Tourism and Road Deaths in the Developing World*, 2010, FIA Foundation for the Automobile and Society, accessed at http://www.fiafoundation.org, 10.
7. George Gurley, "On the Town with a 19-Year-Old Fleet Week Newbie," *New York Times*, June 4, 2016, http://www.nytimes.com/.

Chapter 6: PEOPLE AND TRAVEL

1. "Why We Travel: Oregon" (as told to Seth Kugel), *New York Times*, March 30, 2008.
2. "Floyd County Teen Dies after Car Crash," WYMT, February 8, 2016, http://www.wymt.com/.
3. Jack Kerouac, *On the Road* (New York: Penguin Books, 1991), 100.
4. Ibid., 101.

Chapter 7: MONEY AND TRAVEL

1. Paul Brady, Stephen Orr, Maria Shollenbarger, and John Wogan, "Everything You Thought You Knew About Safari Is Wrong," *Condé Nast Traveler*, June 24, 2015, http://www.cntraveler.com/.
2. Albert Camus, *Notebooks, 1935–1951* (Cambridge, MA: Da Capo Press, 1998).

Chapter 8: BAD INFLUENCES, GOOD TRAVELERS

1. Ross Borden, "African Safari Perfection: A Look Inside Singita's Resorts in Kruger National Park," MatadorNetwork.com, April 22, 2014, http://www.matadornetwork.com/.
2. Kristin Winet, "Hilton Budapest: In the Midst of Hungary's History," Hotel Scoop, September 14, 2016, http://www.hotel-scoop.com/.
3. Contact page, Hotel Scoop, http://www.hotel-scoop.com/contact/.
4. Thomas Kohnstamm, *Do Travel Writers Go to Hell?* (New York: Three Rivers Press, 2008), 3.
5. United States Department of Labor website, http://www.dol.gov/whd/flsa/faq.htm.